Art Writing in Crisis

Art Writing in Crisis

Edited by Brad Haylock
& Megan Patty

Sternberg Press

CONTENTS

CONTENTS

Introduction: Amid Crises

Brad Haylock & Megan Patty

Countless fires burn around the world, literally and metaphorically. From palpably worsening wildfire seasons and distressing data about the warming Arctic to the persistence of systemic injustice and the rise of new breeds of toxic nationalism, twentieth-century narratives of progress today appear hollow from almost every standpoint. Art can encourage us to think awry, drawing upon reason and affect alike, and so help us to understand such crises, but how do we understand art? Here, we might look to art writing—writing that interrogates, explicates, narrates, accompanies, and sometimes *is* art—yet art writing itself is in crisis.

Newspapers and magazines offer fewer channels than ever for independent art criticism, and persistent institutional biases exclude the positions of many: traditional criticism is squeezed between a diminishing suite of established outlets, its own precarious marketability, and the torpor of problematic editorial hierarchies. The proliferation of new platforms promises new opportunities, such as faster publishing timelines, an apparent democratization of access, and an openness to new forms of prose. But these new platforms pose challenges in equal measure, including the ambiguity of markers of quality and veracity, diminishing attention spans in the face of information overload, and a symptomatic trend toward clickbait and away from adventurous or rigorous writing. While we're loath to give airtime to the specter of "fake news," this label clearly signals a new and unwelcome era in the politicization of discourse—one that is, among other things, wholly inimical to intelligent commentary on cultural practice. All of this means that art writing faces profound challenges from within and without.

We have seen new forms of art writing emerge, as well as new channels for its publication and distribution. Collective writing, autofiction, and fictocriticism are enjoying a new or renewed presence in art discourse. Small magazines, literary presses, and independent publishing houses are popping up, fuelled in part by the proliferation of art book fairs around the world, and by small and mid-sized distribution agencies that allow smaller publishers' printed matter to reach beyond local and national markets — an ecosystem that contributes to a diversification of discourse. Amid strong calls for accountability, transformations are afoot in larger institutions, too: in galleries, libraries, archives, museums, and universities, the authors, forms, and subjects of art writing are gradually evolving. On account of these changes, and due to the tenacity of some writers, editors, artists, and publishers, we are seeing a slow trend toward a greater diversity in art writing, along lines such as gender, sexuality, race, and ethnicity, as well as a better representation of blind, neurodiverse, and variously intersectional perspectives, among others. The seeds of change are evident, but much work remains to be done.

There is much writing about writing to be found in the field of literature, and in the field of art we find discussions of related topics such as art history, curating, and the archive, but *writing about art writing* is relatively uncommon. We don't seek here to exhaustively survey existing scholarship in this domain, but there are, in different ways, a few important precursors to this book. These include: the influential Writing Art series of MIT Press, initiated by Roger Conover in 1991; Justin Paton's enduringly popular *How to Look at a Painting*; Jarrett Earnest's book of interviews with critics, *What It Means to Write about Art*; Kimberly Drew's politically charged *This Is What I Know about Art*; and the edited collection *Spaces for Criticism: Shifts in Contemporary Art Discourses*, with which our present volume shares many concerns.[1]

In this book, authors from a wide range of standpoints offer perspectives on art writing, its crises, and the ways in which art and art writing might help us to grapple with manifold other quandaries. With the book already in development, the COVID-19 pandemic hit, disrupting "the old normal" around the world, and the Black Lives Matter movement erupted in the US, challenging systemic racism anew. These momentous events partly heightened the salience of the book's theme, and partly threw a new and unflattering light on the entire enterprise, since writing about art writing seemed less important when raw survivalism was the order of the day. Nonetheless, we pushed on. Necessarily, several chapters squarely address the events of 2020–21 and their recent aftereffects.

To aid the reader in navigating the volume, we offer here very short synopses of the chapters that follow.

Setting the scene, **Justin Clemens** unpacks the term "art writing," the dichotomous practices it evokes—*writing-about-art* and *writing-that-is-art*—and the tensions and slippages between these. **Kalia Brooks Nelson** examines the legibility of Black art writing among broader discourses in the US and beyond. **Boris Groys** describes the changed register of art in the face of the spectacle of terror. **Paul James** and **Brad Haylock** explore the ways in which art and art writing can help us to apprehend otherwise imperceptible global phenomena and planetary-scale threats. From the standpoint of a New York frozen by the pandemic, **Dan Fox** offers a behind-the-scenes view of his time as an art magazine editor, and his hopes for the future of art criticism. **Barry Schwabsky** reminds us of the importance of self-critique in any critical project, and its particular importance for art criticism in the face of an art system in transformation. **Taylor Renee Aldridge** and **Jessica Lynne** offer an evocative personal conversation championing Black, feminist, and lesser-known histories, and reflect upon the importance of new platforms for art writing. **Ben Eltham** laments the demise of art criticism and the public intellectual in Australia and elsewhere amid forever-changed media landscapes. **Bella Li** and **Justin Clemens** interrogate the murky grounds on which art, writing, and the contemporary meet. **Maria Fusco** offers a savvily slight and perfectly aimed broadside against scriptorial complacency. Weaving vignettes across literature and personal history, **Sarah Gory** offers an account of fictocriticism and its contributions to art writing. **Fayen d'Evie** and **Lizzie Boon** recount the experience of listening to a Bill Fontana installation in a San Francisco museum, and propose ways to experience a work through sensorial writing and publishing. **Maddee Clark** proposes three ways to decolonize the art world, including editorial strategies. In a multi-threaded, collaboratively authored text, **Sara Kaaman**, **Jessica Gysel**, and **Katja Mater**, editors of *Girls Like Us* magazine, at once describe and perform the collective work that underpins their publication. **Megan Patty** offers a short history of museum publishing, its duties and challenges, and the work to be done in the sector toward better representation of diverse voices. With **Flavin Judd**, son of artist Donald Judd, we discuss Judd's writing practice and its relationship to his art, the task of disseminating Judd's writings, and the intersections of art, writing, and politics.

Anna-Sophie Springer and **Caleb Waldorf** survey the potentials and the pitfalls of the digital domain, notably the impact of distributed platforms and collective approaches to art publishing. We interview **Astrid Vorstermans**, who reflects upon her roles and responsibilities as a publisher of art writing, with a focus on historical changes in the field and her collaborations with cultural institutions. Against the backdrop of art markets and the ecosystem of art book fairs, **Freek Lomme** unpacks the perils of distribution for independent publishers. **Rachel Marsden** focuses on the significance of photobooks as a type of discourse in China, and the kinds of critical practice they make possible. Lastly, in the context of radical disruptions to the cultural landscape during the COVID-19 pandemic, **Nikos Papastergiadis** and **Hou Hanru** discuss the impact of Zoom upon artistic production, and the futures of museums and readerships following a year without face-to-face exhibitions.

Our own engagements with art writing have taken various forms. In one project, we may be in the role of publisher; in the next, that of author—or editor, designer, researcher, or curator. These different roles have allowed us to engage richly with art writing and its creators, audiences, and economies. In these roles, we have navigated the museum and the market, the academy and the independent press, the artist and the critic. We have encountered many like-minded practitioners engaged with art writing who are similarly inclined to tackle its internal crises and the question of its place in an imperfect world—critical allies who are negotiating and renegotiating the ways in which art writing is produced and reproduced. This book is not a manual for art writing, nor does it purport to offer neat solutions to crises within or outside the field. Rather, it is a broad-ranging interrogation of art writing, from more than twenty standpoints. Ultimately, this collection compels us to ask: who produces the art writing we are reading, under what conditions, and to what ends?

1 On the Writing Art series, see: https://mitpress.mit.edu/books/series/writing-art. See also: Justin Paton, *How to Look at a Painting* (Wellington: Awa Press, 2005); Jarrett Earnest, *What It Means to Write about Art* (New York: David Zwirner Books, 2018); Kimberly Drew, *This Is What I Know about Art* (New York: Penguin, 2020); and Thijs Lijster, Suzana Milevska, Pascal Gielen, and Ruth Sonderegger, eds., *Spaces for Criticism: Shifts in Contemporary Art Discourses* (Amsterdam: Valiz, 2015).

Writing Art Writing

Justin Clemens

Ut pictura poesis
— Horace

L.H.O.O.Q.
— Marcel Duchamp

To misquote Joseph Kosuth: *writing about art is different from writing that is art*. Yet *writing-that* may be strictly identical to *writing-about* when the differences are imperceptible. Let me call this *art writing*. Am I following or quibbling with Kosuth here? Does *art writing* mean *writing-that-is-art* or *writing-about-art*? Do I call it this because I'm writing-about-writing-that-is-art or writing-about-writing-about-art? Or is this itself just writing-that-is-art, or at least wants-to-be-writing-that-is-art? It's up to you to decide. Like Duchamp titled one of his minor works, the relation between art and writing is a hard object, a dart object, an *objet-dard*, the twisted phallic mold of a fake boob. Art writing implies that you can't speak or show the differences between art and writing, differences which are nonetheless absolute. That's where the concept makes the difference. The problem's conceptual. Art — and *art writing*, if there's any real difference between them — is conceptual not perceptual. You can't taste it, see it, smell it, feel it, touch it. Art must be insensible, insensate. Art's a crack-up, an insensible division within appearance between the real and itself. But that doesn't mean art's just conceptual. If it were only conceptual, art would be philosophy. But it isn't. Art is after philosophy, as Kosuth also writes, as well as being after art too — whatever 'after' means. Temporal or spatial or logical succession? But the imperceptibility of art means that it puts such succession into question. After all, art may always already have been there, before we even considered it a concept. It has to be material, materialized. A material concept: art. A belated concept too, since it follows necessarily after the concept, although it doesn't follow at all. In any sense or in all senses. Neon writing, vaginal scrolls, raved pages, post-partum documentation, closet dramas, vanishing notes, white chalk on white boards, scribbling as the defacement of the work that it is. Writing materialized, literalized — literally literalized — not only as letters, but also as letters-as-material, both nothing but material and still letters, that is, elements of possible sense. Art as institution of art? But art is an institution whose *raison d'être* is to exceed — contest, overturn, simulate, frustrate, exemplify — whatever we consider to be an institution. Art writing is the place where art merges most utterly with its other, marks of meaningfulness, marks of knowledge, marks of power. Those marks crisscross everywhere, through everything, since everything is able to be inscribed or written. But art, even composed of nothing other than these marks of possible sense, shows them up as what they are — mere marks — as it moves through them to some elsewhere. Art writing as exposing the conditions of writing; that is, the conditions of meaning without itself being meaning or meaningful. A *kenosis*: emptying. An *ekphrasis*: vividly presenting ways in which another mode of presentation presents itself to *this* mode of presentation. Try tattooing that on your knuckles. But art has more knucklebones than you, however abnormal you might be. It holds the pen funny, and types funny too, and when it writes it simultaneously empties out what it writes, as it shows you how that writing may otherwise have had some meaning if it had not been written by and as art. Notes, signatures, scrawls, instructions, reports, manifestoes, condemnations, apologia, poems, exhortations, explanations, recantations, divagations, art writing is transgeneric. In fact, there's no form of writing that hasn't found its indiscernible double in art writing. By the same token, art writing is always unwriting too — and, however legible, therefore unreadable. You can read it as if it were just *writing-about*, but then you'd be missing the fact of its *writing-that*. Which begs the question: what, actually, is writing? As Jacques Rancière says of Plato's *Phaedrus*: "The written letter is like a silent painting that retains on its body the movements that animate the logos and bring it to its destination."[1] One of the things that art writing can do is show how bizarre a phenomenon writing is. For instance, there are many kinds of writing-systems. Some are ideographic, as are many Eastern scripts. Some are alphabetic, as are European and Middle Eastern forms. Some are neither, like ancient Incan *quipu*, enigmatic knotted octopi of string. Some are not integrally linked to natural languages at all, such as algebra or binary script or musical notation. Each does rather different things: unlike Western alphabets, ideographic writing is not and cannot be identified with transcriptions of the voice, of the spoken word. Yet it is also the case that alphabetic script must be composed of non-semantic elements: one needs to combine different letters to even get a basic unit of sense, whereas a single stroke in an ideographic script cannot help but quiver with promised sense. Dead breath and living image, iconoclastic exhalate of thought or visual expression of world? Read horizontally and downwards, left to right? Or vertically downwards, right to left? You can immediately see that different sorts of writing systems entail different possible ways of envisioning and interpreting the universe. Even the ways your eyes move change depending on your script. The way you look at art, where you start to look, the way your eyes move. The way art is made too. The way art encourages and frustrates the reading eye, with which the looking eye is already secretly involved yet evidently not the same. Art writing cuts your eye or your eyes in at least two. If one starts to get historical about it, things get even weirder. After all, history itself is simultaneously writing history and history writing. Perhaps writing and history are coextensive, given that history itself is already, irreducibly, both the events themselves and the writing of those events. Aside from a set of characters — a finite set of marks, necessarily distinguished as a set from what is not-writing, and distinguished from each other too — and a set of rules prescribing their disposition and combinations, writing requires a surface to be inscribed, and a device to inscribe. Every writer presumes a reader of some kind — whether the writer themselves (a shopping list, for example), or a fantasmatic inhuman addressee (a prayer to a god, for instance). Bone, stone, wax, papyrus, paper, pixels, each accompanied by their particular inscribing implements, and by writing-personages or writing-machines appropriately trained to inscribe and decode, take on multiple forms and project variant genres: hunters' or herdsmen's counts of dead or living animals, temples and tombstones, scrolls and sheaves, caves and codices, find themselves emblazoned with invocations to the gods or the names of the deceased, disquisitions on Being or on Economics, esoteric rantings or scholarly treatises, perhaps enhanced by elite calligraphy or careful font design. Pricks and grooves, strokes and smears, lines and curves. Writing history is a history of artificial lighting and artificial environments. Does one write/read indoors or outdoors? Sitting or standing or lying down? What light sources are available? It is also therefore a history of different modes of psycho-physical comportments. Do you move your lips when you read or write? Is your reading silent or sounded? How long can you write for? Do you sit and think in order to write (Flaubert) or do you walk the mountains to hammer it all into the folds of your brain (Nietzsche)? Writing history is also a history of invasions and control agencies, from blotting paper to editors and censors. And art history is also writing history. From the names of characters on red-figure vase painting to illustrations of myths and literary texts to signatures and titles to texts that appear on the work and as the work — it seems to me that there may be almost no art that has not also simultaneously been a work of art writing. Today, writing has returned to its probable minimal origins in the scoring of bones by achieving its ultimate minimal state with the Turing machine that requires only a binary code to function, yet is capable of inscribing the entire universe in such script. After that? There will still be art writing. Art as writing, art with writing, art that is writing, writing about art, the art of writing, art against writing, art as the epitome or antithesis of writing, even when it's nothing but writing. Continuous creation of differences you can't really perceive or even know how to tell apart. Headaches and problems? Well, *nes* and *yo*, as James Joyce wrote it in *Ulysses*. Or, as Duchamp *scripsit* (but not *dixit*): *there is no solution, because there is no problem*.

1 Jacques Rancière, *The Flesh of Words: The Politics of Writing*, trans. Charlotte Mandell, first pub. 1998 (Stanford, CA: Stanford University Press, 2004), 3.

Legibility Crisis: Race and Contemporary Art Writing

Kalia Brooks Nelson

This essay is being written in the context of social revolution. This may sound like hyperbole, but the list of current events that society is grappling with on a global scale includes: a pandemic outbreak of COVID-19, protests against anti-Black racism, and collective action around environmentalism. The most critical aspect of these three occurrences is that they are happening simultaneously, calling attention to the intersectionality of each of these dynamics as symptomatic of the imbalance human organizations have created on Earth. In 1952, Frantz Fanon wrote: "Every human problem cries out to be considered on the basis of time, the ideal being that the present always serves to build the future."[1] At the current crucial moment, the world's population has to decide if we are going to embody the quality of civility that lends its name to civilization in the creation of a new future, or if we will forfeit this potential for maintenance of the status quo that gave rise to this turmoil in the first place.

Fanon, a psychiatrist and political philosopher writing in the 1950s and 1960s, exemplifies the importance of writing about race and liberation within a global context of anti-racist and postcolonial movements. Although he was not writing about artists specifically, his call to action identifies the space where artists become integral to "restructuring the world."[2] With regard to race and representation, artists model new modes of recognizing Blackness as it has to do with: the self; relationships with others; the prospect of new social, political, and economic forms; geographic and cultural mobility; technological advancement; and the stability of the environment in supporting the human condition. In this context, art writing becomes essential to broadening the discourse around artists' endeavors; as images proceed language, art writers like myself must put words to the radical depictions of race and representation that artists are at the vanguard of.

The term I mentioned earlier, *intersectionality*, coined by Kimberlé Williams Crenshaw in the late 1980s, describes the experience of social and political identification as a combination of factors related, for example, along lines of race, gender, sexuality, nationality, class, citizenship, and religion. Crenshaw, a Black feminist, developed her theory with the awareness that identity positions are not singular constructs but, rather, a combination of experiences. Thinking through this position of hybridity is essential for people from the African diaspora, who had to develop intellectual, cultural, and political property that contained the sensibility of *in-betweenness* — deriving from more than one source or with multiple parts. The transience of this kind of identification is a distinguishing feature of the Black experience, one often made tangible through the aesthetic contribution of Black artists.

Firelei Báez is a painter and installation artist originally from the Dominican Republic whose compositions represent the mixed parts that more accurately portray transatlantic reality. Her work helps the viewer understand how the exchange of materials, bodies, and ideas as a result of the colonial project becomes a currency by which new associations of subjective experience are formed, and traditional histories and typologies are challenged and dismantled. There are myriad themes at play in her work, such as the politics of nationality, race, labor, gender, and sexuality, that directly inform the way the human body appears in the world — as well as the relations of power that are inflicted upon it. Báez's portraits of indistinguishable subjects hint at being female. They contain faces that are anchored by the anthropomorphic clarity of the eyes, and the skin — rendered in the coloration and texture of the landscape; sometimes terrain, other times the sea — connects the Black female body to the surface of the planet. Her mysterious figures are often adorned with elaborate headdresses in the fine detail of latticework, containing a mixture of African, Caribbean, and African American textile iconography. These elegant portraits reveal the combination of biological, economic, cultural, and environmental factors that shape the human form, not in corporeality but, rather, in the imaginary of the transatlantic experience.

The potential for new structures becomes evident when the imaginary is revealed. In her installations, Báez incorporates anthropological, historical, and geographic colonial texts describing the European encounter with the ecology of the Caribbean.

She uses these texts of imperial exploration to call attention to the project of documenting, cataloguing, and storytelling that serves as the basis for scientific and academic knowledge—as well as the European imagination of its colonial subjects in the New World. The composition of a "textual universe" that represented the Caribbean as a "field of learned study" created what Edward Said called an "imaginative geography" that converted the "cultural, linguistic and ethnic" diversity of a vast region into a singular unit.[3] The most important aspect of this realization is that fields of study are "made," and Báez's selection of books shows the viewer the "fictional reality" designed and imposed by imperial power. Báez paints directly onto the pages—darkly pigmented silhouettes, fantastical landscapes, and abrupt markings that make the pages appear water-damaged or burned. Her handling of these texts obviously challenges our conventional understanding of authorship but, more subtly and most impactfully, also asserts the artist's role in unveiling fictional representations that make visible the racist discourse that informs colonial epistemes.

The island of Hispaniola, where Báez is from, was the site of massive ideological upheaval in the New World. It represented, to use the words of Susan Buck-Morss, "the paradox between the discourse of freedom and the practice of slavery [...] within the early modern global economy."[4] Buck-Morss is of course referring to the events of the Haitian Revolution (1791–1804), which gave Haiti independence from France and made it the first Black nation in the Western Hemisphere. Discursively, the Haitian Revolution was in line with the ideologies of freedom and revolution that were a contemporary occurrence in the late eighteenth and early nineteenth centuries, contextualized by the American Revolution (1765–83), and the French Revolution (1789–99).

In practice, the "ideal of universal freedom," enacted "in the richest colony [...] of the entire colonial world," threatened the economic, political, and cultural foundations of imperial European society.[5] The victory on behalf of the slave population, led by Toussaint Louverture and Jean-Jacques Dessalines, over Napoleon's army instigated an existential crisis in Europe, where "racist assumptions" became codified as a mechanism to justify the legal enslavement of Blacks.[6] In another body of work, Báez reconstructs sections of the Sans-Souci Palace in Haiti, originally constructed between 1810 and 1813 as a fortress and monument to military triumph following the overthrow of France. These beautifully rendered architectural fragments signify the utopian and dystopian consequences of colonial geopolitics, especially in the erasure of discordant histories like the one Haiti represents. As such, works like this challenge art writers to think beyond "disciplinary isolation," toward "the constellation of facts" that more accurately portrays the texture of the African diaspora.

Art writing, especially by white critics, has traditionally struggled to articulate and value the intersectional quality of artwork by Black artists. Bridget R. Cooks, in her book *Exhibiting Blackness* (2011), addresses this willful ignorance by providing examples of white critics' reviews of Black art exhibitions in the United States from the 1930s to the 1980s. She points out that art criticism responding to the work of Black artists "call[ed] for a division between aesthetic quality and social politics in order for reviewers to appreciate the art."[7] Cooks also notes that "the expression of Black politics offended critics."[8] This sentiment still rings true today, not only as a distinction of white authorship, but also in the way many Black writers (and curators and artists) are compelled to position the work of Black artists so that it is more palatable to mainstream audiences. It is important to note, too, that Black critics (and curators and artists) have long been engaged in countering the narrow reception that Black artists receive from the mainstream art world. The dynamics at play here have their underpinnings in the racial biases of art history more broadly.

Black artists, by actively engaging with their intersectionality, subvert the essentializing procedures of race and the discourses it informs. They create a crisis of legibility, as we read in the examples of Báez and Cooks above, that initiates new critical dialogues about the apprehension of beauty, diversity of resources, alternative histories, and modes of looking that interrogate the systems of power that define and assign value. This was true for the timeframe Cooks was writing about, as it is true for contemporary artists like Báez. Following the lead of artists, art writing needs to capture not only the formal quality of the work, but also the materials, ideas, and sensibilities that are being used to push the boundaries of the discipline, reinforcing the fact that art comes from and extends into the world at large. The myth of essential unity upholds the operation of racism and, by undermining this, artists create space for new radical affiliations to develop in artistic practice—as well as in cultural and environmental consciousness. Successful art writing too, especially in this time of paradigm shifts, rests on the notion that difference creates a productive opportunity for disparate resources, communities, regions, techniques, and origins to discursively express the plurality of the human experience that will serve as the model for the future.

1 Frantz Fanon, *Black Skin, White Masks*, first pub. 1952 (New York: Grove Press, 2008), xvi.
2 Ibid., 63.
3 Edward Said, "Orientalism," *The Georgia Review*, vol. 31, no. 1 (Spring 1977): 162.
4 Susan Buck-Morss, *Hegel, Haiti, and Universal History* (Pittsburgh: University of Pittsburgh Press, 2009), 23.
5 Ibid., 36.
6 Ibid., 41.
7 Bridget R. Cooks, *Exhibiting Blackness: African Americans and the American Art Museum* (Amherst: University of Massachusetts Press, 2011), 96.
8 Ibid.

The Fate of Art in the Age of Terror

Boris Groys

The relationship between art and war, or art and terror, has always been an ambivalent one, to put it mildly. True, art needs peace and quiet for its development. And yet, time and time again, it has used this quiet in order to, of all things, sing the praises of war heroes and their heroic deeds. Representation of the glory and suffering of war was, for a very long time, a preferred topic for art. But the artist of the classical age was only a narrator or an illustrator of war events — in the old times, the artist was never competing with the warrior. The division of labor between war and art was quite clear. The warrior fought the actual fight, and the artist represented this fight by narrating or depicting it. That means: warriors and artists were mutually dependent. The artist needed the warrior to have a topic for an artwork. But the warrior needed the artist even more. After all, artists were able to find other, more peaceful, topics for their work. But only an artist was able to bestow fame on the warrior and to secure this fame for generations to come. In a certain sense, the heroic war action was futile and irrelevant without an artist who had the power to witness this heroic action and to inscribe it onto the memory of humankind. But in our time the situation has changed drastically: the contemporary warrior no longer needs an artist to inscribe his action onto the universal memory. For this purpose, the contemporary warrior has all of the contemporary media at his immediate disposal. Every act of terror, every act of war, is immediately registered, represented, described, depicted, narrated, and interpreted by the media. This machine of media coverage works almost automatically. It does not need any individual artistic intervention, any individual artistic decision, to be put into motion. By pushing the button that lets a bomb explode, a contemporary warrior or terrorist also pushes the button that starts the media machine.

Indeed, contemporary mass media has emerged as by far the largest and most powerful machine for producing images — vastly more extensive and effective than our contemporary art system.

We are constantly fed images of war, terror, and catastrophes of all kinds, at levels of image production and distribution with which artists with their artisan skills cannot compete. So, it seems that artists — the last craftspeople of present-day modernity — stand no chance of rivaling the supremacy of these commercially driven image-generating machines. And, beyond that, the terrorists and warriors themselves have begun to act as artists nowadays.

Video art especially has become the medium of choice for the contemporary warrior. Osama bin Laden was communicating with the outer world primarily by means of this medium: we all knew him firstly as a video artist. The same can be said about the videos of beheadings, confessions of terrorists, etc. In all these cases, we have consciously and artistically staged events that have their own easily recognizable aesthetics. Here we have people who do not wait for an artist to represent their acts of war and terror; instead, the act of war itself coincides with its documentation, with its representation. The function of art as a medium of representation, and the role of the artist as a mediator between reality and memory, are here completely eliminated. The same can be said about the famous photographs and videos from the Abu Ghraib prison just outside of Baghdad, Iraq. These videos and photographs demonstrate an uncanny aesthetic similarity with alternative, subversive European and American art and filmmaking of the 1960s and 1970s. The iconographic and stylistic similarity is, in fact, striking (Viennese Actionism, Pasolini, etc.). In both cases, the goal is to reveal a naked, vulnerable, desiring body that is habitually covered by systems of social conventions. But, of course, the strategy of the subversive art of the 1960s and 1970s had a goal to undermine the traditional beliefs and conventions dominating the artists' own cultures. In the Abu Ghraib art production, this goal was, we can safely say, completely perverted. The same subversive aesthetics were used to attack and to undermine a different culture in an act of violence, in an act of humiliation of the other (instead of self-questioning, including self-humiliation), leaving the conservative values of one's own culture completely unquestioned. But in any case, it is worth mentioning that, on both sides of the War on Terror, image production and distribution are effectuated without any intervention from an artist.

Now, I leave aside all the ethical and political considerations and evaluations of this image production because I believe that such considerations are more or less obvious. At the moment, it is important for me to state that we are speaking here about images that have become icons of the contemporary collective imagination. The terrorist videos and the videos from Abu Ghraib are impregnated in our consciousness — or even our subconscious — much more deeply than any work of any contemporary artist. This elimination of the artist from the practice of radical image production is especially painful for the art system because, at least since the beginning of modernity, artists wanted to be daring, taboo-breaking, going beyond all limitations and borders. Avant-garde art discourse makes use of many concepts from the military sphere, including the notion of the avant-garde itself. There is talk of exploding norms, destroying traditions, violating taboos, practicing certain artistic strategies, attacking existing institutions, etc. From this we can see that not only does modern art variously go along with, illustrate, laud, or criticize war, as it did earlier, but it also wages war itself. The artists of the classical avant-garde saw themselves as agents of negation, destruction, eradication of all traditional forms of art. In accordance with the famous dictum "negation is creation," which was inspired by Hegelian dialectic and propagated by authors such as Bakunin or Nietzsche under the title of "active nihilism," avant-garde artists felt themselves empowered to create new icons through the destruction of old ones. A modern work of art was measured by how radical it was, by how far the artist had gone in destroying artistic tradition. Although in the meantime modernity itself has often enough been declared passé, to this very day this criterion of radicalness has lost none of its relevance to our evaluation of art. The worst thing that can be said of an artist continues to be that their art is "harmless."

This means that modern art has more than an ambivalent relationship with violence, with terrorism. An artist's negative reaction to repressive, state-organized power is something that almost goes without saying. Artists who are committed to the tradition of modernity will feel themselves unambiguously compelled by this tradition to defend the individual's sovereignty against State oppression. But the artist's attitude to individual and revolutionary violence is more complicated, insofar as it also practices a radical affirmation of the individual's sovereignty against the State. There is a long history to the profound complicity between modern art and modern, revolutionary, individual violence. In both cases, radical negation is equated with authentic creativity, whether in the area of art or politics.

Over and over again, this complicity results in a form of rivalry. Art and politics are connected in at least one fundamental respect: both are areas in which a struggle for recognition is being waged. As defined by philosopher Alexandre Kojève in his commentary on Hegel, this struggle for recognition surpasses the usual struggle for the distribution of material goods, which in modernity is generally regulated by market forces. What is at stake here is not merely that a certain desire be satisfied, but that it also be recognized as socially legitimate. Whereas politics is an arena in which various group interests have, both in the past and the present, fought for recognition, artists of the classical avant-garde have already contended for the recognition of all individual forms and artistic procedures that were not previously considered legitimate. In other words, the classical avant-garde has struggled to achieve recognition for all visual signs, forms, and media as legitimate objects of artistic desire and, hence, of representation in art. Both forms of struggle are intrinsically bound up with each other, and both have as their aim a situation in which all people with their various interests, as indeed all forms and artistic procedures more broadly, will finally be granted equal rights. And both forms of struggle are thought of, in the context of modernity, as being intrinsically violent.

Along these lines, American author Don DeLillo writes in his novel *Mao II* (1991) that terrorists and writers are engaged in a zero-sum game: by radically negating that which exists, both wish to create a narrative that would be capable of capturing society's imagination — and thereby altering society. In this sense, terrorists and writers are rivals and, as DeLillo notes, nowadays the writer is beaten hands down because today's media use the terrorists' acts to create a powerful narrative with which no writer can contend. But, of course, this kind of rivalry is even more obvious in the case of the artist as in the case of the writer. The contemporary artist uses largely the same media as the terrorist: photography, video, film. At the same time, it is clear than the artist cannot go further than the terrorist does, the artist cannot compete with the terrorist in the field of the radical gesture. In his manifesto of Surrealism, André Breton famously proclaimed the terrorist act of shooting into a peaceful crowd to be an authentically Surrealist, artistic gesture. Today, this gesture seems to be left far behind by recent developments. In terms of the symbolic exchange, operating by way of potlatch, as it was described by Marcel Mauss or by Georges Bataille, in the rivalry for radicality of destruction and self-destruction, art is obviously on the losing side.[1]

But it seems to me that this very popular way of comparing art and terrorism, or art and war, is fundamentally flawed. And now I will try to show where I see the fallacy. Art of the avant-garde, art of modernity, was iconoclastic. There is no doubt about that. But would we say that terrorism is iconoclastic? No, terrorism is, rather, iconophilic. The terrorist's or the warrior's image production has the goal of producing strong images—the images that we would tend to accept as being "real," as being "true," as being "icons" of the hidden, terrible reality that is the global political reality of our time. I would say: these images are the icons of the contemporary political theology that dominates our collective imagination. These images draw their power, their persuasiveness, from a very effective form of moral blackmail. After so many decades of modern and postmodern criticism of the image, of mimesis, of representation, we feel ourselves somewhat ashamed of saying that images of terror or torture are not true, not real. We cannot say that these images are not true, because we know that these images are paid for with a real loss of life—a loss of life that is documented by these images. Surrealist artist René Magritte could easily say that a painted apple is not a real apple or that a painted pipe is not a real pipe. But how can we say that a videotaped beheading is not a real beheading? Or that a videotaped ritual of humiliation in Abu Ghraib prison is not a real ritual? After so many decades of the critique of representation directed against the naïve belief in photographic and cinematic truth, we are now ready to accept certain photographed and videotaped images as unquestionably true, again.

That means: the terrorist, the warrior, is radical—but not in the same sense that the artist is radical. The terrorist does not practice iconoclasm. Rather, he wants to reinforce a general belief in the image, to reinforce the iconophilic seduction, the iconophilic desire. And he takes exceptional, radical measures to end the history of iconoclasm, to end the critique of representation. We are confronted here with a strategy that is historically quite new. Indeed, the traditional warrior was interested in those images that would be able to glorify him, to present him in a favorable, positive, attractive way. And we, of course, have accumulated a long tradition of criticizing and deconstructing such strategies of pictorial idealization. But the pictorial strategy of the contemporary warrior is a strategy of shock and awe. It is a pictorial strategy of intimidation. And it is, of course, only possible after the long history of modern art producing images of angst, cruelty, disfiguration. The traditional critique of representation was driven by a suspicion that there must be something ugly and terrifying hidden behind the surface of the conventional, idealized image. But the contemporary warrior shows us precisely that — this hidden ugliness, the image of our own suspicion, of our own angst. And precisely because of that, we feel ourselves immediately compelled to recognize these images as being true. We see things that are as bad as we expected them to be — maybe even worse. Our worst suspicions are confirmed. The hidden reality behind the image is shown to be as ugly as we expected it to be. So, we have a feeling that our critical journey has come to its end, that our critical task is completed, that our mission as critical intellectuals is accomplished. Now the truth of the political has revealed itself — and we can contemplate the new icons of contemporary political theology without a need to go further, because these icons are terrible enough by themselves. And so, it is sufficient to comment on these icons — it no longer makes any sense to criticize them. That explains the macabre fascination that finds its expression in many recent publications dedicated to the images of the War on Terror, which are emerging on the both sides of the invisible front.

That is why I don't believe that the terrorist is a successful rival of the modern artist by being even more radical than the artist. Rather, I think that the terrorist or the anti-terrorist warrior, with their embedded image-production machines, are the enemies of the modern artist because they try to create images that have a claim to be true and real — beyond any criticism of representation. These images of terror and war were in fact proclaimed by many of today's authors as signs of the return of the real — as visual proof of the end of the critique of the image as it was practiced in the last century. But I think that it is too early to give up this critique. Of course, the images about which I am speaking have some elementary, empirical truth: they document certain events and their documentary value can be analyzed, investigated, confirmed, or rejected. There are some technical means to establish whether a certain image is empirically true or if it is simulated, modified, or falsified. But we have to differentiate between this empirical truth or the empirical use of an image as, let's say, judicial evidence, and its symbolic value inside the media economy of symbolic exchange.

The images of terrorism and counterterrorism that circulate permanently in the networks of contemporary media, and which have become almost inescapable for the contemporary television viewer, are not primarily shown in the context of an empirical, criminal investigation. They have a function of showing something more than this or that concrete, empirical incident. They produce universally valid images of the political Sublime. The notion of the Sublime is associated in the first place with its analysis by Immanuel Kant who used, as examples of the Sublime, images of Swiss mountains and sea tempests. Or with the essay by Jean-François Lyotard on the relationship between the avant-garde and the Sublime. But, actually, the notion of the Sublime originates in Edmund Burke's treatise on notions of the Sublime and the Beautiful — and there Burke uses as an example of the Sublime the public beheadings and tortures that were common in the centuries before the Enlightenment. But we should also not forget that the reign of the Enlightenment itself was introduced by the public event of mass beheadings by guillotine in the center of revolutionary Paris. In his *Phenomenology of Spirit* (1807), Hegel wrote that this exposure created true equality among people because it made it perfectly clear that no one could claim any longer that their death had any higher meaning. During the nineteenth and twentieth centuries, the massive depoliticization of the Sublime took place. Now, we are experiencing the return not of the Real, but of the political Sublime — in the form of the repoliticization of the Sublime. Contemporary politics does not represent itself as Beautiful anymore — as even the totalitarian states of the twentieth century still did. Instead, contemporary politics represents itself as Sublime again — as ugly, repelling, unbearable, terrifying. And even more: all the political forces of the contemporary world are involved in the ever-increasing production of the political Sublime, by competing for the strongest, most terrifying image. It is as if Nazi Germany were to advertise itself using the images of Auschwitz, or the Stalinist Soviet Union using images of the Gulag. Such a strategy is new — but not as new as it might seem to be.

The point that Burke had originally tried to make is precisely this: even a terrifying, Sublime image of violence is still merely an image. Even an image of terror is produced, staged — and can be aesthetically analyzed in terms of critique of representation. This kind of criticism does not entail any lack of morality.

The moral dimension relates to the individual, empirical event that is documented by a certain image. But the moment an image begins to circulate in media networks and acquires the symbolic value of being a representation of the political Sublime, it can be subjected to art criticism just like any other image. This art criticism can be a theoretical one. But it can also be a criticism by the means of art itself—as became a tradition in the context of modernist art. It seems to me that this kind of criticism is already taking place in the art context, but I would not like to name names at the moment because it would bring me away from the immediate goal of this essay, which consists of a diagnostics of the regime of image production and distribution in contemporary media. I would only like to point out that the goal of a contemporary critique of representation should be a double one. First of all, this critique should be directed against all kinds of censorship and suppression of images that would prevent us from being confronted with the reality of war and terror. And this kind of censorship is, of course, still here. This kind of censorship, which legitimizes itself by the defense of "moral values" and "family rights," can, of course, be applied to the coverage of wars that take place today—and which sanitize their representation in the media. But, at the same time, we are in need of critique that analyzes the use of these images of violence as new icons of the political Sublime, and of the symbolic and even commercial competition for the strongest image.

It seems to me that the art context is especially appropriate for this second kind of criticism. The art world seems to be very small, closed, and even irrelevant compared to the power of today's media markets. But, in reality, the diversity of images circulating in the media is highly limited compared to the diversity of contemporary art. Indeed, in order to be effectively propagated and exploited in commercial mass media, images need to be easily recognizable for a broad target audience. This makes mass media extremely tautological. The variety of images circulating in mass media is, therefore, vastly more limited than the range of images preserved in museums of modern art or produced by contemporary artists.

Since Duchamp, modern art has practiced an elevation of "mere things" to the status of artworks. This upward movement created an illusion that being an artwork is something higher and better than being simply real, being a mere thing. But, at the same time, modern art went through a long period of self-criticism in the name of reality. The term "art" was used in this context as an accusation, as a denigration. To say that something is "mere art" is an even greater insult than saying that it is a mere object. The equalizing power of modern and contemporary art works both ways — it valorizes and devalorizes at the same time. And that means: to say that, on the symbolic level, the images produced by war and terror are merely art is not to elevate or sanctify them but, rather, to criticize them.

The fascination with the images of the political Sublime that we can now watch almost everywhere can be interpreted as a specific case of nostalgia for a masterpiece, for a true, real image. The media — and not the museum, not the art system — seems to now be the place where the longing for such an overwhelming, immediately persuasive, genuinely strong image can be expected to be satisfied. We have here a certain form of a reality show that can claim to represent political reality itself — in its most radical forms. But this claim can only be sustained by the fact that we are not able to practice the critique of representation in the context of the contemporary media. The reason for that is quite simple: the media shows us only the image of what happens now. In contrast to the mass media, art institutions are places of historical comparison between past and present, between an original promise and the contemporary realization of this promise and, thus, they possess the means and possibilities to be sites of critical discourse. Every such discourse needs a comparison, needs a framework and a technique of comparison. Given our current cultural climate, art institutions are practically the only places where we can actually step back from our own present and compare it with other historical eras. In these terms, the art context is almost irreplaceable because it is particularly well suited to critically analyze and challenge the claims of the media-driven zeitgeist. Art institutions are places where we are reminded of the whole history, of the critique of representation, and of the critique of the Sublime — so that we can measure our own time against this historical background.

1 See: Marcel Mauss, *The Gift: Forms and Functions of Exchange in Archaic Societies* (New York: Norton, 1967); and Georges Bataille, *The Accursed Share: An Essay on General Economy*, trans. Robert Hurley, vol. 1: *Consumption* (New York: Zone Books, 1991).

Art in the Anthropocene: Apprehending Abstracted Crises, Thickly

Paul James & Brad Haylock

The planet is facing manifold crises that are fundamental, comprehensive, and abstracted from the senses. This sensory abstraction, compounded by the non-palpable accumulation of risks, complicates any artistic practice that would seek to apprehend these crises. How, for example, is an artist to represent climate change adequately in relation to its consequences when our knowledge of the process is mediated by statistics, indicators, and monitoring technologies? What images can be used to condense the meaning of the Sixth Extinction when it is a process of moving toward the end, for all time, of multiple categories of being?

Articulating the contours of this condition can begin in written form, by describing how human action over the past half-century has been engaged in interrogating and reconstituting the existential foundations of nature and culture. Against the historical backdrop of many cultures that, for millennia, lived within the limits of the natural world, we can document how, amplifying a more recent and continuing sense of nature as a resource to be exploited, technoscience is now being used to fundamentally remake the elemental constituents of nature. This confluence of forces, the latest stage of the Anthropocene, goes beyond consequential human impact and can be described as a Great Unsettling of both the human and planetary condition.[1] From events such as the splitting of the atom in 1945, which set up the risk of nuclear winter, scientific inquiry has gone deeper into the basis of material existence than ever before: fermions and bosons meet quarks and leptons. Deoxyribonucleic acid (DNA) sequences are harnessed by technoscience and, despite the prevalent language of sustainability, the hyper-exploitation of nature is now dominant. From the initial replication of DNA in a test tube in 1958 and the exploration of the possibilities of in vitro fertilization (IVF) in the 1960s, genetic engineering, screening, and editing are now remaking production and reproduction. We are now even working on genetically reengineering the coral of Australia's Great Barrier Reef in order to "save" it.

Fields as different as agriculture and obstetrics now meet each other on the terrain of machine-measurement and in vitro life-making. In a parallel process, we (humans) have extended our interrogation of the nature of culture in a way that relativizes the meaning of identity, sexuality, truth, knowledge, and emotion. In other words, describing events such as splitting the atom begins the task of pointing to the sources of the unsettling, but apprehending or communicating anything of its full complexity is a different matter entirely.

If that is how a writer might begin the task, then what of an artist? Here, we need to start with the question of the social role of art itself. Writing circa 1974, the late Australian artist, art critic, and theorist Donald Brook set out an influential account that remains compelling to this day:

1. Our apprehension of the world is active, not passive, and art displays an emergent apprehension;
2. Art is only incidentally and not essentially aesthetic, it is concerned with every kind of value and not particularly with beauty;
3. Art interrogates the status quo, it is essentially, and not incidentally, radical;
4. Art is experimental action, it models possible forms of life and makes them available to public criticism.[2]

There is no small irony in the fact that Brook's own life was roughly synchronous with the history of the technoscientific and planetary changes that characterize the present crises. Our argument in this chapter is that, in the context of these crises, the role of art has become increasingly complex—and not only for the artist who would seek to rise to Brook's call for art that is interrogative, radical, critical, and experimental, in the sense of being world-making. Art is caught between, on the one hand, the continuing importance of concrete representations of the world, and, on the other, a discontinuous generalizing abstraction of the social forces that make up this world.

It should be acknowledged that this then places a heavier burden on written interpretation. At the same time that processes unsettling the human condition have become increasingly materially abstracted — culturally, ecologically, economically, and politically — adequate explanations for the bases of these crises are now also increasingly stretched between empirical description and a required conceptual abstraction. Nevertheless, exploring such processes may be relatively more viable for writers than representing or evoking them is for artists. This is because writing has always been a process of abstraction and mediation,[3] while much artistic representation depends on a more direct repertoire of image-making, apprehension, and affect. What does it mean for artists when, although these crises bear back upon the senses in every way, they are not immediately available for sensory apprehension, except as the mediated outcome of abstracted explanation? What does it mean that they are processes rather than events or images?

Even if we can find event-markers, such as the bombing of Hiroshima or the birth of the first IVF baby, these events need interpretation and critique. As much as one might want to say, "I can feel climate change in the hotter sun upon my face," the phenomenal meaning of climate change is a *post-factum* nomination. The same can be said for the concept of "the Anthropocene." The process that names human impact upon the bedrock of the planet is not an event or even a series of events that can be comfortably captured in images or any other kind of representation or expression without textual support. Even the measurable and concrete markers of the Anthropocene exist below the level of immediate awareness: carbon dioxide cannot be smelled, radiation cannot be felt, and the most damaging of the microplastics are effectively invisible.

All of this means that critically minded artists today live in a different object-world than did Goya or even Picasso, and so despite deep continuities they need to do a different kind of work. To point to just one trope: artworks using polar bears as icons of the climate crisis certainly evoke emotions about extinction, but they do not come close to carrying the complexity of what they are intended to represent. For example, Judy Chicago's kiln-dried painting in glass of a stylized polar bear sitting on an ice floe (*Stranded*, from *The End: A Meditation on Death and Extinction*, 2016) depends for its full meaning on its written title and the words scratched on the glass beneath the image: "Every creature on the planet must be hoping that ... our time of awakening comes soon." Roland Barthes described this as "anchorage" — the process by which a reader is guided, by text, toward one interpretation of an image over others, whether by titles, captions, accompanying commentary, or indeed, we would add, by other paratexts.[4]

The common reliance on such textual anchorage by art that seeks to tackle the Anthropocene, particularly the ontological unsettling of the late Anthropocene, points to the radical complexity of the object in question. But we would gently depart from Barthes in two ways. The text that would do such anchoring need not appear on the same page or plane as the image itself. It might include commentary or criticism published elsewhere or elsewhen. And the non-verbal artifact that would be the object of such anchorage needn't be a picture — certainly not necessarily a photograph, which was the type of image in question in Barthes's essay — but might instead be an installation, a performance, a sound work, or any of the other forms or mediums, or combinations thereof, deployed by artists today.

In short, all modern and contemporary art — including abstract, conceptual, auditory, performance, and installation-based works, and their various outgrowths and hybrids — is complexly representational in a way that makes it difficult to adequately embody and project the meaning of a world where the dominant threats and processes have effectively become non-palpable and post-sensory. This, as we argue, makes writing about art, including writing by artists, increasingly important. Writing, including the titling of an artwork and writing within an artwork, allows for abstract connections to be made that would otherwise remain ineffable. It means that we can no longer afford the fay refusal of abstracted interpretation that earlier artists could. Picasso's statement about *Guernica* (1937), for example, that "this bull is a bull and this horse is a horse," is no longer intriguing. "If you give a meaning to certain things in my paintings," he says,

> *it may be very true*, but it is not my idea to give this meaning. What ideas and conclusions you have got I obtained too, but instinctively, unconsciously. I make the painting for the painting. I paint the objects for what they are.[5]

Artists are fooling themselves, and us, when they withdraw into this mystique of the concrete, the directly meaningful, and the palpable. This is not to suggest that it is now incumbent upon artists to *explain* their work. But artists and writers need to work together, we suggest, to develop a repertoire of representations and meanings that begin to address the Great Unsettling. Here, the notion of "working together" does not mean that artistic work and writing must be merged. It means, rather, that we need to address Picasso's consideration that "it may be very true," while maintaining the strengths of the different registers of writing and art, their different ways of working, and an understanding of different modalities of truth. In short, artists and writers alike need to think through the possibilities of representing meaning that currently eludes representation. And some of that work will be mutual.

In this chapter, we discuss a number of ways in which artists are attempting to depict the complexity of the world today. Our examples follow an analytical arc that runs from apprehending *issues* (in the work of Teresa Margolles and Forensic Architecture), through politically specific and affective projects that seek to apprehend *processes* through, for example, the gentle unmasking of the traces of global flows of goods and capital (Walead Beshty), or the documenting of objects and sites typically hidden from view (Taryn Simon), to artistic works that allow us to apprehend *conditions* (as in the work of Patricia Piccinini and Adrián Villar Rojas). It is this last approach that begins to bring the *infrathick* to its most generalized recognition. We suggest that Piccinini remains too much in the thrall of the Great Unsettling—like a two-headed deer caught in the headlights—to take us far beneath the phenomenal surface. Nevertheless, both Piccinini and Villar Rojas give us different ways of seeing this unsettling of the human and planetary condition.

Apprehending the all-but-impossible-to-represent: the *infrathick*

To conceptually capture this abstracted *material* process, one that has been dematerialized only as an object relation, we first turn to Marcel Duchamp's notion of the *infrathin*, an elusive and allusive concept that points to a relational field that can be felt but not quite articulated. The *infrathin* might be described as "the most minute of intervals, or the slightest of differences."[6] Holding that the *infrathin* cannot be defined per se, Duchamp offers only examples of it, the best known of which are "the warmth of a seat (which has just been left)" and the whistling sound made by the brushing together of velvet pant legs as one walks.[7] The concept of the *infrathin* names the liminal traces—the slightest of signifiers at the very limits of perception—of some other thing that is itself infinitesimally small, or subliminally fleeting, or both. There is an echo of the problem of the representability of the Sublime, but, in the case of the *infrathin*, words do not suffice not because the object is so vast, but because it is so slight.

If Duchamp is seeking to describe that which *can be perceived* (however faintly) *but not articulated*, we are talking about something at the other end of the spectrum. His is a phenomenology of instants and interfaces. Ours is an ontology of abstracted relations, in this case disruptions to the fabric of planetary existence. The one: that which can be felt but not named. The other: that which can be named but not felt. Where Duchamp is concerned with fleeting moments, chance encounters, and the singular qualities of things, all too slight or too specific to be fully articulated, we are concerned conversely with phenomena that evade perception because they are too vast, too great in scale, duration, and consequence. These abstracted relations cannot be felt directly except in their instantiation, where each instance is not an expression of the whole, but where naming the whole brings the instantiations into relation for us.

In more concrete terms, an image of a polar bear on an ice floe does not, for example, necessarily express climate change or the Anthropocene, but, in the context of a researched, documented, and named process called "climate change," the symbol of the stranded polar bear as a climate victim can be called into cultural existence. At the same time (and in contrast to Duchamp's *infrathin*), these very real disjunctures *can* be researched and articulated in words—we do so, for example, in concepts such as "the Anthropocene," "climate change," or "the Sixth Extinction." Further, for Duchamp, the *infrathin* is an ineffable moment, whereas what we are seeking to elucidate here is a patterned process that lies *beneath* the surface of phenomenal experience—*infra*, but not thin. Taking all of this into account and drawing on Duchamp's concept, we twist it around to seek to understand the *infrathick*—that is, the deeply embedded contemporary substratum that is all but impossible to represent without a framing conceptual abstraction.[8] Comparisons to the Sublime are relevant, inasmuch as that concept points to suprasensible things, and ominously so, but the suprasensible object of our concern is unlike the archetypal figures of the Sublime in two important ways. Ours is not cosmological, nor nature itself, but the congealed constellation of human action upon nature — the concreted history of the natural-artificial. Its consequence, by now, is deeply ontological, and so equal, at least, to the most diabolical of other-than-human phenomena. Yet, while this is a threat categorically unlike any previously known, it is intensely both imminent and immanent, thus upsetting the classic dialectic of immanence and transcendence.

Comparing earlier forms of existential art

The reference to the Sublime takes us deeper into elaborating the meaning of the *infrathick*, but it also allows us to offer a clearer sense of historical difference. Modern and contemporary art, particularly that which is concerned with human existence, faces a chasm between representation and meaning in evoking the Great Unsettling — across which, we suggest, the entwining of writing and art can offer a bridge. This was not always so in the history of representation, and writing was not always so central to lay knowledge of the meaning of existence. A brief excursus into a different dominant ontological formation, when ways of seeing were constitutively different, offers some insight into the uniqueness of the present chasm between representation and meaning. Integral to *traditional* cosmological ways of seeing was the belief that the physical act of seeing was itself a means of knowing, including knowing the transcendental. Seeing — that is, the embodied act of visual connection between a viewer and an object, including a work of art — could in itself conjure meaning and constitute understanding. One of the most influential traditional theories of this process was Augustine's three modes of vision: *visio corporalis*, embodied seeing through the external senses; *visio spiritualis*, vision by means of the imagination; and *visio intellectualis*, vision that allows us to contemplate God. Medieval theologians added a fourth mode of seeing beyond Augustine's three that underlines our point: the *anagogical*, or ascent to transcendental contemplation *through images* as they relate to the unseen.[9]

Neither writing nor reading was the primary mode of apprehension for many people in the medieval to Renaissance period. But even for those illiterate souls who could never read the scripture nor understand their Latin-speaking priests — hidden, as priests often were, behind rood screens that were covered in images and icons — the movement from *visio corporalis* to *visio spiritualis* was sufficient to understand the ineffable in profound ways. Even the illiterate knew the stories. They lived within an integrated and communicable cosmology. Like Moses gazing upon the burning bush (*visio corporalis*), the laity could look at sacred representations and discern their meanings.

In this historical and cosmological context, non-readers could understand even an inventive artwork such as Hieronymus Bosch's *The Last Judgment* (c. 1482), which appeared to break narrative rules and iconographic conventions. In Bosch's representation of the Apocalypse, the horror of the end times is evoked by reversals and *new* creations, hybrid monsters standing in lizard legs, wearing clothes, and tormenting naked humans. These creatures are the center of a spiritual narrative of twists and turns that encouraged viewers to attend closely not only to what an image depicted, but also, reflexively, to how they themselves navigated the image.[10] This is reinforced by the form of the artwork. From the physical opening of the triptych — noting that the panels of *The Last Judgment* were often closed, with St James the pilgrim traveler depicted on their outside surface — viewers knew that they were traveling from the Garden of Eden on the left to Hell on the right. This spatial movement was part of a well-understood way of reading temporally, and the travel called for an active navigation along different paths where persons could make choices:

> At the very left, in the center of the center panel, a hair's breadth above the place where the viewer's eye enters the image, we see something not depicted anywhere elsewhere in the triptych: salvation. An angel, feathery wings raised behind him, surreptitiously leads a single, naked human man back towards the Garden in the left-hand panel. The presence of the angel and his human charge make one thing strikingly clear: salvation is possible. This moment raises far more questions than it seems to answer, both temporally and morally, especially considering that a few paces behind the angel, a demon aims an arrow at the man's back, suggesting that a moment's lapse will (again) result in a lost Eden.[11]

Three centuries later, classically modern realist artworks continued to remain explicable to lay viewers without heavy anchorage in written explanation. There is no doubt that writing had, by the nineteenth century, become important—from titles, exhibition notes, and announcements of sale to reviews and other commentary—yet, significantly, the subjects of these works remained explicable in terms of the events or objects they represented, even as the artists symbolically extended the meaning of the works beyond the immediate event or drew on earlier cosmological icons. Francisco Goya's *Third of May* (1814) depicts a firing squad of Napoleon's invading army about to kill a Spanish laborer. The painting is deeply symbolic in its references, and although it was painted six years after the event, it would have remained explicable and present to its contemporary Catholic and Spanish viewers. The light shining on the Spanish laborer is reminiscent of the illumination of a saint (from the light of a lamp); the laborer raises his arms in the configuration of a person being crucified. His right hand is marked by a stigmata, a wound such as that which Christ suffered when nailed to the cross. Yet, for all that, the painting is brutally ordinary. It is rough. The man about to be killed is anonymous. Central to the painting, he looks directly at his executioners, while their eyes are not visible. This is telling in culturally specific ways, but we also we know that this simple fact is important to Goya, because in an earlier series of eighty aquatint etchings, *Los Caprichos* (1799), he depicted a world turned upside down, in which the blindness of those who need to see is a recurrent theme.[12] It is thus seemingly no coincidence that Goya chose to launch *Los Caprichos* not in a gallery or a bookshop, as was the norm, but in a pharmacy at 1 Calle del Desengaño (1 Disenchantment Street), Madrid. And he chose the day of the publication as Ash Wednesday, 1799, the last day of the last carnival of the century.[13] In other words, he was depicting a world in upheaval, this time through satire. He knew that his local viewers would know this. The time and place spoke to it.

A century after that, Pablo Picasso's *Guernica* (1937), carrying a number of representative and symbolic lines to Goya's *Third of May*, again responds to a world in upheaval. This time the painting is more abstract representationally, but it continues to use an event as its point of grounding: the suffering of people and animals in the aerial saturation-bombing of a Spanish village on market day, April 26, 1937. The image is bathed in light from two sources, with Goya's lamp overshone by a large eye, a lashed sun with an electric light bulb as its filamented pupil.[14] However, the painting is more symbolically abstract than the *Third of May*, in the sense that it does not describe the literal outcome of bombs. The bull and the horse are rendered semi-abstractly, and the painting contains nothing that directly relates to the town of Guernica, except its paratextual name. Beyond the content of the painting, Picasso had also himself been physically displaced (he would never again visit Spain after 1934 — Fascism intervened). Painting *Guernica* in 1937 in Paris, he was responding to written reports of the massacre in French newspapers and pamphlets. Forty years later, the moment is still in his thoughts: "That death could fall from heaven on so many, right in the middle of a rushed life, has always had meaning for me."[15]

For all of Goya's or Picasso's artistic brilliance, their work was universalized from particular events and places. On the one hand, they still had a cosmology of meaning to work through and against. On the other, the conditions they described did not need post-sensory digital modeling to give shape to the upending of life-worlds. Their time and place spoke to it. If it is true to say that the planet and the human condition are now undergoing a Great Unsettling, characterized by processes that are increasingly materially abstracted and thus not available to the senses except as the figurative expressions of abstracted explanations rendered by scientists and social critics, then what does this mean for artistic representation? It means that existential *political* art has a different object, and so needs to do a different kind of work. Contemporary political art can still draw upon the kinds of repertoires of images and iconographies of meaning that Goya and Picasso drew upon — it has to — but in attempting to represent the unrepresentable it has a much more difficult task than depicting the pain associated with attacks upon particular bodies. The following sections follow this process through the work of some important contemporary artists who follow Donald Brook's call for socially critical art.

Apprehending issues

The artistic practice of apprehending issues is a key orientation of political art, and its remit potentially extends far beyond the didactic or immediate. The practitioners we discuss here as leading exemplars, Teresa Margolles and Forensic Architecture, have very concrete reference points, namely violence or conflict in specific regional and national contexts. Their focus principally lies with the specific issues they document, even as their work points to contemporary global challenges or a more general human condition. In their works, however, we find important examples of the ways in which networks of power and otherwise unseen events can be rendered visible, and the ways in which the written word, as textual anchorage, can support such apprehension.

Mexican artist Teresa Margolles deploys strategies of minimalism and conceptualism, but with a political inflection. Margolles's work tackles death and violence, specifically that related to drug trafficking. While her earlier work was characterized by graphic imagery, much of her later work is extremely subtle yet extraordinarily powerful, confronting viewers with the physical residue of death and violence in ways that are not immediately apparent. In Margolles's work, the written word plays an important role. Words rarely appear in the works themselves, but they would be all but illegible without titles, lists of materials on didactic plaques, or room sheets with explanatory notes. The *World Drug Report* of 2009 observes that the international drug trade had by then already fostered "a criminal market of macro-economic dimensions that uses violence and corruption to mediate between demand and supply."[16] In the performance work *Limpieza* (Cleaning), part of Margolles's exhibition *¿De qué otra cosa podríamos hablar?* (What else could we talk about?) at the 2009 Venice Biennale, silent figures mop the floor at regular intervals throughout the day. An innocuous act, perhaps, but for the fact that the mop buckets are filled — so the didactic texts tell us — not with a cleaning solution but with water obtained by humidifying fabrics previously used to absorb fluids from the ground at crime scenes in different cities in northern Mexico.

The audience thus faces a moral conundrum that is itself a part or an end of the work: to continue through the exhibition, a viewer must walk across a floor that is damp with the residue of dirt and victims' blood. The thin film has the viscosity of an *infrathick* moment. Of course, one quickly realizes that this is not the first time the work has been performed in this space — the floor you are standing on has already been "cleaned" in this way, and so you are already implicated. The experience of this "cleaning," which is anything but, confronts the viewer with the darkest side of the international drug trade, and makes palpable the profound inequalities between wealthier countries, where drugs are consumed, and the Global South, where they are mostly produced and where their production and trafficking are characterized by violence. In the same moment, the consumptive and extractive qualities of art spectatorship, and of other commodities in the Global North, are also drawn into view.

Another work, concealed in an inconspicuous wall safe, is imperceptible in this exhibition but for its textual plaque: *Ajuste de Cuentas* (Settling the Score), a series of pieces of jewelry encrusted not with precious stones but with fragments of shattered car window glass, collected from the site of a car-to-car shooting, a retributive murder, in Culiacán, a city in northwestern Mexico. These and other works by Margolles unmask global flows of goods and power, but the economy in question here is a particularly dark one.

Forensic Architecture is a research agency led by Eyal Weizman, based at Goldsmiths, University of London. Although not an artistic practice per se, Forensic Architecture often exhibits its work in cultural institutions, and so is relevant here. As its name suggests, Forensic Architecture uses techniques of spatial and architectural analysis as tools of inquiry, specifically to investigate human rights violations. The work of Forensic Architecture is presented not only in exhibitions and publications but also in courtrooms and tribunals; the agency is commissioned by and collaborates with partners including branches of the United Nations and various human rights organizations. One of the agency's investigations, *Drone Strike in Miranshah*, first published in 2014, analyses a 2012 drone strike in the town of Mīrānshāh (or Mīrāmshāh), the administrative headquarters of North Waziristan, Pakistan.[17] Working with documentary footage that was smuggled out of the besieged region and later aired on MSNBC, the investigation geolocates and reconstructs, as an architectural model, a ruined two-story building and, in greater detail, the ground-floor room in it in which four people were reportedly killed. The model of the room allows a detailed analysis of events: by studying the blast pattern of shrapnel on the walls, the Forensic Architecture team deduced the precise location that the missile detonated—167 cm above floor level—and so ascertained that the munition was a delay-fuse missile, likely a "Romeo" Hellfire II AGM-114R. The "shadows," where the walls are not damaged by shrapnel, reveal the probable locations of the victims.

Along the way, the investigation also draws attention to the political dimensions of the regulation of imaging technologies:

civilian satellite imagery is limited to a resolution of 50 × 50 cm per pixel—too coarse for a person to be seen from above. The hole in a building caused by the penetration of munitions commonly carried by drones is also smaller than this, so the traces of a drone strike are invisible in non-military satellite images. Created at 1:1 scale in an exhibition space, the reconstruction of the room allows us to appreciate the physical scale of the missile, the angle of its entry, the intensity of the blast, and the traces of lives lost. By experiencing the reconstruction of the room complete with supporting images, videos, and textual materials in an exhibition, we come to understand the specific events examined in this investigation, as well as Forensic Architecture's methodology. More importantly, we come to better understand the horrors of modern warfare, which are otherwise abstracted by fleeting or partisan reportage.

Apprehending processes

We now move to discuss the work of artists who seek to represent broader *processes* by focusing upon particular material expressions of those processes. How, for example, does an artist represent globalizing digital capitalism or the trade transversals of the commodities that have taken over our existential hopes and dreams? Here, the works of Walead Beshty and Taryn Simon provide telling examples and, in both cases, written anchorage is integral to their representations.

Makers' marks or brand names were once enough to signal the place of a thing's manufacture, but, because of the globalization and multilayered outsourcing of production in the twentieth century, country-of-origin labeling has become the norm on goods of all types. (A study of these epithets over time, from "made in Japan" to "made in China," "made in Bangladesh" to "made in Cambodia," and so on, would be a telling history of flows of trade and power in the past hundred years.) The globalization of trade is nothing new, and the global movement of goods, and the implications of this, barely register in the lived experience of consumers today, concealed as they are behind sophisticated service design and the speed of airfreight. The ease with which a product might today circumnavigate the globe is a phenomenon equally prosaic and mysterious, but it also warrants unmasking and reflection, on account of the carbon footprint of such practices, and because long supply chains and geographic distance allow unsavory production processes, including labor-rights abuses and unsustainable manufacturing, to be more easily concealed.

Looking to contemporary artistic practice, we find works that peel away the apparent seamlessness of global logistics and so encourage us to reflect upon such matters. London-born, Los Angeles–based artist Walead Beshty's *FedEx boxes* (2005–14) is a series of sculptures, each comprising one of the eponymous logistics firm's standardized shipping boxes and a cuboid of toughened glass sized to fit precisely inside. The works are sent from the artist's studio to the gallery or museum where they are to be displayed. Upon arrival, the glass forms are carefully removed from their boxes, having invariably acquired cracks, chips, or shattered corners in transit. The battered glass sculptures are displayed atop their weathered and stickered boxes — a deceptively simple formal exercise that makes visible the oft-hidden physicality of the global movement of material goods. What is important here is the means by which Beshty's FedEx works allow such movement to be apprehended. A list of statistics enumerating the scale of global trade would give a certain picture of the situation, but in an age of information overload such figures might be all but meaningless, or at least eminently forgettable. Beshty's works, by contrast, afford an affective apprehension of the improbable ease/friction with which material things today travel. They are human-scale, and so we are drawn into an empathic relation with the objects — we can imagine what it would feel like if our bodies were to incur those impacts that cracked the glass just so. In this way, these works make otherwise abstract global processes legible.

In her photographic series *An American Index of the Hidden and Unfamiliar* (2007), American artist Taryn Simon artfully documents objects and sites typically hidden from view, each of which is central to or strongly emblematic of larger, complex, and often challenging social, political, and economic phenomena. In one photograph, we see the still-glowing frame of a hot-forged Smith & Wesson revolver during production — specifically a .44 Magnum, an iconic weapon made famous by Clint Eastwood in the movie *Dirty Harry* (1971). This image, deceptively simple at face value, evokes the full complexity of the tension between the constitutional right to bear arms in the United States and the nation's persistently high rates of gun violence. In another photograph, an apparently abstract composition, black dots are surrounded by a bright blue glow against a dark background. This captivating image could be a digital rendering or a compositional exercise, until we read that we are in fact looking at submerged capsules of nuclear waste at Hanford, a former plutonium production complex turned waste-storage facility in Washington State, one of the most contaminated sites in the US.

Each of the dozens of photographs in Simon's series, all equally complex and compelling, is accompanied by an extended caption of approximately 150 words, which tells the story behind the image. *An American Index of the Hidden and Unfamiliar* is commonly exhibited as a series of framed prints, but the series is also available in full as a hardcover book. In his foreword to the book, Salman Rushdie rightly notes that "Simon uses text as few photographers do, not merely as title or caption but as an integral part of the work."[18] Although the series is US-centric, as its title suggests, a number of images point to otherwise abstract global phenomena. Among these is an exceedingly plain photograph of orange cables emerging from two holes in a floor and running up a wall. The floor is covered in beige linoleum tiles; the off-white wall is otherwise featureless. The photograph's title, however, begins to reveal what we are looking at: *Transatlantic Sub-marine Cables Reaching Land, VSNL International, Avon, New Jersey* (2007). The caption tells us more: these are underwater fiber-optic cables capable of transmitting more than sixty million simultaneous voice conversations; they stretch from Saunton Sands in the UK to the coast of New Jersey before emerging directly into the headquarters of VSNL International; VSNL is one of fourteen operators of submarine cable systems connected to the continental US; and such cables link all continents except Antarctica.[19]

Simon's photograph reveals part of the otherwise invisible material substrate of contemporary communication technologies. "The point about these cables," Rushdie observes, "is that you might have guessed that such things probably existed but you almost certainly had no notion of where they were, or how many, or how thick, or what colour, until you saw this picture."[20]

Among the many photographs in Simon's *American Index* series, two others warrant discussion here, since they depict otherwise abstract phenomena and processes characteristic of the Anthropocene. In the work *White Tiger (Kenny), Selective Inbreeding, Turpentine Creek Wildlife Refuge and Foundation, Eureka Springs, Arkansas* (2007), we see a big cat who, the caption reveals, has mental retardation and debilitating physical abnormalities. "Due to his deep-set nose, he has difficulty breathing and closing his jaw, his teeth are severely malformed and he limps from abnormal bone structure in his forearms."[21] The caption goes on to tell us about the rarity of white tigers in nature, that "quality" white tigers fetch high prices at market, that all white tigers in the US are the result of selective inbreeding, and that this inbreeding results in high rates of birth defects and mortality among infants. The typically imperceptible excesses of greed-fueled attempts by humans to control nature are thus given a name and a tigrine face.

In another image, mysterious and virtually monochromatic, an almost spherical white vessel on a white support is surrounded by a white haze that might be smoke or might be steam. A silver hose, connected to the vessel, snakes out of the frame toward an unknown origin or destination. This photograph, *Cryopreservation Unit, Cryonics Institute, Clinton Township, Michigan* (2007), shows us the vessel in which the bodies of Rhea and Elaine Ettinger, respectively the mother and first wife of cryonics pioneer Robert Ettinger, lie in cryostasis. Cryonics entails freezing the bodies of the recently deceased in anticipation of advances in medicine that will, at an unknown future time, enable the reversal of death and aging. The caption to this image tells that, as of 2007, the Cryonics Institute, which is licensed as a cemetery in the state of Michigan, held seventy-four legally dead human patients and forty-four legally dead pets in cryopreservation.[22] Cryonics is one of the more audacious practices that would attempt to subject nature to human design. The titles of Robert Ettinger's books — *The Prospect of Immortality* (1962) and *Man into Superman* (1972) — point to the essence of the project of cryonics, but it is Simon's photograph, together with its title and caption, that renders most legible this extreme example of the technoscientific imagination.

Apprehending conditions

Our final category, that of apprehending *conditions*, takes us closest to the *infrathick*. But in choosing two very different artists, Patricia Piccinini and Adrián Villar Rojas, we are also exploring the limits of such apprehension.

In the work of Australian artist Patricia Piccinini, we find a variety of perspectives on the abstracted conditions of the Anthropocene. Across her practice to date, we witness a trajectory from latent technological optimist to detached observer of the arresting corporeality of what might be a near-future posthuman condition. The work *Car Nuggets: They're Good for You* (1998) and the later series *Car Nuggets GL* (2001) are sets of fiberglass sculptures, roughly spherical and roughly a meter in diameter, finished in high-gloss auto paint. While these nuggets are manifestly non-functional, their genus can be discerned from their lines and curves: they are abstract reductions of the styling cues of automotive design. The later series is a souped-up version of the earlier work — each of the *GL* nuggets is finished with pearlescent or metalflake paint, airbrushed flames, pinstriping, or some other special treatment. Piccinini's artist statement for the 1998 work helps us to understand these objects: they "are to cars what Chicken Nuggets are to chickens."[23] They "are not miniature cars or even bits of cars welded together," she continues, "they are essence of car; they are lumps of carness."[24] The speculative collision of categories that we see in the *Car Nuggets* works extends into Piccinini's other works from the period, which more directly express the contemporary process of engendering technological life. *Truck Babies* (1999) is a pair of baby big rigs, stereotypically gendered, one pale pink and one pale blue — again, fiberglass sculptures with high-gloss finishes. Their features are variously shrunken or exaggerated. With oversized headlights-as-eyes, these eminently cute little lorries give tongue-in-cheek form to the social reproduction of animated technology. Here, however, we are prompted to ask a question: is this cuteness adorable, or does the adorable act mask a deeply unsettling technologization of social life and limit any critique of this process?

Whereas these early works by Piccinini are characterized by the anthropomorphization of technological artifacts, most of her work since is characterized by its counterpoint: a speculative vision of the artifacts of the technologization of the human. The question this work raises is also vexing. Can politically detached representation be expressed as empathy for the possible hybrid humanoid creatures of technoscience, or does such representation become empathetic compliance?

In *SO2* (2000), a series of digitally enhanced photographs, a posthuman creature of unknown species and origin punctuates otherwise everyday scenes. It has a body shape roughly akin to that of a squat crocodile, but it has humanlike Caucasian skin, mostly hairless, and long fingers and toes. We see it scurrying in the background as three young (human) boys practice kickflips in a parking lot; then we see it interacting with the young skaters, unthreateningly, seemingly simply curious about them, as they are about it. In another image, it sits prosaically in the front seat of a car alongside a human driver against a suburban backdrop—"waiting for Jennifer," the title of the photograph tells us. Consistent with the method of so many works of science fiction, Piccinini's *SO2* series synthesizes the fantastical and the mundane to compelling effect—the existence of this improbable other-than-human creature is made plausible when rendered in such quotidian settings. This "monster" has a hybrid form similar to those depicted by Hieronymus Bosch in *The Last Judgment*, but it is ontologically very different. Bosch's creatures are the imagined Others of our transcendental nightmares; Piccinini's synthetic organism is a kindred creature, a non-confrontational artifact of our imagined postmodern destiny.[25] Through Piccinini's work, we can apprehend a possible near future of contemporary bioengineering—and so too something of the present—but we are being asked to accept that future as one of cute-confronting diversity. There is no angel offering us an alternative path.

A similar logic runs through most of Piccinini's work since, with her imaginings becoming more lifelike from 2002 onward, in the form of life-size sculptures made of silicone, polyurethane, and hair. They depict life forms that are partly human and partly not, some evidently sentient, some seemingly not, but all of which wholly compel us to question our assumptions about the limits and values of humankind. In *Still Life with Stem Cells* (2002), a young human girl sits cross-legged on the floor, cradling one small, unidentifiable life form in one arm, resting her hand on another, watching a third, smiling, surrounded by a few more. These strange life forms have freckled, human-like skin and wrinkled flesh; parts of them are flabby, but elsewhere their skin is taut over bone structures that look like human spines, elbows, or kneecaps. *Shadowbat* (2019) hangs upside down by two toes that look like human fingers. This creature, too, has wrinkled Caucasian skin. Piccinini's writing tells us that all of her sculptures to date have the same skin, hair, and eye color as the artist.[26] *Shadowbat* is clearly sentient. It has the face of a human child, but with deep-set eyes, large irises, and huge ears. Its head, jowls, neck, shoulders, arms, back, buttocks, and legs are hirsute, but its wings, folded in front of its body, are hairless. Piccinini's sculptures, some almost human, some more markedly other-than-human, extrapolate a truth of our contemporary condition:

that is, almost no aspect of life remains untouched by human intervention. Did these creatures come about by accident or by design? Certainly, their representation points to the dissolution of the occidental division, cardinal for so many for so long, between humankind and nature. However, despite the apparent empathy for Otherness in Piccinini's work, there is no way out, no passage to an alternative Eden — we are either destined for a postmodern world of totalizing hybridity, or we, as the viewers of these works, are cast as unreconstructed modernists fearful of monsters or as having returned to the traditional Manichean world of angels and demons.

By comparison, when the Argentine sculptor Adrián Villar Rojas depicts hybrid creatures, he offers us an ontologically condensed but plural space of intersecting social forms — all-too-animal, all-too-human. He expresses a layered sense of fragile humanity and animality, a world in the end times that needs to find a different path to the future. Much of his work is monumental, and most of it is destroyed after its initial exhibition; other expressions of his work are small and all-but-invisible, based on regularized fleeting rituals that are not publicly announced or not open to the public. In *The Most Beautiful of All Mothers* (2015), pure white, life-size, fiberglass giraffes, wolves, and other creatures — even Picasso's bull — stand on concrete plinths in the Sea of Marmara, just south of Istanbul. It is a mutant ark of animals, clothed in the rich organic/inorganic fabric of other creatures and garbage recovered from the depths of the Bosporus by deep-sea divers.

Villar Rojas's installations depend upon their place in the world, including the place where they are viewed, whether it be the forest floor, the seascape, or the gallery in which an exhibition is located. *The Theater of Disappearance* (2017), for example, uses white and black nylon-printed and polyurethane CNC-milled reproductions of objects from The Metropolitan Museum of Art's permanent collection to make its own meaning. The place becomes like Goya's chemist shop in Disenchantment Street. Villar Rojas's material production of these objects links the once-ordered and catalogued set of human-made items to the contemporary condition of robotization and artificial intelligence. It then dislocates the objects, scattering them across banquet tables. Here, while living humans have left the space, their "presence" is felt in the left-behind objects of their creation, the statues they have made of themselves, and the empty chairs:

> Villar Rojas's installation at the Met is one of the more sublime visions of Armageddon. We don't see the fall of civilisation, just the apparent aftermath: replicas, or partial replicas, of almost a hundred objects from the museum's collection ... Arranged haphazardly across the Met's roof are several dinner tables, rendered in ghostly white, the remnants of a meal still evident, wine glasses overturned as if catastrophe has interrupted celebration. Artefacts that, downstairs, within the museum, have been carefully sorted chronologically, taxonomically and geographically, here intermingle with the aborted feast. The sad, petrified bodies of Pompeii are an obvious reference point. A knight reclines close to a vase. A replica of an otter sculpture stands near the edge of the roof. A thin layer of dust covers the entire installation.[27]

It is as if Villar Rojas is concerned to make apparent what we described earlier as "the concreted history of the natural-artificial." Another site-specific installation titled *Planetarium* (2015) takes up the entire interior of an abandoned ice factory in Khor Kalba, a remote part of the United Arab Emirates (UAE). Here, concrete is stratified with Kalba earth in massive pillars and slabs, mixed with bones, seashells, rocks, detritus, and waste—organic and synthetic—mostly collected from across the UAE. The exhibition spills beyond the main plaza of the building with tons of freshly produced compost forming rows of shoulder-high mounds. Viewers feel the warmth of the decomposition and hear the sound of insects in the soil. One viewer writes in her blog:

> An obnoxiously plastic-y running shoe, bits of fisherman's rope, a child's pink sweatshirt sleeve each were part of a living tower. I was particularly struck by the coolness of the air inside and the sound of birds singing through the open roof juxtaposed with the decaying feathered bodies of two finches laid reverently on the steps of a rectangular sculpture. Ants crawled across the garishly yellow feathers like tiny performance artists.[28]

The work that we want to finish with is *Mi Familia Muerta* (My Dead Family, 2009), a life-size sculpture of a whale. The massive creature is beached in Yatana Forest in Ushuaia, Patagonia, a region at the bottom of the world. The dead whale was finely detailed and made of dark, slate-colored clay that was not fired, making it vulnerable to the weather. (We write in the past tense because the whale has now gone — the carcass decayed and returned to the earth.) A student who made Rojas the subject of her thesis writes movingly about the artwork:

> Displaced from its natural habitat and left to disintegrate on the forest floor, the lifeless mammal in "Mi Familia Muerta" transformed the wooded site into a place of melancholic surrender. A victim of an illogical overlapping of ecosystems, its death was an evident result of its removal from a marine environment. The work's melancholic ambience was heightened by the connotations attached to this endangered species.[29]

Why is Villar Rojas's whale different from Judy Chicago's stranded polar bear? The dead figure of the whale was alive to us as its cracking clay was eaten by fungi and rain. The sculpture confronted us with the ruin of this world now, lying for its time in the forest as if it had always been there. It provided *anagogical* pathways to existential meaning for those with faith, and moments of thick reflection for those with none. Villar Rojas's creatures evoke empathy and mirth, shock, and suppressed revulsion. They have an emotional register that is emplaced and embodied while stretching out beyond their immediate effect. There is something about them that is thickly evocative of the threat of our extinction — and no less so once they are gone.

Propositions for rethinking the bases of artistic expression in these end times

Drawing this discussion to a close, we offer a few basic propositions, thinly. Art, even abstract and installation art, is representational in a way that makes it difficult to adequately embody and project understandings of a world in which the dominant threats and processes have become less palpable and more systematically abstract in their materiality. This makes writing about art, including writing by artists, increasingly important. Writing, including the entitling of an artwork, allows for abstract connections to be made that would otherwise remain ineffable. All art is representational of some aspect of the human or planetary condition, even if its object or methods are characterized by elision, allusion, affect, or abstraction. In other words, all art is a representation of the world, even if it is partial or anachronistic. Some art, however, evokes the complexity of the *infrathick* today. Writing about art contributes to our understandings of this existential unsettling. All of this means that artists and writers need to work together, without diminishing their different registers of engagement, to help foster the apprehension of abstracted crises.

1 Manfred B. Steger and Paul James, *Globalization Matters: Engaging the Global in Unsettled Times* (Cambridge: Cambridge University Press, 2019).

2 Donald Brook in *A Decade at the EAF: A History of the Experimental Art Foundation 1974–1984*, ed. Stephanie Britton (Stepney: The Experimental Art Foundation, 1984), 1. See also the 'About' page of the Australian Experimental Art Foundation (AEAF), archived at https://webarchive.nla.gov.au/awa/20160913143007/http://pandora.nla.gov.au/pan/122387/20160914-0000/aeaf.org.au/about/aboutaeaf.html, accessed December 14, 2020.

3 Walter Ong, *Orality and Literacy: The Technologizing of the Word*, (London: Methuen, 1982).

4 On anchorage, see: Roland Barthes, "The Rhetoric of the Image," in *Image/Music/Text*, ed. and trans. Stephen Heath (New York: Hill and Wang, 1977), 39–41. On paratexts, see: Gerard Genette, *Paratexts: Thresholds of Interpretation* (Cambridge: Cambridge University Press, 1997).

5 Ken Reker, Garry Harley, and Catherine Leisek, "The Intersection of Art and Politics," *Thought and Action*, vol. 33, no. 1 (2017): 69. Emphasis added.

6 Marjorie Perloff, *21st-Century Modernism: The "New" Poetics* (Malden, MA: Blackwell, 2002), 102.

7 Erin Manning, "For a Pragmatics of the Useless, or the Value of the Infrathin," *Political Theory*, vol. 45, no. 1 (2017): 99.

8 In proposing our notion of the "infrathick," we riff, too, on Clifford Geertz's "thick description," except that his rich and nuanced descriptions are ontologically thin. Clifford Geertz, "Thick Description: Toward an Interpretive Theory of Culture," in *The Interpretation of Cultures: Selected Essays* (New York: Basic Books, 1973), 3–30.

9 Cynthia Hahn, "Vision," in *A Companion to Medieval Art Romanesque and Gothic in Northern Europe*, ed. Conrad Rudolph, 2nd ed. (Hoboken: Wiley Blackwell, 2019).

10 Hannah Kagan-Moore, "The Journey through the Judgment: Affective Viewing and the Monstrous in Bosch's Vienna Last Judgment Triptych," *Preternature*, vol. 5, no. 2 (2016): 133–158.

11 Ibid., 151.

12 Andrew Schulz, "Satirizing the Senses: The Representation of Perception in Goya's *Los Caprichos*," *Art History*, vol. 23, no. 2 (2000): 153–181.

13 Victor I. Stoichita and Anna-Maria Coderch, *Goya: The Last Carnival* (London: Reaktion Books, 1999).

14 Robert Rosenblum, "Picasso's Disasters of War: The Art of Blasphemy," in *Picasso and the War Years: 1937–1945*, ed. Steven A. Nash (New York: Thames and Hudson, 1998).

15 Pablo Picasso in an interview with Simone Gauthier, 1967.

16 Antonio Maria Costa, "Preface," *World Drug Report 2009* (Vienna: United Nations Office on Drugs and Crime, 2009), 1.

17 See: https://forensic-architecture.org/investigation/drone-strike-in-miranshah, accessed December 14, 2020.

18 Salman Rushdie, "Foreword," in Taryn Simon, *An American Index of the Hidden and Unfamiliar* (Göttingen: Steidl, 2007), 8.

19 Simon, *American Index*, 63.

20 Rushdie, "Foreword," 5.

21 Simon, *American Index*, 55.

22 Ibid., 67. As of December 7, 2020, the Cryonics Institute website lists 173 "deanimated" patients in cryopreservation, mostly anonymous, presumably all human — the patient list appears not to have been updated since August 2018, and information regarding the number of pets in cryostasis seems not to be available. See: www.cryonics.org/ci-landing/patient-details/.

23 Patricia Piccinini, "Untitled," http://www.patriciapiccinini.net/archives/pp2/cc/text.htm (n.d.), accessed December 14, 2020.

24 Ibid.

25 Rosi Braidotti and Patricia Piccinini, "Your Place Is My Place: Rosi Braidotti in Conversation with Patricia Piccinini," https://www.patriciapiccinini.net/printessay.php?id=110, 2019, accessed December 14, 2020.

26 Patricia Piccinini, "Some Thoughts about My Practice" (2020), https://www.patriciapiccinini.net/printessay.php?id=112, accessed December 14, 2020.

27 Oliver Basciano, "Adrián Villar Rojas," *Art Review*, September 29, 2017.

28 http://dannawrites.com/the-abandoned-kalba-ice-factory-becomes-an-installation-site-for-sharjah-biennial-12/, accessed December 27, 2020.

29 Mina Juhn, *The Fiction of the Fabricated Ruin: Memory and History in the Work of Adrián Villar Rojas*, Honors Thesis in Art History (Wellesley, MA: Wellesley College, 2013), 12.

April to July 2020

Dan Fox

The time capsule

It was the first April of the pandemic. Lockdown had turned New York mute, save for the emergency sirens and birdsong. The city's galleries and museums were empty. Its morgues were full. The airplanes that took art professionals to do art business had stopped flying over my neighborhood. Fairs and exhibitions were canceled. All that was left to do was talk, which was fine since talking is something art professionals love to do. Curators broadcast online conversations with artists at home for Instagram TV, in which they asked earnest questions, such as: did the artists consider making kombucha to be part of their practice? And: are notions of solitude in art inherently political? Zoom conferences addressing Art and The Crisis were convened with the solemn urgency of United Nations emergency summits. A secular rosary was repeated: Art Is Necessary in Times Like These. Now More Than Ever. Artists Are Important. Now More Than Ever.

Industry people talked and industry people died. Industry people lost their jobs: visitor services staff, museum educators, security guards, janitors, art handlers, preparators, docents, studio managers, editors, and others already living one shove from the cliff edge of flat broke. Employees of commercial galleries were furloughed then fired. I fretted about writing gigs evaporating. Worrying about my finances in a field that feigns disinterest in money while chasing after it wasn't a novel feeling. But I was new to the freelance rollercoaster, and was therefore relieved when Megan and Brad emailed inviting me to contribute a chapter to this book. They wanted a personal view from quarantine. Thoughts on art writing and limbo. On whether criticism might suggest ways to think through the catastrophe. It was just three weeks into New York's lockdown, and the book was scheduled to be published more than a year later. My essay would be a time capsule for a changed world.

The same week that Megan and Brad's invitation arrived, an academic journal also asked me to write about art in These Uncertain Times. The journal was supported by two major institutions and yet somehow could not offer a fee. It is common in the visual arts to receive invitations to work for free. They come with cap-in-hand apologies about budgets, appeals to the higher calling of The Discourse, and a fairy dusting of flattery. But The Discourse is an expensive club to join. To survive as an art writer untethered to academia or another job, it helps to be wealthy, to be married to someone wealthy, or to be good at living on free coffee at exhibition press views. I wanted to ask the journal editors what they thought would happen if I invited a plumber to come and fix my leaking sink and told the plumber I had no money to offer but that I was deeply honored to enable their vital contribution to my apartment.

Megan and Brad had offered a fee for contributing to their book. Given the circumstances, they offered to pay half of it up front. I was taken by the decency of this gesture. As ideas for the essay came and went, I kept returning to it. I was noting all the heartfelt calls to support artists as the pandemic ate the economy. Noting the petitions against museum staff redundancies. Friends in other fields, in film and music, organized fundraisers to aid furloughed cinema employees and empty gig venues. Nobody was interested in helping art writers. Who supports the supporters, I wondered? I read an op-ed in *Artforum* authored by the people behind the Cinema Worker Solidarity Fund in New York:

> After years of thinking of the workplace as a "family," especially in the cultural sphere, we might wonder: In what family are members exiled from the clan the second they become liabilities to the household's bottom line?[1]

It felt beside the point to write about the value of criticism when so little value was placed on the people who wrote it.

I felt a tug of loyalty to my old profession. I say old, because I was not long out of a two-decade job as an editor and staff writer for *Frieze* and, since leaving, one of my goals had been to take a break from writing about art. I was burned out and looking for something new. Time to make way for people younger than me, people different to me. I now read art criticism only rarely. I got more sustenance out of novels and screenplays. Essays about anything but art.

It wasn't that I had fallen out of love with art, as happens to some who have been in the game too long. Nor had I taken a reactionary turn against it, another symptom of exhaustion. I even wanted to start making art again, something I had done before I was a writer. I'd enjoyed the process of making magazines. It had been an education. I admired my colleagues. Many freelance writers I worked with were an inspiration. I took pride in producing beautifully designed publications. Pay was lousy but regular, and I learned to write on the job, and I got to travel to places I never imagined I'd visit. I was wined and dined. Got to meet the best and the worst and the most absurd people in the field. Made friends for life. Unless you were born into a world of art and its cultured citizenry, the experience of getting to visit big galleries in big cities for a living was a gift.

The problem began when I noticed I was unable to see art anymore. Slowly, over a number of years, the view had become obscured by the growing industry. At a certain point, all that was visible to me when I visited an exhibition were careers in motion. Big white spaces hung with institutional politics and organized in line with reputation management and business networks. The system had become increasingly self-obsessed, convinced of its own importance in society. (Or self-conscious about accusations of inaccessibility, over-selling the case for its relevance.) The job of the editor-critic had always involved keeping one eye on the system's workings, on the trade audiences who bought advertising, provided advance information, and enabled access to artists. I knew and respected people who enjoyed the intrigues of the industry — tracking who worked where, deciphering the ley lines of influence and money. But the scene had come to mean more than the art. It's common to experience nostalgia for periods in life when everything felt exciting and full of potential, and I'm wary of suggesting that the art system was "better" when I signed up in my early twenties. It wasn't. I simply felt out of sync with what it had become. Misaligned with its priorities.

The ecology

It's hard to know where to start discussing my experiences as an art critic. Difficult to separate the act of writing from the art world in which it happened. "Art worlds" would be more accurate, for they encompassed a plurality of groups and interests, even if certain names and organizations got disproportionate attention. I can only describe my narrow, partial history. I worked at the noisy end of the anglophone art magazine trade, where the institutional sector met the art market met the grassroots-run-on-a-shoestring met the academy met the VIP trashset. Don't believe anyone who claims to know how the machine functioned.

Everyone had their clear sightlines and their blind spots. Nobody had a complete overview, no matter how plugged in they were. It was a snarl of tangled wires and jury-rigged circuitry.

It's impossible to talk about art criticism of the last twenty years without talking about what curating has done to it. It's the messianism that I remember most. In the early 2000s, upwardly mobile curators claimed their profession was going to save the world. Issues in urbanism, archives, philosophy, war, architecture, ecology, history, sociology, science, democracy, technology — you name it — could all be resolved with an exhibition in a small Belgian town, a symposium, and a smartly designed catalogue. Back then, truly endemic problems — sexism, racism, class — were swept into subcategories of exhibitions addressing vague concepts about the Global Contemporary Imaginary, or some other nebulosity presented with an impressionistic wash of seriousness. The world-saving was weighted toward Western Europe and North America. Even when Western curators said they were interested in notions of the Global South — and they were always "interested in notions of" something, the "notions of" providing a buffer from actually getting involved — I got the faint sense that it was only to prove how the Rest of World were fans of, say, European modernism or US Conceptualism, when the narratives were far more complex than that.

I witnessed professionals in the field proclaim, against all howling conflicts of interest, that critics had lost their power and that curators were now the best placed to write on art. Only they truly understood the artists because they'd curated their shows. I recall one evangelist lecturing me that only curators knew how to review other curators' exhibitions. Criticism would happen in heavy anthologies and at multiday conferences that the rest of us with full-time jobs had neither the time nor the money to attend. I noticed more hyphenates appearing in the pages of magazines. Artist-curators, curator-critics. I wondered if freelance curators writing reviews might be tempering what they wrote in order to preserve professional relationships. Old-school curators, who came to the job through scholarship rather than the post-grad curating course path, tended to be solid, sometimes excellent, critics. Many of the new-breed curators were terrible writers. I know this because I edited dozens of them when they wrote for *Frieze*, when their copy would come in weeks late, blitzed on jargon, addled with grandeur, with instructions that edits go through their assistants because they were too busy to answer an email themselves. My colleagues and I would wonder why we bothered, then our employers would remind us that these were now the power brokers.

As the world-saving middle managers enjoyed their imperial phase, the character of art publishing broadened. Printed matter bloomed: zines, artists' books, broadsides, chapbooks, pamphlets, comics. Reissues of out-of-print artists' writings. Hand-risographed books about forgotten activist collectives. Collections of ephemera. Poetry and fiction. Art books about rare art books. Small presses sprouted like daisies and book fairs became popular. Amid this genuine and welcome enthusiasm for independent publishing, a softer label, "art writing," crept in. The tag rendered it hard to generalize about "the state of criticism" because it was harder to establish what, specifically, was meant by "art writing," even if certain metrics were clear: that the field was predominantly male and overwhelmingly white.

The invisible writing work of editors — the scaffold literature of picture captions, pull-quotes, headlines, decks — provided a unifying tone for criticism published in magazines. Sober, cool, scholarly. But criticism was many things. It was done by art historians burrowing deep into their specialisms. Stalwart journalist-critics, at least those who still had columns in the dwindling number of newspapers with art sections, produced weekly reports from the latest shows. Market watchers crunched the numbers in auction analyses. This wasn't criticism but, like criticism, it revealed a lot about taste and economics. Artists wrote too, the best with imagination, lucidity, and wit. Magazine review sections featured intelligent writing by younger critics and curators at the start of their careers. Here you would also find the art-speak drones who reviewed shows in a plod-plod of deathly, exsanguinated language. (Why use one word when you could use three neologisms and a tautology instead?) They sat alongside the aspirationally world-weary, who affected to write like Fran Lebowitz or Gary Indiana but were never as funny and pithy. The professionally jaded shared space with hard theory types, from the "if it hurts it's good for you" school of sanctimony. They saw it as their duty to admonish everyone else for their complicity with the neoliberal hegemony. They were the sort who'd tell me with disdain that reviews in *Frieze* were "descriptive," as if describing an artwork was somehow beneath them, or didn't involve qualitative decisions. As if it was inconceivable that their description-free analysis of an end-game painting show in Cologne was incomprehensible to anyone who hadn't seen it.

There were the literary essayists — or the "belle-lettrists," as they were referred to by the hard theorists, who despised them for their bourgeois sentimentalism. As I was never much of a theory-head, I loved what they did. Here were writers who had cut their teeth on music, literature, or movies. They brought personal, experimental approaches to criticism. Writing that made me laugh, that gave permission to talk about art in a voice that didn't sound like it was being asphyxiated in a seminar room. I took lessons from music writers and from memoirists. Tried making short video essays that combined criticism with the moving image. I looked to novels that played with form; literature suggested many possibilities for writing about art that were rarely explored. These sorts of writers had always been found in art magazines, but there seemed to be a new influx of them in the mid-2000s. In some cases, such as with music critics, the migration to art publications was because titles in their own fields had been demolished by online business, going bust at a rate that art magazines — buffered from financial trouble by luxury fashion advertising or the support of academic institutions — were not yet experiencing. (High-quality print still had cachet at this time.)

Everyone played a part in the ecology. Bracingly austere writers balanced those who made playful references to pop culture. Recondite poetic types made mystic pronouncements while reporters looked for The Story. Something looser, less bothered by older orthodoxies of criticism, was flourishing, because no one believed writers had power anymore. There existed a handful of art-world-famous critics, mostly US academics associated with *Artforum* and *October*, whose words carried weight. But I sensed from conversations with writers working outside the university walls that their authority was on slow fade. In *Frieze* we ran fiction, essays on overlooked historical figures, think pieces on left-field topics, paeans to pop culture. You could try things out. There was freedom in the shadows. You could make mistakes. (I will never forget the trouble we got into from our publishers when we once devoted an entire issue to poetry — a commercial disaster in their eyes.) One day I hope someone publishes an Anthology of Critics' Regrets — I'd have a lot to contribute.

Variety didn't mean criticism was free of fashions. Editorial work gave me an aerial view of these. For example, when editing some twenty or so reviews for a given issue, I would notice certain writers or books referenced repeatedly. When I began working at *Frieze* in 1999, for a good year Joris-Karl Huysmans's symbolist novel *À Rebours* (1884) was mentioned in every issue. Why, I have no idea. Perhaps a new English translation had been published. Maybe it was *fin de siècle* cosplay. Slowly Huysmans disappeared, replaced by Jorge Luis Borges, an old standby. Then there was a back-to-critical-theory phase with a whole lot of Giorgio Agamben and Jacques Rancière. The Invisible Committee had a brief moment. Chris Marker's films *La Jetée* (1962) and *Sans Soleil* (1983) were guaranteed to be mentioned once in every issue for at least a decade. Science fiction was a hardy perennial, especially J. G. Ballard, Philip K. Dick, Ursula K. Le Guin, some 1990s throwback love for William Gibson, then, into the 2010s, many nods to Margaret Atwood and Octavia E. Butler. When auto-theory grew popular, Maggie Nelson's name appeared frequently. As issues of race became more pressing in art circles, you'd notice Édouard Glissant and Stuart Hall namechecked alongside Fred Moten, Claudia Rankine, and Audre Lorde. White art professionals who had never once mentioned James Baldwin could be found quoting Baldwin like they'd been raised on him.

Similar trends could be seen at a sentence level. I remember how "riffing" was popular for a while. A lot of "limning" was going on, too. If an artwork was modest and hard to fathom, it was "poetic." "Performativity" repeated itself to the point where it had escaped Judith Butler's original definition. "Radical" turned up so frequently that it gained a banal respectability. And so much "referencing" you'd be forgiven for thinking that all artists did was browse Wikipedia. Periodically, there would be a new "turn": the social turn, the pedagogical turn, the archival turn. These sounded to me like road directions or a sudden illness. Trends suggested an atmosphere of shared ideas and demonstrated good intentions to better understand urgent topics. Yet they set narrow parameters. Who wanted to read the same books as everyone else, be guided by the same intellectual lights? Which begged the question: why would you want to write criticism in the same way as everyone else? Conventions in art writing perpetuated ingrained structural attitudes. Unfortunately, in order to take them seriously, the industry preferred its art critics to sound like art critics.

The content churn

I would hear dealers, curators, even artists, make sweeping generalizations about the poverty of criticism. They'd moan about how bad the writing was in magazines that they also boasted about never reading. Press them on the rancor and it usually turned out to be because they weren't being covered in those magazines, or they hadn't gotten the editorial return they presumed they'd get for their advertising money. Admittedly, part of the trouble was that the speed of traditional criticism was failing to keep up with the speed of business and the explosion of exhibitions, fairs, galleries, and biennales. Magazines — most of which were staffed by small teams — found that the specialist territory they had once easily covered had now expanded beyond their reach. One positive effect was that editors at the major European and US art publications were pushed out of their local comfort zones in search of writers from Africa, Asia, and Latin America, territories that these magazines had overlooked for too long. There was more to cover, and an increasing percentage of readers was as interested in the industry news — who was working where, which galleries were representing which artists, and so on — as they were with ideas.

Criticism was sucked into the content churner. The big shows — the Venice Biennale, documenta, the São Paulo Art Biennial, Gwangju Biennale, Whitney Biennial, and so on — all had to get covered, along with the blockbusters and the small-but-talked-about exhibitions. As readership grew online, so did rapid-response reviews of the key biennales, published on opening day. They were designed to attract website traffic and did nothing for thoughtful writing. When hundreds of artists were in a show, reviewing was reduced to list-making. Deadline-stressed authors could overlook significant works or miss the point entirely. These online volleys would be followed up later with a more reflective take in a magazine's print edition, written by a heavyweight name who would have been afforded ample time and a bigger fee to think about their response.

It was vital to keep track of the new faces, or "emerging artists" — a label that made me think of cute animals waking up to spring after hibernation. As an editor, I knew what I had to do before I even saw the work. I would notice an artist's name start appearing in group show listings. Writers would start pitching reviews of those shows. The name would get dropped in conversation at private viewings, where everyone would nod knowledgeably even if they hadn't themselves heard the name before. Soon the artist would have a solo exhibition in a small but influential gallery, and I would notice reviews starting to appear in the right places. Sometimes I would catch one of these artists at this point, commission a review, and feel good about the magazine keeping up with the game. Occasionally I'd be told later that I had covered them "too early," meaning that nobody noticed, or "too late," meaning that the magazine did not appear to be on the pulse. The affirmation mechanism that rolled these young artists off the conveyor belt always remained misty to me, glimpsed only in fragments I could not quite put together even as my job involved pulling certain levers on the machine. And while it was necessary to run a tight line in futurology, it was also advisable to keep up with the latest Historically Important Artists. These were either dead or nonagenarian, and in the latter case presumably curious as to why nobody had cared until this point. There were times when I wondered if simply running a list of names on the magazine's cover would be enough to pass for critical conversation. It used to be the case that traveling to big shows or fairs would provide introductions to new work. By the 2010s, the system turned over at such a fast rate that you had already seen the art before you arrived. (Foreshadowing the pandemic, there was speculation that online images were becoming a substitute for seeing the real thing, yet some artists' work remained resolutely local, refusing absorption into the global biennale-fair circuits, and it remained important to visit places in person to get the full sense of a scene.) Reputations were built on an echo chamber of consensus and a fear of saying "I don't know." I don't know that artist. I don't know that show. I don't know what you assume I should know in order to have your respect.

I began working at *Frieze* shortly after leaving art school in Oxford and moving to London. I was broke and could not get a paying arts-related job without prior experience, but to obtain that experience involved doing unpaid work. Thanks to friends letting me sleep on the floor of their apartment, I was able to take an internship at the magazine, answering the phones, dealing with the mail, processing subscriptions. The position offered fifty pounds a week, a free lunch and my weekly Tube fare. In the late 1990s, the art industry was smaller, and the pace of production was less hurried. There were perhaps a dozen commercial galleries and artist-run spaces in London. Tate Modern had not yet opened. Phone, letter, and fax were used more than email. Artists would pop by the office in Soho, usually to drop off prints or transparencies of their work if we were covering them, as this was the pre-digital standard for documentation. The friendlier ones would stay for a chat. Gossip, anecdotes, gripes, and enthusiasms. Opinions on fashion and design, books and music. As the 2000s progressed, I observed how often art industry technocrats framed artists as seers, as quasi-holy visionaries whose moral compass was magnetized by an ethical good far greater than that of average persons. Artists would revolutionize the world and must be listened to. By then I knew too many artists to believe this fantasy. I agreed with Simon Martin, who observed in his 2006 video essay *Carlton* that artists are people who "look like everyone else, worry about their weight, book foreign holidays." I did not believe in the veneration of everything artists did, like parents doting on children. In artists' novels, artists' poetry, artists' bands, artists' furniture, artists' cookery books. In the sophistry that lent sloppy work the excuse that its sloppiness was intentional and made from a position of criticality. Playing the "artists' X" card always brought to mind a man I once met who had spent his life working as a gas fitter but who told me, as if confessing an embarrassing secret, that he wrote poetry. Why was there no interest in gas fitters' poetry? We are all special and we are all dull, but artists, it seemed, could never be wrong. If you doubted anything they did, the etiquette was to say you were In Two Minds, that you needed to Go Back and See the Show Again, that you needed to Think About It. Anything, so long as you avoided direct disagreement with the consensus. Disagreement made you unmutual, bad for the community. There were artists who attacked or satirized the system, but because artists were respected oracles they could speak truth to power and let everyone else continue to conduct business as usual.

The inflating balloon

During the mid-2000s, my colleagues and I wrote a series of satirical letters in *Frieze*, based around a fictional jet-set curator called Jean-Philippe Obu-Stevenson who lived in a Herzog & de Meuron–designed apartment in Schiphol Airport. For the first couple of issues featuring the letters, several people thought Jean-Philippe was real. Some did not find the caricature amusing. Then, around the time of the 2008 economic crash — I'm hazy as to exactly when — the paint job began to flake on the curator-savior juggernaut. As the word "curating" off-gassed into popular usage — everything was "curated" now, from your sock drawer to your grocery cart — the mania around the profession settled. Jean-Philippe retired.

I recall hearing earnest conversations about how the crash would be "good for art," provide a reset, allow us all to get back to real, authentic pursuits. That didn't happen. The crash barely touched the art industry. More galleries and fairs started. More parties were thrown. There were more collectors, curators, and people with jobs the necessity of which was unclear. By the mid-2010s, the conversation had inflated to hyperbolic proportions. I noticed how this affected language. Institutional vocabularies became disproportionately self-important. Professionals started to sound like diners in a noisy restaurant trying to make themselves heard. Every show was Significant. Landmark. Every gallery's program was Interesting. Every collector was Great. Have you seen their collection? So Great. Every artist was The Most Important of Their Generation. Such an Important Voice. One art dealer in Los Angeles declared to me, in all seriousness, that he was The Most Important Gallerist of His Generation. Throughout that decade, my morning inbox would be filled with around seven hundred emails. That is a conservative estimate. Some 90 percent of them would be press releases for Very Important Events and Proud Announcements. The sheer number made it hard to believe they were Very Important at all.

Identity politics and activism slowly returned to center stage among artists. A reaction to a global shift to the right in politics. Maybe a way to push against what art industry expansionism represented, to make it easier to sleep at night because that system still paid the bills. At the same time, museum didactics and press packs continued to talk of "strategies" and "tactics" in art, which persisted from older days of heroic modernism. Perhaps this was a result of their employees having been trained on university art history or curating courses, or perhaps it was simply an industry convention that provided a comforting muzak of seriousness. Artists were here to Interrogate You, Challenge You, Force You to Confront Your Assumptions. They were right. You were wrong. Embedded in this language was a persistent undertone of violence and subjugation that was at odds with institutions professing to be champions of justice and equality. Later in the decade, as greater transparency was called for, it would not seem so odd. Museums with board members in private security staged shows about protest, identity politics, and the inequities of capitalism. “Up With the People!,” they shouted, as they upped admission prices and fought staff efforts to unionize. Purge your Preconceived Notions of job security and equal opportunity! So Great. So Important.

Strange distortions and cross-breeds emerged in the terminology. Socially engaged projects — inclusive, publicly minded — were described in argot that few without specialist training could understand. The space of public language — wall texts, handouts, and catalogue essays — was used by professionals to demonstrate their knowledge to each other as much as to their audiences. Terms from the fields of art history and museology, which suggested scholarly reserve and cooled you down with icy objectivity, flowed freely from respected journals into press releases about satellite art fairs and private museums. It became common to joke about not understanding what press releases meant. Nomenclature taught in exclusive academic institutions, for use and distribution through a privileged professional field, became the lingua franca for a system increasingly geared toward the veneration of collector and patron money. The tone was technical and paired well with mid-century modern furniture. Site-specific, post-studio, referential, research-based, project-based, text-based, lens-based. Practice, survey, monograph. Use of the third person was regularly mistaken for a sign of ethical probity: the viewer, the visitor, the audience. High-toned “X-ing the Y” formulations were common: “Mining the dialectic,” “Exploring the real.” Everything was Critical. Everything had the definite article: The performative, The curatorial, The contemporary.

Artists’ interests diversified wildly as many went deep into researching fields of recondite knowledge and complexity. Critics had to become generalists, or flash specialists in specific subjects. One week, it was postmodern dance. The next, artificial intelligence, Soviet-era architecture, the Factory Records label. It was The Age of Explanation. Every show came with a contextual essay and talks program. This didn’t happen at the cinema, or when I went to a concert, or bought a novel from a bookshop. In these fields, it was assumed that the audience was comfortable understanding the work by themselves. Art exhibitions generated a vast para-industry of interpretation. Text was everywhere, so much so that I began to wonder if anyone was reading it. Even as an editor, I didn’t have time to get through the glut of print that arrived on my desk each day. It struck me that the heft of a catalogue, the sight of words arranged on a page, with The Right Name attached so as to demonstrate that the subject was worthy of attention from The Right People, was all that was required. A picture of writing, an image of criticism.

The fantasy league

Major media outlets would regularly run stories about the contemporary art world that fixated on astronomical auction prices and what Jeff Koons was going to do next and which celebrities went to Art Basel Miami Beach. Profiles of the newly forming caste of Euro-American mega-galleries — Gagosian, Hauser & Wirth, David Zwirner — and their super-rich clients. That was the art world as far as journalists were concerned, and art critics were just shills for a giant money-laundering scam. That world seemed a galaxy away from the one I lived in. They never covered artists struggling to get by on adjunct teaching jobs, gallerists who couldn't afford the rent on their spaces, provincial art museums doing sterling work with little cash and scant recognition. Even as the standard Euro-American narratives of modernism were being dismantled, they ignored cities and countries with different perspectives, histories, economies. New York and London were everything. (The trade magazines made some efforts to look farther afield but were hampered by a combination of big-city parochialism, the pursuit of advertising revenue, and limited resources.) Those who were already disenfranchised from the art world for reasons of class, race, gender, or sexuality continued to be ignored in favor of The Big Men of Big Sculpture, whose works now served as garden gnomes for The Big Men of Big Finance. Until the pandemic hit in 2020, only a few, save for a handful of activist groups, talked about how the economic boom of the art system had left a lot of its workers behind.

Writers helped generate value around artists. I found it perplexing that institutions — and it was often those with directors earning six- or seven-figure sums — seemed able to produce beautiful catalogues but unable to pay writers adequately, if at all. This created an impossible economic situation for freelancers who were earning less than what the cheap wine cost for a private viewing. It ensured criticism was a class game. Only those who could afford to write could do so, greatly narrowing the range of perspectives brought to bear on art. Commercial galleries, less constrained by budgets, generally made a better effort to pay writers fairly, and I met smart dealers who appreciated the work that critics did. But, in the mid-2010s, the bigger galleries saw fit to start their own in-house magazines to promote their activities, rather than support the independent art media at a point when the publishing industry was already struggling to stay alive.

The expanding interest in contemporary art was ironic where *Frieze* was concerned. Its sister company ran a growing portfolio of successful art fairs, pouring large quantities of accelerant into the system. As editors, we worried about our autonomy when the Frieze London fair first began, although the excitement it generated in the city was heady. Our employers did their best to protect the magazine's independence. When, for instance, a savage review of an exhibition at a powerful US gallery was published the day that the second iteration of Frieze London opened, the gallery threatened to close its booth and walk out. Our bosses stood up to them and defended the firewall between the magazine and the fair. We could be quite intransigent as editors, and possibly caused more headaches for the fair organizers than they did for us, but, for the most part, we had to live with cognitive dissonance. We organized a talks program for the fair, presenting artists and thinkers whose work we admired. People accused us of giving commerce an intellectual gloss. As the years passed, I found it increasingly alienating as we fought to maintain the integrity of editorial work on the magazine while the art fair transformed the market. It was disheartening to hear collectors and gallerists refer to *Frieze* as the in-flight magazine of the art fair, even though the magazine had existed for over a decade before the event began. Especially as the magazine's cultural capital had attracted people to the event in the first place. In my final years as a *Frieze* employee — when the business was sold to a large US entertainment company — I would spend as little time as was demanded of me at the fairs, and then play truant. I had played a part in its growth and now, as a critic, felt surplus to requirements, shut off by the money, depressed by the entitled behavior I saw. I'd go for walks in the park, or drift around town with friends who had nothing to do with art, to ground myself. It was a strange sensation to be at the epicenter of something yet feel disconnected from it.

During my first week as the *Frieze* intern, I took a call from a world-famous European painter phoning to cancel his subscription. He was upset by a review we had just published, written by a younger artist and fan of his work. It was well-written but opened with a long, clever paragraph hinging on a metaphor involving this painter drinking his own urine. I could see why he was unhappy. The incident felt charmingly old-fashioned, the kind of spat you'd read about in an artist's biography. Later, as the industry expanded, people got lost in showbiz. Friendships and relationships became insidiously conditioned by social status in the art hierarchy. Power encouraged pettiness. On more than one occasion, a negative review in *Frieze* caused a gallery to punish the magazine by dropping advertising. Over time, I built up a small collection of postcards sent to me by a powerful museum curator who complained bitterly and sarcastically if he got less than full marks in a review. Success — and the pursuit of it — turned some artists into brats, insisting on approval of articles before publication, treating magazines as personal PR services. You could work hard for weeks on an essay, put all your intellectual and imaginative effort into reading an artist's work, and never hear a word about it upon publication — unless the artist or their representatives disagreed with your opinion. So much for the discourse. One famous artist became angry at me at his private viewing for having had the temerity to write that his videos reminded me of film director Andrei Tarkovsky's work. Another minor player phoned to insist, threateningly, that I should consider committing suicide after a mildly critical piece had been published about an alternative art school he was involved with. I didn't even write the damn thing.

But the self-involvement of some only served to underscore the graciousness of others. Late one year, in the early 2000s, I received a package in the mail. It contained a handwritten letter from an older artist whose work I had just written about in *Frieze*. The letter read like a short story. It described how he had received the magazine through the post, opened it, and saw that the feature "felt good," before taking a long stroll. He described the weather, the winter light, the atmosphere of London that day, before returning home, pouring himself "a glass of green chartreuse," and settling down to read my work. Included with the letter was a copy of a book he had made some decades earlier, inscribed to me "with empathy." In that moment, I realized what it was that I wanted from the labor of criticism: dialogue with fellow travelers. Fifteen years later, I still think about that letter.

Artists' tantrums — now there's a genre — made for a good story when they weren't straight-up abusive. But, cumulatively, all the career narcissists playing out their Fantasy League Art

World dreams made the act of writing criticism feel like pissing in the wind. It was art we were pursuing, not the cure for cancer. The hyperbole made it hard for me to take anyone seriously. The world was on fire. It was melting from pole to pole, and my writing was burnishing the value of objects for other people to make their fortunes on. I had power, but it increasingly sat uncomfortably with me, and there were limitations on what my colleagues and I could do. I found I could not in good faith continue writing about art from that position. I had to find a different way to look at art again.

The dread quiet

If the pandemic was having any effect on art criticism, we were too close to see it during those first couple of months. Which is not to say that there weren't a few measurables. Writing work was falling off. Review sections withering. Magazines struggling to survive a precipitous drop in advertising. Critics with nothing new to see casting their nets elsewhere. During the dread quiet of COVID-19, if you were not an essential worker, if the breadline didn't force you to leave the house, the mandate was to shelter in place. The virus was not going to stop art from being made. I suspected that the voices telling us how necessary art was were actually concerned with the necessity of art being distributed through the channels they knew, to observe the protocols of professional visibility.

I liked to imagine all the work that was being made with no audiences, in private. Things made without the anxiety of what people might think. For some art professionals, quarantine meant sourdough recipes and time with the kids. Making space for values to be reset. I think others just wanted to get back to a pre-pandemic normal that had served them well. They were the ones who looked to reenact familiar rituals in digital VIP viewings for physically canceled art fairs, or who drove to the wealthy Hamptons enclave outside New York where mega-galleries had begun opening mini-outlets for the summer — if not for perpetuity. Tragically, for many the experience was one of financial insecurity, trauma, death. For that reason, discussions of art-and-the-pandemic felt wrong. Not where energy should be directed.

Unable to visit galleries and museums, to be a body in space, art writers had to confine their scopophilia to digital photographs, postcards, printed images in books. They shared reading recommendations. Perhaps this put more of an emphasis on the written rather than the visual experience of art. A sense of physical scale and somatic contact was missing. This made the importance of language as a record of art seem all the clearer. Some venues used the opportunity to stream film and video works from their collections online. A few enterprising artists circulated spreadsheets containing links to artists' videos and classic avant-garde movies, like bootlegs passed under the table. This was the closest many of us were going to get to seeing A Real Artwork for a while. The disquieting thing was that these works shared the same screens as *Tiger King: Murder, Mayhem and Madness* (2020) on Netflix and George Floyd's murder by cops from the Minneapolis Police Department.

The Big-P Problems

In early June, a widely shared tweet marveled at how, in a matter of weeks, people in the US had gone from baking bread in quarantine to demanding defunding of the police. At the start of the year, democracy protests convulsed Hong Kong, a plague of locusts hit the East African continent, Australia was burning, and the Amazon rainforest was in flames. Half a year later, the world was still ablaze and now there was a pandemic, mass unemployment, and a revolt against systemic racism.

Across New York, protestors marched day after day, night after night, in hot weather and in thunderstorms. It would have been nice to say that the contemporary art world went from sharing lockdown recipes to putting itself at the service of change, but that was not quite the case. If the art system had relevance with respect to the protests, it was not because it was leading conversations around racism and injustice, but because it embodied those problems, despite imagining itself to be a progressive corner of culture.

The industry calendar was shot to pieces. No fairs to attend. No biennales. Time stopped being an agent of control. On social media, I glimpsed artists with savior complexes itching to make Iconic and Moving monuments to unfolding crises. To paint the icons before the church had been built. With little art to see, attention turned to structural issues. Museums laid off more staff, which only exacerbated demands to face up to problems of representation, labor rights, leadership ethics, economic disparity. Of straight-up racism. As the Black Lives Matter protests spread across the US, social media accounts sprang up calling individuals and institutions in the art industry to task for discrimination. Museums issued tepidly worded statements deploring injustice and inequality and explaining how they had a lot of listening and work to do. Some did so without even mentioning race at all. Eyeballs rolled. Everyone wanted to talk about accountability. All the exhibitions, the conferences, the panel discussions, and the in-conversations promising solidarity with future revolutions — implying that museums would help deliver us to a kinder, fairer society — had turned out to be just that. Talk. It was hard to take their professed politics seriously at all. Institutions promised to change, but whether they would do so remained unclear.

The divisive symbolism of public monuments thrust art history into the headlines. Questions of the "How Can You Write About Art When X Is Happening?" variety flew around. The hard-to-swallow truth was that ignoring X was what, in part, allowed art to flourish. X had always been happening to someone, somewhere. In criticism, Big-P Politics felt like a corrective to the art industry's ghastly excesses, even though it puzzled me as to why anyone would look to art magazines for primary information about bigotry and systemic discrimination. But the danger arose that if you weren't explicitly addressing Big-P Problems in your art writing, then it might be assumed that you were not sufficiently engaged. It seemed as if people had forgotten that it was possible to have a personal hinterland in which you did political things — say, volunteer work — that you did not have to declare publicly in your Professional Art Life.

Megan and Brad's book deadline arrived in July. I couldn't see beyond the end of the week, let alone the horizon of art history. It was getting hot and the mood of the city was strange. For a couple of weeks leading up to the Fourth of July holiday weekend, fireworks were set off all day, every day. Nerves were frayed, people wanted to let off steam. Paranoia grew about Donald Trump's threats to discredit the coming November presidential election. Stories of audacious art industry fraud were reported, although this was hardly surprising. Information circulated about how the most powerful galleries in New York had received federal aid from the US government. Jeff Koons had too, the media announced. The news came as those same galleries fired swathes of staff. Rumors circulated about layoffs at art magazines. New York cautiously began to reopen. A few galleries were open by appointment, but museums remained shuttered that summer. The virus was spreading fast across the rest of the country.

The hopes

Whatever disappointments taint my feelings about the art industry, it is important to state that many who wrote regularly over the last twenty years continued to believe in the value of art criticism. They were courted to write up shows then ignored, told by other professionals that nobody read their work. Still, they remained dedicated to the act of recording and interpreting art. I admired this tenacity in many writers, even if we disagreed about style and method. There was optimism in the commitment. These writers provided collegiality and encouragement that enriched me no end. We read each other's work and cheered each other on when nobody else would. They might have teased me for my sentimentality, for my featherweight scholarship, but they gave me an education that no master's degree could match.

I wondered if the season of change precipitated by the virus might be the time for critics to ask to be paid fairly for their work and to be recognized for their contributions as interpreters, readers, translators, as useful antagonists and sympathetic observers. It was the moment to ask of the art system: why should I respect you? Why should I give you my time and labor? I began to hope that the pandemic would ventilate the system of its hyperbolic gasses. Maybe there would be fewer claims to revolution from institutions that are structurally invested in things never changing. Talk of social justice and mutual aid might not just be a passing art industry fashion. Curators and artists might begin to correspond with critics about the substance of what they write, beyond fact-checking or petulant disagreement. There were signs that the field of criticism could become genuinely more diverse, an opportunity for the publishing business to take a long hard look at its own structural biases.

But those were only hopes. I told myself this would be the last occasion I would write about art criticism for a while.

1 Thomas Beard, Ed Halter, Nellie Killian, and Sierra Pettengill, "Cut. And Action.," *Artforum*, May/June 2020, https://www.artforum.com/print/202005/thomas-beard-ed-halter-nellie-killian-and-sierra-pettengill-on-the-cinema-worker-solidarity-fund-82816.

Critical Localism
Barry Schwabsky

Exhibition reviews and similar critical writing on contemporary art assume an already-existing public: people who like to look at art. From this public, the critic attempts to carve out a second, more particular, one: those who like art who also might like to read about it.

But criticism is vain unless it is also, at least implicitly, self-criticism. That is, it will inevitably mean the application of one's own tastes, desires, knowledge, energy, wit, enthusiasm, lethargy, experience, and so on — everything that goes to make up what is called "subjectivity" — to works that someone else has proposed as being "of art," but if in the process it does not end up eliciting a heightened critical awareness of the limitations of that subjectivity, then what good has it done?

If you're a writer, then you're probably often asked the question: "Who do you write for?" And even more likely, you've probably asked that of yourself. Luckily, a quick answer comes readily to hand: "I write for myself." Fine. But that raises a deeper question: "Who's that?" Here comes the limited nature of subjectivity again; I am not transparent to myself, so self-knowledge is just as partial as any other.

That's why, even writing for oneself, one needs readers, or at least the idea of readers. As you imagine who may be reading your work, you're imagining yourself in relation to them. Sitting alone in a room, writing turns out to be a quintessentially social activity. Yes, I write for myself, but I also write in and to and sometimes against a context.

The problem with context is that it eventually includes just about everything. Here I can only recall the words of Henry James:

> The art of representation bristles with questions the very terms of which are difficult to apply and to appreciate; but whatever makes it arduous makes it, for our refreshment, infinite, causes the practice of it, with experience, to spread around us in a widening, not in a narrowing circle. Therefore it is that experience has to organise, for convenience and cheer, some system of

> observation — for fear, in the admirable immensity, of losing its way [...] Everything counts, nothing is superfluous in such a survey; the explorer's note-book strikes me here as endlessly receptive.[1]

In order to put some temporary practical boundaries on this endlessness, I limit my sense of context here to the pressing question of the critic's role — even of what might be called the market for criticism. Immediately, it appears that the situation of the art critic has changed a lot in recent years. The most apparent change, and the most discussed, is evidently just one of the little aftereffects of a much more widespread problem, namely the decline of print magazines and newspapers. This is partly down to a decrease in readership, but, more so, to an even more dramatic decline in advertising revenue as the ad business has moved online with a vengeance. Just as in the music business, where the transition from modes of distribution based on physical media (vinyl, then CDs) to downloading and then streaming has ended up undermining the economic position of musicians while producing enormous profits for the platforms through which their work is circulated, so too the increasing dominance of online publications has worked to the benefit of Google and social media companies while weakening the position of publishers and the writers they work with. What travels through the ether now is the individual article, detached from the editorial context of which it was nominally a part.

This also means that, as well as each publication being in competition with others for advertising, writers are also in competition with their colleagues for the clicks that are so important to their publishers. When I started out as a critic in the 1980s for publications like *Arts Magazine* in New York, *Flash Art* in Milan, and *Artscribe* in London, my editors and publishers could have only the vaguest intuition of how my individual contributions helped their bottom lines. Now, any magazine with an online presence can see from minute to minute how many readers have landed on my articles compared to those who've been attracted to other things — and therefore (since ads are now sold per page view rather than for the magazine as a whole, with the advertising for each view sold via an automated real-time online auction) they can see how much (or how little) money I've made for them.[2] Needless to say, no publication has ever offered to pay me, instead of a flat rate per article, a percentage of their take from the publication of my work — something more like a royalty. But such a thing would seem to be inherent in the logic of the situation — and it would probably diminish the income of most writers still further, just as for most musicians the royalties from streaming have turned out to be a fraction of what they were earning from vinyl and CD sales.

In all this, as I've said, the small pond inhabited by art critics is just a microcosmic reflection of vaster changes that have overcome the whole realm of journalism. But art is a peculiar system all its own, quite different from the economic systems of businesses based on mass sales. It's a deep-pockets market and, as a result, it responds to different social forces than does an industry like publishing. And art criticism is in the strange position of being at once part of the publishing world and part of the art world, which obey completely different economic laws. One simple way to illustrate this is: If a commercial gallery asks me to contribute an essay to an exhibition catalogue they're putting out, I will ask for a rate of $2.50 per word — thus, for an essay of three thousand words, I would want a fee of $7,500. That means that if they are printing one thousand copies of the catalogue (which is more than usual, by the way) then I am getting $7.50 for each one, most of which are in any case going to be given away rather than sold. (Most galleries don't publish their catalogues online, which suggests that it's irrelevant to them whether anonymous readers have access to them; publishing an exhibition catalogue is about having something you can put into a prospective collector's hand as you look them in the eye.) But any gallery that's paying for a big catalogue with a substantial essay is probably selling the works they're showing for upwards of six figures — so my fee of $7,500 shouldn't look like more than a rounding error to the cost of mounting their exhibition (though that hasn't prevented any number of deep-pocketed but short-armed gallerists from trying to bargain me down on my rate — and sometimes I'll let them do it; it just depends on how eager I am to take on the project, that is, on how much fun I think it would be to write on their artist). By contrast, *The Nation* pays me $1,000 for an article of the same length. It has a circulation of about 150,000 in print (which includes digital access) plus about a tenth more in digital-only subscriptions. Non-subscribers can also read my articles in *The Nation* online; a paywall comes up only once you've read five articles in a given month. So that's all to say that for every potential reader of my article in *The Nation*,

I'm paid less than a penny, as opposed to the $7.50 I get for each pair of eyeballs passing across my catalogue essay. As to how many hits my articles get when they're published online, I've never asked. Maybe I'm afraid to know. As for *Artforum*, where I contribute mostly short reviews of about six hundred words, the $200 fee means the per word rate is the same as that of *The Nation*, though since the readership of *Artforum* is smaller, that means a better compensation rate per reader.

The idea of being paid per reader may sound odd, but it is essentially how online publishers are paid and perhaps no odder than any other way of determining compensation for a writer's work. What all that I've told you should indicate, however, is simply that it would never have been possible to make a living solely as a writer of art criticism for magazines. Part-time work as an editor has helped, as has teaching and lecturing, but, fundamentally, it has been writing for exhibition catalogues — that is, with a less distant relation to the art market than a thoroughly critical stance would seem to require — that has enabled me to live as a freelancer for nearly three decades. For all that, I believe I've preserved my integrity, and my commitment to criticism as a project.

I should make it clear that I am not complaining about my pay at *The Nation* or *Artforum*, any more than I am complaining about the paucity of readers for my catalogue essays. I'm simply pointing out the very different kinds of economies at work at, on the one hand, the oldest continuously published weekly magazine in the United States, a left-wing stalwart that is hardly fertile soil for the sort of luxury goods advertising that floats, say, *The New Yorker*, and that only continues to squeak by thanks to donations; and, on the other, in writing for galleries, which flourish to the extent they succeed in turning art into merchandise. The fact that so many people can read what I write for *The Nation*, and that they needn't be connected to the art world to do so, is in itself invaluable to me. In a sense, I can say that my writing for exhibition catalogues subsidizes my writing for magazines, by which alone I would not be able to survive. And to have a regular soapbox at a publication like *The Nation* is in itself a privilege because it means that I get to talk about art to a readership that is wide awake, educated, and curious, but not with a specialized or professional stake in art. It makes me feel like I have the chance to open some eyes. I'm not preaching to the choir.

And that's another thing: when I write for *Artforum*, I am a member of the choir, just one of many regular reviewers, alongside countless occasional or one-off contributors; at *The Nation* — where I am not the only person who writes about art but I am the only one who does so steadily, month after month, with a spot on the masthead — I serve as a soloist. I have different responsibilities there. *Artforum* as a whole conveys an implicit picture of what contemporary art is and can be — an implicit picture with which I need not agree, even as I add my little bit to constructing it — and if I can make sure that certain things are not expunged from that picture, or that they are given slightly more emphasis in it through my writing than they otherwise would, I am satisfied. I know that just as I can take the *Artforum* view on art with a grain of salt while continuing to learn a lot from it, so can most of the magazine's readers, who, like me, are likely to be active participants in the art world who can judge what they read (and what's left out) with some perspective.

Peter Schjeldahl, in a poignant valedictory essay, recently explained his way of choosing the subjects for his column in *The New Yorker*:

> I assess art by quality and significance. The latter is most decisive for my choice of subjects, because I'm a journalist. There's art I adore that I won't write about, because I can't imagine it mattering enough to general readers.[3]

I work a little bit like that when I write for *The Nation*, but at *Artforum*, where I assume no general readers tread, I'll push for what might not matter to my colleagues every time. But I would also have wanted to remind Peter that, in art, taking a longer view, quality *is* significance, and therefore we critics should shoulder the responsibility of sometimes imposing our sense of what matters on our readers; we should believe that some of the things we adore can become important to our readers, general or specific, thanks to the passion and lucidity with which we expound them. Elsewhere, Schjeldahl has defined the work of art as "a unique, usually handmade physical object, worthless in itself, around which ideas propagate and dreams are spun."[4] If we writers can't pretend to spin some of those oneiric webs out of our own linguistic spinnerets, then of what use are we?

Sure, the reasons to be pessimistic about any critic's influence on what counts in art today are myriad, and I realize that many colleagues might dismiss as tilting at windmills my call to claim such power. In a certain sense, taking the exhibition review as the paradigm for our work, we've accepted the idea that we always come after the fact. Whoever has the power to exhibit an artist's work, whether that's a dealer or a curator, has already been accorded substantive agency in crystallizing its public; the critics can only assert themselves by making a second cut, ignoring some of what the galleries and museums are proposing, and talking up some of the rest.

And that talk seems to be getting cheaper by the year. In today's globalized, multipolar art world, creating an international reputation is a massive commercial and institutional undertaking, and any reputation that's not international barely registers as a reputation. That's partly a cause, partly a consequence, of the rise of a new breed of world-spanning mega-galleries, with Gagosian (Athens, Basel, Beverly Hills, Geneva, Hong Kong, London, New York, Paris, Rome, San Francisco), Hauser & Wirth (Hong Kong, London, Los Angeles, New York, Somerset, St. Moritz, Zurich), Pace Gallery (Geneva, Hong Kong, London, New York, Palo Alto, Seoul), and David Zwirner (Hong Kong, London, New York, Paris) in the lead. But even though a majority of galleries continue to remain rooted to one spot in one city, that mono-local appearance can be deceiving. Many feel it necessary to internationalize themselves by way of participation in fairs — "the central driver of the modern-day art market," according to the journalist Andrew Goldstein. A couple of years ago, Goldstein published an interview in which the longtime New York dealer Jose Freire announced that after taking part in seventy-eight fairs in seventeen years — "as many as eight fairs in a year," according to Freire, "and as few as two or three" — he would no longer participate.[5]

But Freire (who has since closed his gallery altogether) may have been pushing against the tide. The fairs, and the big international galleries, continue to dominate the art market. And then the ever-increasing number of biennales and other recurrent, large-scale international exhibitions dominate those parts of the art circuit that are putatively insulated from the market. These extravaganzas, Charles Green and Anthony Gardner claim, "have come, since the early 1990s, to define contemporary art" and "have drawn local practitioners into ostensibly globalized networks of art-world attention and financial support, publicizing regions or cities previously deemed 'peripheral' to the metropolitan centers."[6] In this context, art essentially functions as a form of mass entertainment whose public subvention implicitly carries the demand that it convey an edifying social message. But in this situation, as one artist perhaps cynically phrased it, "artists, it seemed, could do nothing else except carry on the trend of divulging the local to an international audience."[7] Many of the artists who have been taken up enthusiastically by the biennale circuit, seemingly in constant motion from one big exhibition to another, are only loosely if at all connected to the gallery system — though, as uncommercial as their works may appear, gallery representation can usually materialize once a certain prestige has accrued by way of multiple showings worldwide — while artists who thrive in the market ecosystem of galleries, fairs, and auctions appear to be persona non grata at the biennales. The works of, say, Brice Marden or Damien Hirst may be exhibited all around the world, but when was the last time you saw one in a biennale? Those artists may have nothing else in common, but they share this — shall I say? — apparent unbiennalability.

The two systems — the market system and the biennale system — may be distinct, but their differences make possible their complementarity. What they share is an accent on the importance of global mobility. Thus, as art historian and critic Lane Relyea pointed out in his book *Your Everyday Art World* (2013):

> Those without the time, money, and institutional backing to travel constantly are finding it next to impossible to join the elite who can experience the development of today's most important careers and bodies of work firsthand and in the flesh, and thereby talk about it comprehensively, with authority. The hierarchy is not between this city and others, between New Yorkers and the rest. It's between those who can entrust their gallery or other business to a well-enough-paid staff while they're on the road all the time, or [...] who can travel or freelance without fear of offers drying up, and those who can't.[8]

Under this dispensation, Relyea observes, "mobility serves as the very medium through which particularly oppressive forms of hierarchy now assert themselves."[9] He cites sociologists Luc Boltanski and Eve Chiapello, who say that, under what they call the new spirit of capitalism, "the immobile are exploited in relation to the mobile."[10]

What Relyea does not add is that, in comparison with all the other available subject typologies offered by the art world — artist, dealer, curator, collector — it is the critic who is generally the most localized, the least mobile. For those who have a steady venue for their writing, the venue itself serves to localize them. Consider, for instance, the names of the most prestigious and widely read general interest US publications to regularly feature art criticism. There's *The New Yorker*, already mentioned, and *The New York Times*. In both cases, the name speaks for itself. My own main outlet, *The Nation*, by its title suggests a wider remit — though not wide enough to fulfill the art world's implicit demand for a global perspective — but it's also a New York–based publication and its budget does not allow for the kind of travel that, if Relyea is correct, would be necessary for an authoritative position within the discourse of contemporary art (though I take advantage of other travels to write occasionally in *The Nation* about exhibitions in cities like London or Berlin, or to cover events such as the Venice Biennale or documenta). In a magazine like *Artforum* — which, significantly, carries the word "International" under its masthead, as until recently did its Milan-based competitor *Flash Art* — we individual reviewers primarily cover a local beat so that the magazine as a whole can reflect its international reach. An international overview is impossible without the observations of individuals embedded in local situations, even if their supposed synthesis is imagined to take place elsewhere, above our heads.

An interesting point that Relyea does make is that, over the years, art magazines have come to find art historians more attractive as contributors than independent art critics. This is something he is particularly well placed to notice, having himself crossed over from the hardy band of critics to the better shaded groves of academe. His explanation for this is not the one I'd have thought of at first — the fact that someone already making a living by his or her work at a university can better afford to work for the relatively low pay offered by art magazines than someone trying to make a living solely by writing. Rather, he suggests, the reason has at least in part to do with the overriding demand for global connectivity: "The critic, when compared to the historian, looks isolated and unconnected," whereas art historians "are abundantly hyperlinked" thanks to their "transcontinental academic archipelago of professionally linked colleagues, sites, and organizations, with their cross-advertised conferences and symposia, through which to travel, mingle, connect."[11]

What Relyea says is plausible, but maybe exaggerated. The distinction between critic and historian is pretty blurry, as his own case suggests. And the extensive networking of art historians may not be that well linked to the rather different network that counts as the art world. One doesn't get the sense that many art historians actually get off campus very much — even those whose specialty is the contemporary. Art critics may be less directly connected to their immediate peers than are art historians, but I suspect a thorough sociological study would prove that they are much better connected to artists, and also to dealers.

No, if the critic has a natural competitor within today's art world, it is not the art historian but the curator, and in particular the independent curator whose relatively autonomous position, not bound by terms of employment to any of the various institutions they might work with, seems closest to that of the freelance critic. The difference is that the work of the curator is to gather all the resources of the institution (above all its budget) in the service of a project that is, admittedly, quasi-critical — but only quasi, insofar as it has to do above all with *presenting* works of art, where presence is an absolutely binary instance: something is either present or not. The work of the critic, on the contrary, is only binary at the level of the choice of subjects. One might decide to review an exhibition or not, for example, and the choice to say nothing about a certain exhibition, a certain work, a certain artist is certainly as much a part of the critical process as the decision to say something. But there is a vast range of nuance available to the saying, a whole register of implicit or explicit judgment and of affective ambiguity and polyvalence that can be communicated by the critic's prose to exemplify the ways that — to paraphrase Schjeldahl — ideas are propagated and dreams spun. By comparison, the texts that curators write to justify their positive choices, their decisions to exhibit *this* rather than that, usually seem at best dutiful and informative. And those texts clearly remain secondary to the exhibition presentations they serve.

In Relyea's account, the merely individual and subjective cast of the critic's work tells fatally against it in the current state of things. I wonder whether that might have been truer, however, when he was writing *Your Everyday Art World*, which was published in 2013, than it is today. It's not that the neoliberal system

Relyea was concerned about then has fundamentally changed; in fact, it has propagated itself so successfully that it seems on the verge of consuming itself. Rather, it's that the decentering of the art world has by now so clearly gone hand in hand with an increasing concentration of reputational prestige and market power in the hands of such a small number of players that an inchoate desire for something else is becoming more general. Just as a dealer such as Freire reached the point where he was ready to drop out of the art fair system that he'd been cultivating for years, artists and others are questioning the likelihood that the current art system as a whole can ever realistically work for them. As I've suggested elsewhere, our current situation may have parallels with that of early nineteenth-century Paris.[12] That was the time when (as Harrison and Cynthia White explained back in 1965) the established art system — the École des Beaux-Arts, the Royal Academy, and the annual salons — began to break down because of its inability to meet the needs of the many participants who'd been attracted by the very success of that system, leading to the eventual formation of a new counter-structure that the Whites called the dealer-critic system, which dominated the art world until recently.[13]

With the breakdown of the dealer-critic system, we seem to have arrived at a dealer-curator system, or perhaps it can be called a fair-biennale system. And yet this new system seems to lack staying power. After just a couple of decades, it already seems obsolescent. What will replace it? No one knows. The COVID-19 pandemic seems at once to have accelerated the consolidation of the market, fomented an inchoate desire for more localized art scenes, and at least temporarily put a period to the flourishing of biennales and fairs — a set of contradictory indications.[14] But in a situation in which the old is dying and the new has not yet been born, there are worse resources to call on than the questioning and self-questioning that is at the beating heart of critical thinking as it is informed by the specificity of local knowledge.

1 Henry James, "Roderick Hudson," in *Literary Criticism: French Writers, Other European Writers, The Prefaces to the New York Edition*, ed. Leon Edel and Mark Wilson (New York: The Library of America, 1984), 1039.

2 A recent news article gives a clear and concise explanation of how the process of auctioning an online advertisement works: "The page itself, through the use of digital trackers, collects data on the reader. Then, the page sends this user information up the pipeline along with a certain set of rules, such as what kinds of ads it's willing to show, and at what price. An ad exchange then instantly

arranges an auction for the space and the user, often seeking the highest bid among ad buyers who have also pre-entered their preferred targets, prices, and what their ads look like. Once this whole process takes place — in a matter of microseconds — the ad appears." See: Sam Dean, "California is rewriting the rules of the internet. Businesses are scrambling to keep up," *Los Angeles Times*, December 26, 2019, https://www.latimes.com/business/technology/story/2019-12-26/california-internet-data-privacy-law.

3 Peter Schjeldahl, "77 Sunset Me," *The New Yorker*, December 23, 2019, https://www.newyorker.com/magazine/2019/12/23/the-art-of-dying. Luckily, the valediction turned out to be premature; as this goes to press, Peter has been writing up a storm.

4 Peter Schjeldahl, "Dealership," *The New Yorker*, February 2, 2004, https://www.newyorker.com/magazine/2004/02/02/dealership.

5 Andrew Goldstein, "Team Gallery's Jose Freire on Why He Is Quitting Art Fairs for Good," *Artnet News*, March 5, 2018, https://news.artnet.com/market/jose-freire-art-fairs-interview-1235624. See also: Andrew Goldstein, "'I'm Not Larry Gagosian — I'm Just a Loser With a Gallery': Team Gallery's Jose Freire on the new zero-sum art market," *Artnet News*, March 6, 2018, https://news.artnet.com/market/team-gallerys-jose-freire-on-the-zero-sum-art-market-1235933.

6 Charles Green and Anthony Gardner, *Biennials, Triennials and documenta: The Exhibitions That Created Contemporary Art* (Oxford: Wiley-Blackwell, 2016), 3.

7 Walid Sadek, "Peddling Time When Standing Still," *The Ruins to Come: Essays from a Protracted War* (Pully, Switzerland: Motto Books, 2016), 90.

8 Lane Relyea, *Your Everyday Art World* (Cambridge, MA: MIT Press, 2013), 13.

9 Ibid., 13–14.

10 Ibid., citing Luc Boltanski and Eve Chiapello, *The New Spirit of Capitalism* (London: Verso, 2007), 363.

11 Relyea, *Everyday Art World*, 183–184.

12 Barry Schwabsky, "When Downtown Was Up," *The Nation*, March 16, 2017, https://www.thenation.com/article/when-downtown-was-up/.

13 Harrison C. White and Cynthia A. White, *Canvases and Careers: Institutional Change in the French Painting World* (Chicago: University of Chicago Press, 1965).

14 For further reflections on art after COVID-19, see Barry Schwabsky, "What Are Art Galleries For?," *The Nation*, July 1, 2020, https://www.thenation.com/article/culture/future-of-galleries/.

This Is How You Tell the Truth

Taylor Renee Aldridge
& Jessica Lynne

This text is an essay on friendship and criticism and the refusal of silences. It is an essay about wayfinding. It is not a manifesto; it is a guide, a marker, and a testimony. It is a place to which we may return. It is an ongoing process of naming ourselves for ourselves.

Dear Jess,

Lately, I have been thinking about the potential pitfalls and unmitigated risks involved in intersubjective critique. What does it mean to make a public critique about a community that you belong to, one that you are deeply invested in and implicated by? How do we make critiques within our own spaces of intimate and familial relationships? Recently, I rewatched *Black Is... Black Ain't* (1995) by the late filmmaker Marlon Riggs. The film poses questions about the impossibility of describing Blackness in a definitive manner, the histories and nuances of Black American ontologies, and the gendered dynamics that persist within this culture.

Notably, there is a segment that considers a Black feminist perspective and the marginalization of Black women that has occurred, chiefly throughout the Black Arts Movement, in an effort to advance the well-being of Black life. With the help of commentary by iconic political figures such as Barbara Smith and Angela Davis, Riggs posits that many of the mid-century civil rights movements were misogynistic at their core. As we know now, there was an insistence, instigated by Black men and even some women, that Black women's rights were not to be prioritized over Black men's rights. There was a desire to redress the emasculation of Black men, which occurred throughout the Middle Passage across the Atlantic and during chattel slavery, by reclaiming the power of the phallic, as put frankly in Riggs's film. For some of the figures within the Black Arts, Black nationalist, and civil rights movements, Black male patriarchy was a liberatory aspiration.

Cultural critic Michele Wallace—who wrote *Black Macho and the Myth of the Superwoman* in 1979, which exposes the insular violence perpetuated by ideologies of Black patriarchy within the aforementioned movements—is featured in the film, reflecting on the contributions she made in the book, and the extreme backlash she experienced from the Black community because of it. Essentially, in *Black Macho and the Myth of the Superwoman*, Wallace made visible the unsaid, yet well-known, fact of misogyny that existed within these political movements. She did so to the chagrin of some of the Black community, and even her own mother. Additionally, Robert Staples published a scathing response to the book in *The Black Scholar*, titled "The Myth of Black Macho: A Response to Angry Black Feminists" (1979), which purported that the book was an all-out attack on Black men. In *Black Is... Black Ain't*, Riggs asks Wallace about the harsh treatment she received from the Black community after the release of her book. "And you were punished," he says. "And I was punished," she concurs. In this moment, her stoic presence takes a pause, and she reflects on the reality of the punishment; her body deflates slightly, and her eyes sadden. "I'm still being punished," she declares.

There is a shame that appears to wash over her in the exchange, which remains indelible on my mind. A shame that is not necessarily prompted by regret but rather a disheartening, because the community that she wrote to and for did not appreciate her offering. As a critic who thinks of criticism as an "act of love," as Wallace did, there is a fear that sometimes greets me when I dare to offer perspectives of dissent—especially as a self-identified Black queer woman. As you know, some of my critiques have been lauded as querulous rather than well-thought-out analyses. These comments are often entangled in a gendered and racialized schema, which I think is not unrelated to the critiques of Wallace's work.

In the exchange with Riggs, we are able to witness Wallace's disposition as a pariah. This particular moment in the film alerts me to a larger set of concerns and questions that I have been thinking about regarding accountability, punishment, and intersubjective critique. *Who among us is allowed, or not allowed, to critique and hold people accountable without retribution? What has it meant for us to grow up in a culture that defers to punishment to resolve conflict, injustice, and dissent? How does punishment manifest and settle in our psyches and bodies?*

Taylor,

There is much at stake in our work. I would like to think that this is a sentiment once held by the late Marlon Riggs and perhaps still embraced by Michele Wallace. When I say that I am a Black critic who has something to say to Black people, I recognize that this also means that not everyone will like what I have to say, most of all my own people. 2020 has been a year of reckoning, as crisis has (re)shaped many interpersonal and institutional relationships. For my own part, this has meant better understanding the scope of the tasks I assign myself as a critic. When I say tasks, I mean that I aim for my writing to refuse the ease of infantilization, and to exist within the traditions and communities of Black people who have long worked to name the ever-present harms that surround us. I would like for my role as a critic to be one that is not afraid to move toward liberation.

I begin this way because this is how I have always understood Riggs and Wallace and Smith — unflinching in their truth telling, because there has always been so much at stake for us. To reflect on their legacies is to reflect on the terms by which we tell ourselves the truth. In *Black Macho and the Myth of the Superwoman*, Wallace tells the truth. I think this is what critics should always do. Of course, the presumption in this assertion is that truth exists as an objective point along an objective line. Wallace's refusal of the position that asserted the primacy of straight, Black male leadership or authority at the helm of quests for freedom was a truth telling that frightened, enraged, and disrupted. Black feminism(s) is a truth telling that frightens, enrages, and disrupts. It is also the best lens through which I hope to write. I read your offering and I think: what does it mean to tell the truth to ourselves?

The expectation that Black critics and other critics of color, or critics who occupy a position outside dominant culture (read: white, straight, male, cis), "put on" for artists who share similar identity markers is high. There is value in representation, I know, but it is not the thing that will save us. Early on in my career, I felt as if I needed to champion all the artists who looked like me because I was so afraid that the nebulous, arbitrary boundaries of "the canon" (itself an exercise in nationalism, as Toni Morrison notes) would suffer with this omittance. But on what grounds does the canon of Western art history become truth, anyway? And what of the art that declares a position to which I am fundamentally opposed? What of the art that proposes a (world) framework that I want to trouble? Even if it is created by someone who looks like me. And so, we must tell the truth. Especially to ourselves.

I think that each generation of Black critics has to confront these questions. If given the chance, I would ask Wallace in what ways she took shelter in the wake of a backlash that can still be felt a generation later. That is, how did she remind herself of the urgency of her truth?

In our work, we get so close, embedded in a writing practice that is attempting to see entire constellations beyond the singular object, performance, literature itself. It is this myth of distance to which I keep returning. Does it actually exist? Are we lying to ourselves with any sort of attempt to chase it? The critic I was told I needed to be and the critic I actually am are on opposite sides of a long, long spectrum because, in fact, I do not think it possible to imagine freedom and be invested solely in a shallow game of representation. That would be dishonest. That is not my work. What, then, does it mean to move away from the fear of retribution? Does it always haunt? Or is there the possibility of refuge on the other side of radical honesty?

Dear Jess,

When I think of truth telling, I think of Detroit.

Detroit, as you know, is my hometown, and one of the Blackest cities, demographically, in the United States. It is a city that is primarily composed of descendants whose families traveled north during the Great Migration. I heard an intuitive call to return to this place in 2014, after several years of study along the northeast American coast. (Sometimes the land and its people call us.)

During my return, between the years of 2014 and 2020, I experienced a coming of age that required radical honesty. The city had just declared bankruptcy, one of the largest municipalities ever to do so in the world, and its remaining inhabitants — primarily poor Black people — were left without the basic resources needed to survive, such as water, proper education, housing, and healthy food. So many lost their lives, homes, families, and work; Detroiters were grieving so many things. I often say that the impending end of the world that we have all been anticipating this year happened in Detroit first, in 2014. With the exception of the pandemic, the year we're having now, in 2020, is quite similar to the environment people were living through in 2014 Detroit. Through the lens of Detroit's economic decline, I was able to witness firsthand how the "American Dream" is made possible through Black suffering. After the 2008 recession, Detroit died so that America could live.

Through the extraction of resources and extreme loss, Detroiters reimagined and rebuilt new worlds that were self-sustainable and unexploitable — instituting community gardens, providing mutual aid, and creating power sources independent of the State. I returned back home to encounter this vibrant autonomous ecosystem in a primarily Black enclave that was left for dead. (This should not at all be romanticized.)

It was under these conditions, and through my encounters with the elders and community organizers of this place, that I learned the necessity of radical truth telling, and the freedoms it affords us. There was this pervasive acknowledgement that the State does not care about or for us, so how can we care for ourselves? I learned that truth telling is the result of experiencing so much grief. There is a wising up, an admission, and then a submission to what is. From there, we might gesture and speculate about possible futures, but first we must acknowledge what is in front of us before we can move forward. Being mystified about our realities does very little for our survival.

It was during this sojourn home, under these conditions, that I became a critic. I learned from fellow Detroiters the radical vulnerability required in telling the truth — a truth that was also born out of love and the desire for a more livable world. In Detroit, I was exposed to the ways in which Black suffering is usurped in and outside of art spaces, used to incite savior complexes among the white and wealthy. After these same groups had intentionally divested from the city, they returned to reinvest in it after Black Detroiters had worked to prove its viability. I recognized, then, that there is a currency generated through the dispossession of Black subjects in and outside of the capital-A Artworld that directly benefits whiteness. My time back home is where I analyzed these structures, named and exposed them as a critic.

You mentioned the haunts of retribution that come along when we tell the truth, but there are also things that haunt when we do not tell the truth. An irredeemable silence that may cost a life, may marginalize a person or practice, and may compromise a livelihood. These things were far more important than protecting myself from retribution.

It was during my time in Detroit that our friendship and work relationship budded, when we would come to create the only platform dedicated to criticism from Black perspectives. It has become a site where we insist on truth, and encourage our contributors to do the same. I believe our work together has been able to sustain itself because of our kindred desire to elicit freedom through critique. Our friendship has made my work possible. It is through your encouragement that I have been able to persevere in this work of truth telling. When it gets hard, and the potential harm that comes from refusing silence bears heavy on my body, I find great solace in your affirming words and grace, Jess. I imagine that being seen and affirmed by Riggs and others in her community is what allowed Michele Wallace to persist in doing the necessary but undesirable work of being a critic who does not lie — who is critiquing out of love. Where I find sanctuary as a critic is in you, and in others in our collective who commit to veracity and valor in this work.

Taylor,
I have only just now begun to take myself seriously as a writer. There are many reasons for this, and they are reasons that you and I have discussed the world over. As a young person, the distance between the type of writer I wanted to be and the type of writer I was, was significant. (Here is another spectrum, I suppose.) And in the ways that I imagine everyone does when they aspire to a thing, I became enamored with writers who were my best models of bravery, form, storytelling, and community. These writers moved through the world with an attention to *their people*. I mean this here both in the broad sense and on the very intimate level of interpersonal relationships. Writers like Toni Morrison or Bessie Head or Ntozake Shange or Barbara Christian or Una Marson. There are clear lessons I take from them as writers, and yet I am often most in awe of the way they loved their people and, as you say, found sanctuary in one another.

I am thankful that this is also our story and the story of those who are in community with us.

Of the many presumed roles of the critic, the position of distance is the one to which I can't quite commit. This is why, as I mentioned in my first missive to you, I keep returning to the myth. It fascinates me no end. The women who I have named above, and their contemporaries, have shown me otherwise. I think about lineages often and selfishly, about where I might hope to fit. And more than lineages of "art" criticism, which respond to a dominant narrative about culture, I am most invested in the lineages of the Black women writers who have shaped this world. They have taught me how to look, how to listen, how to tell the hard truths, how to imagine *more* and *beyond*. What gave me great hope as a young person still gives me hope today when I think about what it is that our work means and might one day signify. I am not in a position to make definitive declarations, but it feels pleasurable to wonder and to move within the lessons and words of these women.

I see this in you and am reminded of this whenever you talk about Detroit. (I almost wrote *Black Detroit* but that would be redundant.) This city, *your people*, offer not just solace in the face of an empire intent on crushing us, but also their communion brought you to a new place in your own truth telling efforts. And though I know that all skinfolk are not kinfolk, it is also worth saying that Black people are always teaching the world how to get free. It is not glamorous work. It is exhausting. It is always in contention with this world that has emerged after 1492 (to loosely borrow from Sylvia Wynter). We do it for a world to come. Like you, this realm is where I have learned to find myself as a critic.

As we compose this epistolary essay, we are also honoring the twenty-fifth anniversary of Toni Cade Bambara's transition. Toni, who taught us that the dream is real and that we must write just as we must hit the streets. Dream. Write. Be *out there*. What a potent summation of what it means to be honest, to tell the truth. Our readers will not know this, but earlier this year we wrote to one another in the season that honors Octavia E. Butler and June Jordan. They, all of these women and all of our elders, are guiding us, Taylor.

Our friendship is one of magnificent dreaming, strategizing, and building. I love how our people have taught us that this is a function of criticism, of response, of naming a future. And you are right — the haunting of silences just might be that much more frightening when truths are not spoken. I find shelter in your friendship because I know that this is a relationship that cannot only be defined by our work. This is a lesson I glean from your Detroit and the writers we study. Writing is an exercise of constant sharpening. So too is friendship, for me. So too is world making. I am thankful we have embedded ourselves in all three terrains.

Clive James Is Dead, Alas

Ben Eltham

Clive James is dead. The Australian poet, memoirist, critic, and television presenter died in November 2019. Many mourn him, myself among them.

Unusually for a writer, James was genuinely famous, as befits the investigator of fame in the twentieth century, one of his most fertile explorations.

I don't think the man himself would baulk at grandiose statements about the end of an era, and we can perhaps see such a closure approaching. Along with Robert Hughes, Barry Humphries, and Germaine Greer, James was one of the big four Australian expats that made their name in Britain and the United States in the 1960s. Their success in letters and performance testified to the fertility of the Australian talent pool, but also to the superficiality of a staid and hidebound colonial culture. Now James and Hughes are dead and, with Greer and Humphries aging, a certain idea of postwar Australian culture — of Anglo-American culture, really — is plainly in eclipse.

What was that world? In a word, it was the middlebrow, a world that has gained in posthumous lustre as the indignities of 2020 have multiplied. It was the world of late print as much as late capitalism, a world where newspapers were still the unquestioned vehicles for political dialogue and debate, where magazines and books were a genuinely globe-spanning big business, where newspaper empires made more money than movie studios or television networks, where Oprah Winfrey was the most powerful book critic in the world's biggest book market, and where two print journalists could bring down a US president.

James bestrode this world as a rumpled critical colossus, a man equally at home translating Dante as titillating British television with Japanese game shows. As Adam Gopnik observed in an obituary in *The New Yorker*:

> From start to finish, what kept it all unified was that double gift: the delighted appetite for art, the capacity for its accurate appraisal. Usually, a critic with the first gift is charming but slight, "middlebrow," while the other kind

> can be tiresomely fastidious. With James, the tension between his entertainer's brio and his star student's brine became the keynote for his œuvre.[1]

The term "middlebrow" is generally traced to the 1920s. It was supposedly first used by *Punch* as satire, and it was a term of contempt for the Bloomsbury set (Virginia Woolf decried it in an unpublished letter to the *New Statesman*, declaring that she would take a pen knife to anyone accusing her of the term).[2] But it became an ongoing subject of fascination for two generations of critics, literary theorists, and sociologists.[3]

Middlebrow really got a kick along in the postwar era, as Americans like Dwight Macdonald turned their guns on the Babbitry of the middle-class masses. After the French sociologist Pierre Bourdieu surveyed 1,217 French citizens on their taste in books, television, fashion, and food, it became possible to assign precise socio-cultural metrics to the various classes. In the France of François Mitterrand, the Australia of Bob Hawke and Paul Keating, the Britain of Margaret Thatcher, or the United States of Ronald Reagan, the middle classes were dominant, and so was their middlebrow taste.[4]

The late twentieth century was not only characterized by the "cultural logic of late capitalism," as Jameson argued.[5] It was also the hey-day of mass middlebrow culture. By the late 1980s, the Western cultural industries in their entirety were essentially a washing machine of middling culture, where global media corporations co-opted fashionable ideas of postmodernism and cultural studies, and mashed them up.

Late high postmodernism was a medley of high, low, and middle, in a riot of colors and genres: Quentin Tarantino and Jean Baudrillard, Michael Nyman and Madonna, surf wear and Jean Paul Gaultier, Donna Tartt and David Foster Wallace, Robert Venturi and Frank Gehry, edge-city exurbs and cavernous video stores, slip dresses and ecstasy, terrible chinos and third-way neoliberal politics. The dominant musical culture was hip-hop. The dominant medium was television. Cyberpunk was a utopian future, rather than a dystopian now. All of it, you could argue, was middlebrow.

James was not himself a postmodernist, of course, and he would have been horrified by the appellation of middlebrow. He was rather a kind of remnant modernist, a revanchist of mass literacy. James was a gadfly and a bon vivant, but also an unusually voracious reader. He was a man who believed that the riches of literature were available to any thinking citizen, but sufficiently flexible and funny a modernist to effortlessly navigate the shoals of mass culture. But isn't that the point of middlebrow?

That world is gone now. Looking back at it from the 2020s, the late-century high tide of the baby boomer lifeworld seems to have more in common with the nineteenth than the twenty-first century — a world in which, as critic Guy Rundle wrote recently, with only four stations on television and a couple of newspapers in any big city, it was still eminently possible to know precisely the content of the national debate. "Well, that was mass culture, that was what it was," he wrote in an obituary for singer Glen Campbell. "Its heyday? About 1970 to 1995, one generation."[6]

Walter Benjamin famously argued that Charles Baudelaire was the last lyric poet to have European repercussions. James wouldn't have much truck with that; he didn't much like Benjamin, notoriously for an otherwise polyglot celebrant of central European genius.

But you could equally say that James's death represents the death of a particular mode of criticism. James could well turn out to be the last middlebrow critic to have a mass audience; his successors, such as *The New Yorker* critic James Wood, the English food writer A.A. Gill, or Australian critics and commentators such as Guy Rundle or Helen Razer have, at most, niche appeal. That's not to say there aren't still literary stars, of course. But they're not critics.

When writing her time-slice history of the year 2001, Phillipa McGuinness went back through the old newspapers from the year to get a better idea of what was occupying the zeitgeist at the time.[7] What really stunned her, she told me while writing it, was just how much zeitgeist there was. Compared to the shrunken samizdats of the late 2010s, the newspapers of 2001 were bloated phone books. I remember what it was like in the early 2000s, just before the internet avalanche hit. The daily newspaper was a heavy roll — *two* fat heavy rolls on Saturday — from which the plastic would have to be carefully unpeeled, after which the big folds of newsprint would flop onto the kitchen table with a satisfying *thunk*. My dad liked to spread them out and read them section by section, always with a nice cup of tea.

They were full of criticism — cultural criticism of the déclassé Birmingham School variety, pop sociology, gender studies (was John Howard really winning a fan base of young voters?, or ruminations on the "metrosexual," say, or the vexed question of whether the career woman could have it all). There were lots of reviews, and acres of newsprint devoted to this or that celebrity author or musician. I remember my first feature commission for Brisbane-based daily newspaper *The Courier Mail*—a three thousand worder on hip-hop as a cultural phenomenon, complete with interviews with cultural theorists and cultural studies academics.

The world of mass-market criticism has vanished too, evaporated with the classified ads. Maybe we won't miss another longform essay on the latest Radiohead album, but it is indubitably gone. Arguably, the prominence of criticism was already eroding by the end of the century, even before the widespread penetration of the internet through everyday life. Highbrow criticism, of the Leavisite or Bloomian variety, was in truth always a niche pursuit, typically exercised by the high priests of literature in their ivory towers. The fragility of memory elides what we have lost. The mass culture period after the Second World War allowed obscure academics or working critics to move from the review pages and the liberal arts university into positions much closer to the mainstream. Mass media allowed such figures as Kenneth Clark, Raymond Williams, and John Berger to make documentaries that reached a wide audience of thinking citizens. Now that he is largely a set text for undergraduate students, it's easy to forget that Williams was once a major figure in middlebrow British culture, and that *Keywords* (1976) was published as a trade paperback with a huge print run.[8] The 1980s were a time when an art critic like Robert Hughes could become a television star.

Around about the time that Williams released *Keywords*, Clive James established himself as an extremely popular television critic, and was on the way to becoming a genuine television star in Britain, hosting a variety show that was simultaneously bawdy, erudite, and very, very funny. I remember watching late-night reruns of it with my father as a teenager; we both thought he was hilarious. There was something about James's rumpled and self-deprecating TV persona that was immensely charming, even if it concealed (or archly celebrated) both a first-class mind and a first-class ego.

It's difficult to imagine such riches in the present day. Current criticism looks more like the criticism of Baudelaire's or Balzac's time than that of James's or Hughes's: scrappy, precarious, and unpopular. Where criticism retains a last fingerhold on the popular mind, it is in the few holdover publications of the now-vanished golden age of the mature baby boom — such as *The New Yorker*, where Gopnik's obit was published. In Australia, the situation is even further advanced; the body of criticism is now firmly senescent. Looking across the Australian critical landscape in 2020, the steady erosion is impossible to ignore. There are fewer places to write thoughtfully about art and culture, fewer artworks being discussed, and less critical discussion overall. Specialist arts pages at major newspapers such as *The Australian*, *The Sydney Morning Herald*, *The Age*, and *The Australian Financial Review* have been slashed or even eliminated altogether.

Specialist publications are not picking up the slack. Although there is excellent work being done at smaller publications like *Meanjin*, *Overland*, *Sydney Review of Books*, *Discipline*, *The Lifted Brow*, and, less frequently, *Australian Book Review*, it's becoming increasingly clear that the broader critical horizon is contracting.

A telling example is the decline of specialist arts writing on the national broadcaster. The Australian Broadcasting Corporation (ABC) was once the first place most Australians came to for discussion and debate about arts and culture. It was, for instance, an ABC broadcast in which A.A. Phillips first put forward his ideas about "cultural cringe." By the 1970s, as Peter Timms recognized, ABC Radio National had established itself as a preeminent public service broadcaster specializing in longer-form discussion and critical debate (Timms argued in 2004 that Radio National was "virtually the only non-print media forum for art in this country").[9]

In our time, the ABC's cultural content is diminished from its glory days.[10] Gone are the prime-time arts programs of the 1990s, or the funky documentaries of the 2000s like Marcus Westbury's *Not Quite Art*. The problem was already worrying ABC staff in the mid-2000s, when they commissioned accomplished cultural studies academic Liz Jacka in 2004 to examine the state of ABC arts programming.[11] Since then, the trend has further declined. By the 2010s, the ABC found itself without a specialist arts program on its primary free-to-air channel.[12] In 2017, after a series of funding cuts from the federal government, the ABC took the knife to Radio National, slashing a number of specialist programs.

Perhaps more alarmingly, a lot of historical ABC arts content has disappeared in recent years, including eleven years of *At The Movies* with film critics David Stratton and Margaret Pomeranz, not to mention the entire ABC Arts online portal. These disappearances represent thousands of reports, reviews, and critical essays, including Stratton and Pomeranz's reviews of hugely important Australian films such as Warwick Thornton's *Samson and Delilah* (2009). Some of those were the only reviews of small-budget Australian features on the public record. Key articles and reviews from noted Australian critics Alison Croggon and Dan Golding have also vanished, apparently into the netherworld of the ABC digital archives.

Unfortunately, we do not have a robust quantitative picture of just how much criticism has been pruned from Australia's public sphere since, say, the year 2000. A thorough and rigorous content analysis of the trend is very much needed; perhaps the Australia Council for the Arts could look to fund such a study. But we do have quantitative data on the number of paid writers and journalists in this country, via the Australian Bureau of Statistics (ABS). These figures are telling. Comparing data from the last three Australian censuses, we see wholesale job losses for journalists and writers, particularly in print — exactly the space where critics once plied their trade. Jobs for print journalists, for instance, declined by around a third between 2006 and 2016, according to the ABS.

Employment for writers and print media workers, by occupation, 2006–16	**2006**	**2011**	**2016**
Author	2,548	2,599	3,342
Book or Script Editor	251	1,726	1,396
Classified Advertising Clerk	812	657	217
Copywriter	1,018	1,456	2,038
Newspaper or Periodical Editor	4,844	5,059	4,388
Print Journalist	6,306	5,510	3,827
Radio Journalist	671	603	468
Technical Writer	2,114	2,560	2,922
Television Journalist	1,059	1,123	1,002
Other journalists and writers	2,693	3,830	4,516
Proofreader	449	389	295
Total Writers and Print Media Workers	**23,765**	**25,472**	**24,411**

ABS data for "writers and print media workers" for the last three censuses.
Source: Australian Bureau of Statistics micro-data.

We also know what writers in Australia are typically paid, thanks to a long-running and detailed study by Macquarie University cultural economist David Throsby. Using a survey to establish a robust cohort of professional artists working in Australia,

Throsby and his coauthors' data shows that pay for writers is low and declining.

Median incomes of Australian writers, 2014–15 financial year	Median creative income	Median creative and arts-related income	Median income (all sources)
Writers	$4,500	$6,600	$35,000
All artists	$6,000	$15,500	$42,200

Median incomes for writers in Australia, 2014–15.
Source: David Throsby and Katya Petetskaya, Making Art Work.[13]

As Throsby's figures demonstrate, half of all writers in Australia in the year 2014–15 earned less than AU$4,500 from their writing, and less than AU$6,600 from "arts-related income," which takes into account activities such as writing workshops, festival appearances, and other income related to their craft. The poverty line for a single person in Australia in June 2015 was AU$26,912.[14] This means that most writers in Australia cannot make enough money to sustain even a meagre living from their work. In short, the available data establishes a firm empirical record of a declining sector.

Conversations with a number of prominent critics in Australia lend qualitative weight to the assertion that critical coverage is shrinking. This tallies with what we know of the precarious and insecure nature of writing, particularly specialist non-fiction writing like criticism. Distinguished critic Miriam Cosic, a former arts editor at *The Australian*, told me that she thought arts coverage and criticism has declined. So had the standard of the critical conversation, she noted, with pieces getting shorter and the standard of critical debate eroding. "Serious criticism isn't a short buyer's guide with a star rating attached," Cosic told me.

> It provides historical and social context, assessment from an educated and experienced point of view, and even gives food for thought to someone who can't go: a discourse, in other words ... Sadly, I think the erosion of arts journalism as well as criticism in Australia — dwindling space in the print media, younger cheaper staff, pressure for clickbait, and the prevailing taste for instant, easy entertainment — is endangering the very concept of art today.

In a recent paper on the state of Australian performing arts criticism, celebrated Australian critic and novelist Alison Croggon made similar points:

> Arts journalism, and particularly arts criticism, has been one of the major casualties of these seismic shifts in the media industries. The specialist, niche readership meant that they were among the first to reduce or disappear under the reign of the bean counters and the laser-accurate reader stats of the data revolution. In Australia, only newspapers that value the aura of prestige that comes with the arts—such as News Ltd.'s *The Australian*, or Schwartz Media's *The Saturday Paper*—keep a strong arts section. Elsewhere, longform arts journalism has all but vanished from the mainstream press.[15]

Does this matter? One valid question that could be asked in light of this data is whether the decline of critical discussion is necessarily a bad thing, either for the arts themselves or for our society more broadly. I think the answer is yes, on both counts. Criticism matters to the health of culture because it plays a pivotal role in nurturing audiences and developing taste. Criticism assists innovation, not only by helping audiences find new work, but also by encouraging artists to take risks. Good criticism fertilizes the cultural soil and tends to the artistic garden. It evaluates, reasons, and judges. As Noël Carroll observes in his short but perspicacious book *On Criticism* (2009), the business of criticism is *precisely* "providing qualitative evaluations of works of art."

> The association of criticism with evaluation corresponds to the origin of the concept. The term "critic" derives from the Greek *kritkos*—one who serves on a jury and delivers a verdict [...] A *kritikos* can issue a positive as well as a negative verdict. Likewise, an art critic in the relevant sense can offer constructive as well as destructive criticism.
>
> For me, the primary function of the critic is not to eviscerate artworks. Rather, I hypothesize that the audience typically looks to critics for assistance in discovering the value to be had from the works under review. The common reader expects guidance from the critic concerning what is worthy in an artwork. We hope to grasp the value or significance that the critic intends to point out to us.

> This is, in fact, our leading reason for consulting critics, despite the fact that the title sometimes carries more negative associations [...] the plain reader more fundamentally regards the critic as a skilled discriminator of quality in her chosen domain [...] that is, as someone who is also expert in the sense that she is adept at backing those verdicts up with reasons.[16]

Carroll is surely correct to argue that the essential feature of good criticism is reasoned evaluation. And I think he's also right to point to the places where that reasoned evaluation typically takes place: publications—vehicles for the presentation of reviews and critical essays. (That's not to say that criticism has to be written, of course; there are wonderful podcasts and television shows devoted to criticism.) This is particularly true for popular criticism, the kind that can reach a wide audience, the kind that Clive James wrote.

What happens when we abandon any genuine attempt at assessing and evaluating work? The result is not necessarily a critical desert, in which work is no longer critically discussed. It is more likely that the result is rather an impoverished cultural discussion, in which crude quantitative metrics (such as box office or book sales), or raw emotive expression (such as social media pile-ons), are substituted for genuine engagement with artworks themselves.

Another possibility is a degradation of our critical sphere, of the kind that we have seen in our political sphere lately. You don't have to be a follower of German philosopher Jürgen Habermas to see the degeneration of our critical faculties as the harbinger of a darker, less tolerant, and more violent political world. The replacement of considered judgment with emotional fanaticism is a noticeable phenomenon of the way large movie studios now plan and script their superhero melodramas. In a darker sense, such degradation was also the genesis of the game culture controversy known as "Gamergate," and the neo-fascist energies it heralded.

As Charlie Warzel argued in *The New York Times*, after the original Gamergate controversy:

> Five years later, the elements of Gamergate are frighteningly familiar: hundreds of thousands of hashtag-swarming tweets; armies of fake Twitter accounts; hoaxes and

> disinformation percolating in murky chat rooms and message boards before spreading to a confused mainstream media; advertiser boycotts; crowdfunding campaigns; racist, sexist and misogynist memes; YouTube shock jocks; D-list celebrities hand-wringing about political correctness on Twitter; Milo Yiannopoulos, Steve Bannon and Breitbart; Candace Owens.
>
> Gamergate's DNA is everywhere on the internet, and the ubiquity of Gamergate's influence has even spawned a winking trope: Everything Is Gamergate.[17]

Perhaps not quite everything is Gamergate, but it's no coincidence that many of the tropes fought over by the denizens of Reddit and 4Chan are cultural symbols. In this respect, the contemporary moment shares a weird symmetry with the original media and cultural analyses of critical thinkers such as Antonio Gramsci or Stuart Hall.[18] Right-wing fury coalesced around the symbolism of *Star Wars* characters; it appropriated a cartoon frog as an alt-right symbol; it used the tools of media studies against the leftists it accused of imposing "social justice" norms. Even Cathy Young, a center-right defender of Gamergate — because, of course, there are some — describes the event as "the first rebellion against the politicization of popular culture by the 'social justice left'."[19] Warzel observed:

> Five years on, no lesson feels more prescient than the fact that its supposed central premise — a broad reckoning regarding journalistic ethics in video games — was based on an easily (and frequently) debunked lie.
>
> Gamergate is occasionally framed as a battle for the soul of the internet between a diverse, progressive set and an angry collection of white males who feel displaced. And it is that, too. But its most powerful legacy is as proof of concept of how to wage a post-truth information war.[20]

It's possible to see the eclipse of criticism as part of a broader trend in our techno-culture, a trend away from slower, considered, and more thoughtful analysis and critique toward a hastier, hotter, and more emotional style of reaction. As British political economist Will Davies argued in his 2018 book *Nervous States*, the sudden advent of world-spanning social media platforms (augmented by the ever-greater influence of older but still-powerful media like cable television news) has created a new type of public sphere, one in which untruths and hatreds can rapidly proliferate.[21] The decline of criticism is not the cause of such maladies, but it is a symptom.

James was onto all of this, of course. His last monograph was, fittingly, a return to the television criticism that had made him justly famous, and which may end up being his truest legacy. In *Play All: A Bingewatcher's Notebook* (2016), James produced a late masterpiece in a minor key, peppered with his customary brio and wit. *Play All* was characteristically optimistic about the television shows it considered.[22] As Gopnik observed in his lovely obituary:

> In his popular work, he didn't sell out; he sold *up*. Along with many other remarkable people of his generation — Jonathan Miller, slightly older, who died in the same week, was of the same kind — he took it for granted that all strong ideas could be made lucid to a large audience, and that if there was one that couldn't, it might not actually be that strong an idea.[23]

Myself, I wonder. The world that James inhabited — the world of easy mass literacy, of free movement between the center and the periphery, of endless material abundance, of the availability of high culture to the middle classes, and of the unquestioned centrality of mass culture — is rapidly vanishing, along with the economic structure that held that edifice upright. What has replaced it is a world much closer to the disorder and pathologies of the first decade of James's life and, as *Cultural Amnesia* sagely predicted, an incipient source of coming nightmares.[24]

James wrote about binge television when it was already the last gasp of a vanishing culture. Middlebrow was a cultural logic of middle-class dominance. But the reign of the middle class is over, overmastered by tech platform neo-feudalism, the middle classes enserfed to the billionaires atop the social hierarchy. This is not a post-global phenomenon, exactly, as these trends are international. But in Donald Trump's United States, Boris Johnson's England, and Narendra Modi's India, we can see the end of the globalist dream of the 1990s. Vanishing with it is the mass literacy James took for granted, heralding the dusk of the humanist republic of letters that he championed.

1 Adam Gopnik, "Clive James Got It Right," *The New Yorker*, November 30, 2019, https://www.newyorker.com/culture/postscript/clive-james-got-it-right.

2 Virginia Woolf, "Middlebrow," in *The Death of the Moth* (London: Hogarth Press, 1942), 113–119.

3 I am indebted in particular to the work of Beth Driscoll on the postwar middlebrow. Beth Driscoll, "The Middlebrow Family Resemblance: Features of the Historical and Contemporary Middlebrow," *Post45* (July 2016), http://post45.org/2016/07/the-middlebrow-family-resemblance-features-of-the-historical-and-contemporary-middlebrow/.

4 Pierre Bourdieu, *Distinction: A Social Critique of the Judgement of Taste*, trans. Richard Nice (London: Routledge & Kegan Paul, 1984); Dwight Macdonald, *Masscult and Midcult: Essays Against the American Grain*, ed. John Summers, (New York: New York Review Books, 2011).

5 Fredric Jameson, *Postmodernism, or, The Cultural Logic of Late Capitalism* (Durham: Duke University Press, 1991).

6 Guy Rundle, "*Love Serenade*: Glen Campbell and AM radio," in *Practice: Journalism, Essays and Criticism* (Carlton: Black Inc., 2017), 245.

7 Phillipa McGuinness, *The Year Everything Changed: 2001* (North Sydney: Penguin Random House Australia, 2018).

8 Colm McAuliffe, "Radical Broadcasts: Raymond Williams on TV," *The Raymond Williams Society*, June 24, 2018, https://raymondwilliams.co.uk/2018/06/24/radical-broadcasts-raymond-williams-on-tv/.

9 Peter Timms, *What's Wrong with Contemporary Art?* (Sydney: UNSW Press, 2004), 102.

10 The following discussion of ABC arts programming draws on an article I wrote in 2018 for *Crikey*. Ben Eltham, "How Much Should the ABC Be Investing in Australian Arts and Culture?," *Crikey*, November 29, 2018, https://www.crikey.com.au/2018/11/29/how-much-should-the-abc-be-investing-in-australian-arts-and-culture/.

11 Liz Jacka, "'Don't Use the A-word': Arts by Stealth at the ABC — a Latourian Analysis," *Cultural Studies Review* 13, no. 1 (2007): 50–69, https://doi.org/10.5130/csr.v13i1.2154.

12 Amanda Meade, "ABC Revives Arts Coverage with New Show," *Guardian Australia*, June 12, 2014, https://www.theguardian.com/culture/australia-culture-blog/2014/jun/12/abc-revives-arts-coverage-with-new-show.

13 David Throsby and Katya Petetskaya, *Making Art Work: An Economic Study of Professional Artists in Australia* (Strawberry Hills: Australia Council for the Arts, 2017), 74.

14 Melbourne Institute for Applied Economic and Social Research, *Poverty Lines: Australia, June Quarter 2015* (Parkville: University of Melbourne, 2015), https://melbourneinstitute.unimelb.edu.au/assets/documents/poverty-lines/2015/Poverty-Lines-Australia-June-2015.pdf.

15 Alison Croggon, *Platform Papers 61: Criticism, Performance and the Need for Conversation* (Sydney: Currency House, 2019), 17–18.

16 Noël Carroll, *On Criticism* (Abingdon: Routledge, 2009), 14–15.

17 Charlie Warzel, "Everything Is Gamergate," *The New York Times*, August 15, 2019, https://www.nytimes.com/interactive/2019/08/15/opinion/what-is-gamergate.html.

18 A point recently made by Will Davies in a range of publications. See: William Davies, "Why Can't We Agree on What's True Anymore?," *The Guardian*, September 19, 2019, https://www.theguardian.com/media/2019/sep/19/why-cant-we-agree-on-whats-true-anymore.

19 Cathy Young, "(Almost) Everything You Know About GamerGate Is Wrong," *Arc Digital*, September 6, 2019, https://arcdigital.media/almost-everything-you-know-about-gamergate-is-wrong-c4a50a3515fb.

20 Warzel, "Everything Is Gamergate," 2019.

21 William Davies, *Nervous States: How Feeling Took Over the World* (London: Jonathan Cape, 2018).

22 Clive James, *Play All: A Bingewatcher's Notebook* (New Haven, CT: Yale University Press, 2016).

23 Gopnik, "Clive James Got It Right," 2019.

24 Clive James, *Cultural Amnesia: Notes in the Margin of My Time* (London: Picador, 2007).

Another False Start: Some Chronotopes of Art Writing in the Present Age

Bella Li & Justin Clemens

"In the winter of 1992," the journalist Janet Malcolm writes, "I began a series of interviews with the artist David Salle."[1] The essay that resulted from these encounters, titled "Forty-One False Starts," was first published in *The New Yorker* in 1994, twenty-five years ago, and more recently republished in a collection of essays on artists and writers, also titled *Forty-One False Starts* (2013). Ostensibly a profile of the contemporary (and still contemporary) artist David Salle, Malcolm's essay provides a useful entry point for our own: an inquiry into the nature of the ill-defined grounds on which art, writing, and the contemporary world meet.

"Forty-One False Starts" raises, as its centerpiece, the seemingly solid figure of the artist as a proxy for understanding the artwork: a perceived nexus of relation that animates, in the simplest view, our fascination with artist biographies. Somewhere within the body of the artist, after all, is the material "start" of the work. As the title suggests, however, while the essay gives the reader forty-one beginnings, each of them turns out to be false. Salle, introduced to us forty-one times in varying locations and circumstances, at various stages of remove, is sometimes "the painter David Salle" and very rarely simply "David Salle." Most often he is "the artist David Salle." This phrase, repeated until the four words merge into one proper noun, is an echo that gives an impression of increasing distance, an increasingly unbridgeable gap, between the reader/viewer and the subject of our gaze. "The artist David Salle" recedes, and is finally nothing more than a smooth surface, a sounding board for ideas about contemporary art, about the artist's role in society, about the artist's relation to capital, about appropriation and originality, about the relationship between artists and writers, writers and other writers, about the whole complicated machine of cultural production ... among other subjects.

With its labyrinthine weave of thematic continuities and discontinuities, the essay constitutes, in Malcolm's inimitable way, the playing of a kind of trick on the reader (who is reading, presumably, to gain entry into the inner life and inner sanctuary of the artist David Salle). Malcolm alludes early on to "Salle's hermeticism, the private, almost secretive nature of his interest and tastes and intentions,"[2] and it is this privacy — both of the artist and the artwork — that her essay, while purporting to expose, actually works to keep veiled and inscrutable (the veiling and inscrutability being precisely what gives it infinite potential value). No sooner does a door open into a room in which we glimpse the artist seated in his studio, or attending an exhibition opening, than the door, often abruptly and unceremoniously, closes. We are given a brief space to collect ourselves before another door opens and we enter again, with increasingly diminished hopes of finding what we were looking for in the first place.

If Malcolm is enacting a game of cat and mouse, she is only following in Salle's footsteps. She weaves her way not only through her own in situ encounters with the man, which start to take on the atmosphere and substance of dream (recurring scenes, sometimes with slight variations in dialogue, subtle shifts in lighting and perspective), but also through the numerous other interviews and articles and reviews written about Salle and/or his work. Throughout "Forty-One False Starts," Malcolm is fully aware of her writerly role in the performance piece that is "The artist David Salle"; one that unfolds in the real time of writing (or so it is implied) through Malcolm's appropriation of Salle's own method:

> He told me that he never revises. Every brushstroke is irrevocable [...] He works under the dire conditions of performance. Everything counts, nothing may be taken back, everything must always go relentlessly forward. Mistake may be fatal.[3]

And yet this ethos of relentless forward motion, identified as a central component of Salle's praxis by Salle himself, is undermined, in Malcolm's writerly representation of it, by the "real" subject of the essay, which emerges once the "false" subject recedes. This subject — which is also the true subject of the present essay — is the chronotope of the false start.

In a classic essay titled "Forms of Time and of the Chronotope in the Novel," the twentieth-century Russian critic Mikhail Bakhtin introduces the eponymous concept in this way:

> We will give the name *chronotope* (literally, "time space") to the intrinsic connectedness of temporal and spatial relationships that are artistically expressed in literature [...] What counts for us is the fact that it expresses the inseparability of space and time (time as the fourth dimension of space). We understand the chronotope as a formally constitutive category of literature.[4]

Bakhtin's examples of chronotopes are extremely varied. There is the criminal trial, for instance, which densely organizes plots and characters around its own determinations. Or, again, such figures as the rogue and the adventurer, the prostitute and the parvenu, are all instances of chronotopes insofar as they introduce into the world of their fictions certain expectations and regularities, certain zones of available action and movement, of verisimilitude and preposterousness. Under this description, what we usually think of as "persons" or "events" are chronotopes, just as much as are recognizable locales. Bakhtin gives several examples: "the heroes of chivalric romance are *individualized*, yet at the same time *symbolic*."[5] That is, when we are presented with the Red Cross Knight we already know the sorts of things that are going to have to happen in the time-space he incarnates; by contrast, the rogues, clowns, and fools of popular medieval literature are deindividualized-yet-determining figures of a public manifestation. The key aspect is that they establish and incarnate specific relationships of time-space in their own way. A chronotope is a kind of literary widget — a small, stolid, solid, and stable set of steps — which gets plugged into forms of writing to shape and order a narrative.

In the chronotope of the false start, we see a kind of dissimulation at work: in English, the word "start" means a beginning; in the case of Malcolm's essay, the beginning of a study of an artist. But it also refers to a *start*, to a physical spasm, a bodily reaction to something *before one knows* what one is reacting to. A start is at once reactive and anticipatory; at once the potential beginning of attentiveness and also its rupture or interruption. As the philosopher Giorgio Agamben remarks of the word *studium* (Latin for study):

> It goes back to a *st-* or *sp-* root indicating a crash, the shock of impact. Studying and stupefying are in this sense akin: those who study are in the situation of people who have received a shock and are stupefied by what has struck them, unable to grasp it and at the same time powerless to leave hold.[6]

A start, then, is also always a *stop*. It is, moreover, inevitably false, insofar as it promises a continuation that it never delivers. But it is false in another sense too, in that it promises to reveal a cause that it nonetheless covers up. A start is a false start because it never gives rise to a real process, simultaneously withdrawing any commitment to an explication of its cause. Yet, paradoxically, a false start is by the same token also a true start insofar as it still gives you a start. And that true start is a re-start, a starting-again, simultaneously multiple, divergent, and intensely repetitive. A sort of ethics is at work here: not just to start once, but to start again and again, the repetition of the "again" being bound to the powers of the false. The doubled falsity of the chronotope of the "false start," which entails an ethical relation to the praxis of beginning or "winding up" (to introduce a shadow that will become more substantial later in our piece), is not only the fulcrum of Malcolm's essay, but also a constitutive feature of the timespace we find ourselves in: our own (writing) present.

In seeking out the dimensions of this present, and the tripartite relationship between art, writing, and the contemporary that may or may not illuminate it, we might wonder about the status of the common syntagma "contemporary art." Is "contemporary art" itself a chronotope? Can it illuminate, or be illuminated by, the chronotope of the false start? Is contemporary art a kind of stop-start? Or is it a creature of another kind altogether?

In an essay titled — helpfully, for our purposes — *On Contemporary Art*, novelist César Aira argues that what we conceive of as contemporary art exists in an ever-expanding, ever-present present: one that is, in reality, the past.[7] Literature (writing about art) inserts contemporary art back into history and, by tethering it to the mass of other artifacts we call "culture," imbues it with depth, complexity, meaning. Literature exerts, in this view, a positive influence on contemporary art, provides gravity to counteract its (real or perceived) weightlessness and formlessness.

If we read not only the content of Aira's essay (which is actually, like Malcolm's, a series of mini essays or fragments), but also the particulars of its production as an artifact, we find that there is something about writing about contemporary art that is in fact necessary to guarantee the latter's *true* contemporaneity. Aira's *On Contemporary Art* is part of a series by US publisher David Zwirner Books, going by the moniker The *Ekphrasis* Series (emphasis in the original). To quote the series blurb in the back pages:

> By bringing back into print important but overlooked books [...] and by commissioning emerging writers, philosophers and artists to write freely on visual culture, David Zwirner Books aims to encourage a richer conversation between the worlds of literary and visual art. With an emphasis on writing that isn't academic in the traditional sense, but compelling as prose, and more concerned with subject matter than historical reference, *ekphrasis* invites a broader and more varied audience to participate in discussions about the arts. Particularly now, as visual art becomes an increasingly important cultural touchstone, creating a series that encourages us to make meaning of what we see has become more compelling than ever. Books in the *ekphrasis* series remind us, with refreshing energy, why so many people have dedicated their lives to art.

Let's attempt to parse this blurb. To begin with, one of the phrases that stands out is: "broader and more varied audience." Which implies that art writing (by which is meant art criticism?) is too academic? Too stuffy? Limited to a small audience by virtue of its (un)literary style? Conversations about art, this seems to be saying, need to occur out past the strictly patrolled shores of the art world of not only artists (and primarily perhaps not artists at all), but also of curators, cultural institutions, critics, consumers, and the nefarious market in general, into the boundless waters of the General Public, where everybody else is swimming and maybe having a better time. As practitioners of poetry, a marginal art form, we feel extreme sympathy for this gesture toward a luminous General Public that most likely couldn't care less. We ask ourselves, for instance, who precisely would be buying a David Zwirner Book from The *Ekphrasis* Series, and the answer we come up with is: mostly artists, curators, cultural institutions, critics, consumers, and perhaps the nefarious market in general.

This demarcation of the "art world" from the rest of the world is a consistent feature of writing about art. In the sixth "false start" of "Forty-One False Starts," Malcolm tells us that she and Salle had originally met because Salle had proposed she write the text for a book of his work. She questions her suitability for the project:

> When I told him there must be some mistake, that I was not an art historian or an art critic and had but the smallest acquaintance with his work, he said no, there wasn't a mistake. He was deliberately looking for someone outside the art world, for an "interesting writer" who would write an unconventional text.[8]

What is occurring when a well-known writer, such as Malcolm or Aira, is commissioned or cajoled to bring their "outside" expertise to bear on the obscure and obscured "inside"? What is imagined or hoped for, usually by those who are doing the commissioning or cajoling, is some kind of act of "reseeing," to couch this in visual terms. This "reseeing" is not valued for its optical perspicuity (that is, "seeing" to the truth), but for its time-shifting abilities: as a way to bring the work of contemporary art — held in abeyance in the purgatory of a continuous present, which also bleeds into the past — properly into the present through the introduction of visible divisions in time (its seeing is tied to the eye, which is tied to a body, which is embedded in social/historical reality). In this manner, art is *re*started through a piece of writing.

And yet, as the operations of contemporary art are characterized by an always delayed temporality — always lagging behind the "real" present — and the maintenance of spatial boundaries, between "art" and its others, that nevertheless long for dissolution, to *write* about contemporary art is therefore to both engage with it and also to threaten its extinction. In order to achieve the former and avoid the latter, what occurs, as we have seen with Malcolm's essay, is an occlusion of the subject itself via an endless circling, in which the circling becomes the focus. In Aira's essay, for instance, the final fragment begins: "To end where I began" (the start is the full stop; the stop, once again, returns us to a start).[9] This is not, however, the end of *On Contemporary Art*.

After Aira's last words (punctuated by the date of composition—2010, almost a decade before its publication in The *Ekphrasis* Series—as if to inadvertently prove Aira's point about the pastness of the "contemporary"), we are presented with another essay by another writer, Alexandra Kleeman. The tone and style of Kleeman's afterword appears, in fact, to be far more in line with the aim of the series: that is, to present less "academic" and presumably more "accessible" writing about art (Aira's writing is pretty academic, if we are going to hand out labels). Writing about the experience of standing in line to see an unnamed and "recently deceased artist's final installation" (at an unnamed museum, in an undisclosed time and place), Kleeman's point, in the end, is that the artwork itself is not the point:

> It occurred to me that perhaps the line we were standing in was the point of the whole thing. Our line, like a swaddling cloth, encircled the entire work and set it apart from the busy metropolitan background. From within it, we generated an aura of anticipation that colored the world rosily. We set in motion stories about the work's contents [...] and these stories were unrecorded, not transcribed, irreproducible, the ghostly effects of the absent object. In this sense, the work generated experience within us, narrative experience, even if it refused to be made available to us as stimulus.[10]

Just as in Malcolm's essay, where the ostensible figure of the artist recedes into the background and becomes only a means to an end, here Kleeman presents us not with the artwork that is her ostensible subject, but with a story or series of stories generated by sheer virtue of its existence. What such instances of writing about art, in our contemporary moment, reveal is that the chronotope of contemporary art is, like the chronotope of the false start, a dissimulation. "Contemporary art," as Aira argues, has become an all-encompassing term for any art produced after 1970. To speak of "contemporary art," then, is to attach the adjective "contemporary" to the wrong noun; which is to say that it is to not speak of the *contemporary* at all.

Let's return again to The *Ekphrasis* Series blurb, which employs words like: "more [...] than ever" and "increasingly." Such (marketing) phrases are tied to subjacent presumptions of a false continuity—a process of "increasing," of "more and more"—

that are precisely refused by Malcolm's declaration of false starts. These gesture with the vocabulary of urgency toward the *now*. Which is what, exactly? If we have been speaking of circling, we must admit that we ourselves have been tracing a groove around a question that needs to be addressed directly, however many times we may need to start and start again in our address: what constitutes "the contemporary"? The contemporary, it seems to us, is a world characterized absolutely by two global phenomena: the extreme material effects of climate change and the materially based (in the form of servers, cables, etc.) but seemingly immaterial sphere of the internet. The node of this inquiry is really situated here, in the hollow of the contemporary world in which we are firmly stashed, in which we are seemingly trapped between the hell of a shattering and crumbling biosphere and the heaven of a limitless cyberspace that seemingly transcends space itself—of all which we are the authors and masters and victims.

What is the place of art in this contemporary world? What is it that we can ever "understand" about artists and art in general? Would that in turn even help us to understand the contemporary world? And where does writing—literature, fiction, poetry—fit into all this? If our inquiry in this essay is, as it must be, about *this* contemporary, where does this leave us? Are we happy to stand around in queues telling stories to strangers? What about the environmental catastrophe that's happening (always in some other place) while we're swapping anecdotes?

Yet it is also the case that the very vastness and complexity of the situation denominated by such indices seems at once so material as to be unrepresentable, and so immaterial as to constitute an abyss of simulations and derivatives. It is as if Francis Bacon's famous dictum—the seventeenth-century English Lord Chancellor, not the Irish artist—that "knowledge is power" has been resoundingly falsified. Today we have something like absolute knowledge coupled with absolute impotence, absolute urgency coupled with absolute confusion, a sort of temporal and topological derangement without currently attestable directions.

If the question of representation lies somewhere near the center of our inquiry, then the figure of the chronotope assumes greater significance, as both an epistemological and ethical tool. A chronotope is a literary image—a unified assemblage simultaneously sensible and symbolic—that establishes a singular mixture of space and time in a narrative. The forest, the desert, the hotel, the dump, the gallery: *timespaces* that delimit movements, characters, events. An inside is delimited from an outside or outsides — the American forest from the city of London, for instance. That delimitation is itself a relation of sharpness and vagueness, inscribing zones of possibility and impossibility, likelihood and improbability. Chronotopes are therefore at once generic — you can pull them in and out of various stories — yet non-algorithmic, insofar as they don't ever absolutely determine the course of a story. If a genre is a kind of narrative that is legible insofar as one recognizes its stock status, and a myth is a kind of narrative that makes a claim for a non-generic special status, then a chronotope is also what separates myth from genre within a fiction in the course of its elaboration. This might seem contradictory or unclear; surely myth and genre share chronotopes? Aren't all the aforementioned places, the forest and desert and so forth, at once indifferently mythic and generic? Bakhtin's point, however, is that a chronotope is not simply a regulative aesthetic idea, an image, figure, or locus; it is also an operator that puts the ideological status of its own projections into question. A chronotope does something odd to the status of the narratives in which it is deployed, insofar as it is at once essential to the narrative, and yet works to undermine the narrative's own claims. This is why Bakhtin can remark that "it is precisely the chronotope that defines genre and generic distinctions."[11]

Paradoxically enough, under the conditions of the contemporary — disaster capitalism at the limit of ecological viability — the commodification of everything is absolute (it is utterly *generic*), but only insofar as this stock status can continue to pass itself off as special (as *myth*). As Karl Marx might put it, the commodity form — its "fetishism" — is the *myth* of capital. Nonetheless, some commodities try to separate themselves from myth (which can never be entirely achieved) by exposing their own generic nature. Art is one of the central practices in contemporary culture where such an attempted separation is often made. For Bakhtin, the novel's deployment of chronotopes attempts a non-doctrinaire exposure of something that goes beyond existing limits by separating genre and myth in the course of its own elaboration. The novel is therefore the imaginative *genre as anti-genre* par excellence. Its power is linked to its own contradictions, to its ceaseless struggle against those myths which, to the very extent it succeeds in rendering them generic, also fails because it thereby creates a new myth — the myth of its own singularity.

In his extraordinary children's book *The Mouse and His Child*, first published in 1969 (and therefore almost exactly contemporary with Aira's demarcation date for contemporary art), Russell Hoban tells the story of two little windup tin mice, father and son.[12] When we first meet them, in a plush toyshop just before Christmas, the mice are joined at the hands; when wound, the father swings his son up and down while dancing in a circle. This little constrained performance is their very *raison d'être*. They are purchased as Christmas ornaments and, year after year, are brought out to be carefully wound up by the parents to dance by the glittering tree before being carefully packed away again. One year, the boy mouse, overwhelmed by the sentimental vision of a doll's house — which reminds him of his first warm memories of the toyshop in which he first came to consciousness — inadvertently lets out a tiny sob while dancing for the delectation of the family. The pet cat, startled by the strange and sudden sound, knocks over a vase of flowers which crushes the pair — and the now-useless mice are thrown out together in the trash. There they are discovered by a tramp going through the garbage, who dusts them off, winds up their battered-but-still-functioning mechanism, and sets them down on the side of the road, farewelling them with the injunction: "Be tramps." So, the chronotope goes: two tin mice with one winding mechanism are on the road. Where are they to go when they know of nowhere to go? How will they go when they can only go when wound up? What are they to do when they can no longer do what they were made to do? The course of their wandering will literally be long and winding.

But it will also be an unwinding: after the accident, the mice no longer dance in a circle. The father now pushes the child in an off-kilter line, so that the latter — like Walter Benjamin's famous interpretation of the little image *Angelus Novus* (1920) by Paul Klee — moves forever backwards into a future that he cannot see. The pair cannot wind themselves; they can only stop and start in accordance with the dictates of their mechanism. For better or worse, then, they are at the mercy of the various passersby they encounter. One of these is the literally demonic rodent Manny Rat, lord of the dump, who salvages just such mechanical toys so that they will work for him as slaves amid the wastes. Forced into Manny's service, the mice work with other faltering tin recruits.

Everywhere they toil in the dump, they come across empty discarded cans of Bonzo Dog Food, which bears on its label a dog with a chef's hat carrying a can of Bonzo Dog Food, on which there is a dog with a chef's hat carrying a can of Bonzo Dog Food — and so on, to infinity. This *mise en abyme* — literally a putting-into-the-abyss, a term that derives from heraldry, here repurposed for commercial advertising and branding for pet food — gives rise to another emblematic and enigmatic injunction that echoes throughout the book: *what's beyond the last visible dog?* An allegory of contemporary art is put into play.

Through their unwilling part in a failed bank heist, the mice manage to escape their rodent tormentor, only to be thrown into the perils of the natural world. In the course of their adventures, the mice meet, in addition to the malevolent rats, fellow lost windups such as the snobby elephant and the performing seal, a fortune-telling bullfrog, a blue jay journalist, warring shrews and wood mice, predatory weasels, horned owls (one of which eats the weasels), and many other creatures — all caught in the endless carnage of hunting and fleeing and killing and eating, nature "red in tooth and claw." Pursued by the relentless, furious Manny Rat, the windups flee through the wilderness.

At one point, they are lucky enough to meet Mr and Mrs Crow, who turn out to be actors with the Caws of Art Experimental Theatre Group (previously the Caws of Art Classical Repertory Group), and a frowsy parrot, escaped from her human owner, who has renamed herself Euterpe (after the ancient Greek Muse of music). Euterpe now acts as the repertory for the Caws. The company is presenting a play called *The Last Visible Dog*, written by the enigmatic and elusive playwright C. Serpentina (later revealed to be a turtle), which, for the cognoscenti, is a kind of parody of Samuel Beckett's play *Endgame*. As Euterpe sets the scene:

> *The bottom of a pond: mud, ooze, rubbish, and water plants. Two tin cans, standing upright, half buried in the mud at centre stage. At stage left, a rock. A head rises from one of the tin cans. It is the head of Furza. The head of Wurza rises from the other tin can. Gretch enters stage right and crosses to the rock.*

The play does not go well. The incensed audience, upset by its experimental tenor, heckle and then attack the players. The rabbit playing Gretch is killed by irate weasels; after much argy-bargy, the crows and parrot are saved by an impromptu comic performance from the windups, and they escape to perform another day. "That's show business," comments Euterpe, reflecting on the debacle. "But look how far we've come!," replies the child. "And think of all we've done! We got out of the dump; we came through the war safely; we saved the Caws of Art." Although their journey has hardly begun, Hoban makes it clear that, without at least a detour through the world of art — however brief, unimpressive, or farcical — there will be no subjective movement, only natural process, animal or mechanical: what the great seventeenth-century English Puritan poet John Milton (perhaps rather depressingly) named "a universe of death."

There are a number of significant resonances of the pun Caws-Cause. According to the *Oxford English Dictionary*, the word "caws" can be:

1. Of a crow, rook, raven, or other bird: to make its characteristic harsh sound; to utter a caw or caws;
2. Of a person: to make a harsh sound likened to that of a crow, rook, raven, etc.; to talk loudly or foolishly;
3. Of a person: to utter or express (esp. something foolish or trivial) with a harsh sound likened to that of a crow, rook, raven, etc.; to utter in a grating or prattling manner.

As for "cause," there could hardly be a more significant philosophical and scientific term. Indeed, the significances of the word are so extensive they can hardly be listed here. Among the major senses are:

1. That which produces an effect; that which gives rise to any action, phenomenon, or condition;
2. A person or other agent who brings about or occasions something, with or without intention. (Often in a bad sense: one who occasions, or is to blame for mischief, misfortune, etc.);
3. A fact, condition of matters, or consideration, moving a person to action; ground of action; reason for action, motive.

A cause is something that necessitates or contributes to a material action, but it is also a particular project in whose name one seeks to act, to bring about, or transmit something that is not-entirely-physical. The etymology of the word comes through French from the Latin: a matter of interest or legal controversy, a charge or case brought against a person, and so on.

But there is more: if *caws* sounds like *cause*, it also sounds like *cores* and *coarse* and *course*. The word *core*—perhaps itself deriving from the Latin *cor* for heart, or perhaps rather from *corps*, the French for body, or *cor*, the French for horn (as in cornet)—can speak of the heart of a fruit, a disease in sheep, a central part of an object that is excised. What is *coarse* is ordinary, common, mean, rough, harsh, or rude. A *course* is a movement, a circulation, a run, or running.

Hoban's homophones thereby explicitly stop and start upon the mobile and entangled lines between meaning and meaninglessness, between sound and sense, between reason and foolishness, between motivation and action, between mind and body, between art and technology, between the rough and the smooth, between movement and rest. The mice here are the chronotopes of the narrative, insofar as their situation sets the parameters for all the action that follows. As the book proceeds, the mice develop clearer ambitions and directions: they need to be separated, they need to become self-winding, they need to acquire a territory.

The dream of autonomy thereby literally becomes a kind of *homing device* in the novel. One becomes "self-winding" (personally) and acquires "territory" (external property) in order to live without dependency and fear. But perhaps *autonomy*—literally, self-law—is not quite the right term. The chronotope of the tin mice makes the reader's point of identification these mass-produced, fragile, and precarious artificial creatures created merely for momentary distraction, and the adventure itself these creatures struggling to become something other than their own nature—commodities made only to be sold, and whose sale immediately diminishes their value—other than as private fetish for the delectation of others. To escape the automatisms of nature and design—from the doubled chains of what philosophy calls "efficient causes," in which one action directly effects another, like billiard balls bashing together, and "final causes," the ends for which a thing was made, as a hammer was made for hammering—the mice can only get there through a hazardous sequence of start-stops. It turns out that false starts can sometimes turn out to be true ones—just as can the stops.

To speak of false starts, which are also always full stops, we are also always speaking of endings. Janet Malcolm's *Forty-One False Starts* ends with the following fragment:

> One day, toward the end of a conversation I was having with the painter David Salle in his studio, on White Street, he looked at me and said, "Has this ever happened to you? Have you ever thought that your real life hasn't begun yet?"
>
> "I think I know what you mean."
>
> "You know — soon. Soon you'll start your real life."[13]

At the conclusion of an essay that has, in its fragmentary, repetitive nature, begun to resemble more dream than reality, Malcolm steers the reader toward an important understanding: the knowledge that art, no matter how closely it shadows and responds to reality, is first and foremost dream. And that "real life" begins, with absolute necessity, where art ends. In *our* contemporary reality, what is required is something that art can (and must) draw our attention to the necessity of, but which it cannot and should not be held responsible for: change itself. Art, by its very nature, can only dream and dream better; the burden for seeding change rests in the hands of we who made the world in which we live *now*. We all work under the dire conditions of performance, a performance that has no rehearsals and no reprise: it is the first, last, and only. Everything counts, nothing may be taken back, everything must always go relentlessly forward. Mistake *will* be fatal.

We would like to add a spoiler alert: *The Mouse and His Child* has a happy ending. But it doesn't end with the glittering restoration of a destined imperium, a utopia of pleasure and power and privilege. It ends, rather, back in the dump where the windups and a very heterogeneous group of friends, including a now-chastened Manny, restore a trashed doll's house and open it as a "hotel" — in what seems to be a non-commercial sense of the word — named The Last Visible Dog, with a sign consisting of a rectified Bonzo Dog Food label and a pendant reading *Migrants Yes*. In addition to welcoming visitors from absolutely anywhere, it also becomes a place for art and performance, where even the Caws can now present the full version of their experimental play without being killed and eaten.

The book thus represents at least four different ways of thinking about art. Art as a light mechanical performance to entertain one's masters, whereby the performer will be immediately discarded when they can no longer entertain. Art as an experimental laboratory that offends the audience, and which cannot be sustained without potential damage to its practitioners. Art as a mode of self-discovery that necessarily presents the damaged self in a distorted and imaginary form. Art as a festive practice integrated into the lifeworld of an open community. If *The Mouse and His Child* may conclude by seeming to affirm the last of these possibilities, it nonetheless suggests that all are necessary stops in a world of false starts, that the thought of art is literally vital for life.

Contemporary art drives through its endless differentiations and repetitions in the guise of change, the form of which does not itself change. What (art) writing — whether wrought as an apparent exposé of an artist, or a pedagogical book for children — may tell us is precisely this: "contemporary art" does not designate a true false start; it is not a chronotope, but a myth. From within the turbulence of this myth, however, a separation might still be made that returns us to what we all might share of the generic, to a space in which we can find not only the potential for harboring dream, but also a properly hospitable relation to ourselves and others. In the midst of an apotheosis of waste, it's time for another false start.

1 Janet Malcolm, "Forty-One False Starts," in *Forty-One False Starts: Essays on Artists and Writers* (Melbourne: Text Publishing, 2013), 12.
2 Ibid., 4.
3 Ibid., 7.
4 Mikhail Bakhtin, *The Dialogic Imagination: Four Essays*, ed. Michael Holquist, trans. Caryl Emerson and Michael Holquist (Austin: University of Texas Press, 1981), 84.
5 Ibid., 153.
6 Giorgio Agamben, *The Idea of Prose*, trans. Michael Sullivan and Sam Whitsitt (Albany: SUNY, 1995), 64.
7 César Aira, *On Contemporary Art*, trans. Katherine Silver (New York: David Zwirner Books, 2018).
8 Malcolm, "Forty-One False Starts," 7.
9 Aira, *On Contemporary Art*, 46.
10 Kleeman in Aira, *On Contemporary Art*, 55.
11 Bakhtin, *The Dialogic Imagination*, 85.
12 Russell Hoban, *The Mouse and His Child* (London: Faber & Faber, 2000).
13 Malcolm, *Forty-One False Starts*, 38.

The Critic as Gesture or: John Malkovich's middle name is Gavin

Maria Fusco

The critic as gesture is a frustration with exhausted modes of critical engagement within our elite, cultural world, expressed in writerly form.[1]

Gesture here is defined as an act that is *motivated*.[2] What is loitering behind the invocation of an act that is motivated are the subjects who are acted upon and the direct causes impelling such subjects (ourselves), to experience a desire sufficiently pressing enough to affect scriptural change through our belief in simple marks on a page.[3] The obvious question this motivation elicits, therefore, from the mouths of first-world textbooks is: What's so wrong with the way I write anyway?

An answer to this, understandable enough, question would be: I don't like it. Another answer: The way you write is not precise enough. Another answer: Your job is to dismantle, not to build. Another answer: I don't want to be colonized by you *again*. Another answer: You don't own that, put it back where you found it. Another answer: The language of history is contagion, not antidote.[4] Another answer: The way you write hides the way you write.

Language-games must be accosted in each dark alley in which they lurk.[5] It is not sufficient to be able to simply *voice* a proficient echo of an historical form (however hilarious this might be), because this demonstrates only proficiency. Whilst it is the wish of all of us who are self-conscious and precocious enough to want to be witnessed publicly as being proficient, finally we cannot place trust in, nor shit from the great arse of, this vainglorious instinct.

As with the physical action of employing a lever, it is essential to depress when we wish to elevate.[6] Accurate navigation is a perilous yet patent responsibility of the analytic enterprise. This invocation of navigation does not agree that legislative plans are always fit for purpose. Rather, navigation here describes precision of intent, exposing the ethical responsibility of the deeds of the writer to our reader, or if we are very lucky, to our readers, plural.[7] It's grand to live alone on a small island, tending our inky crops, as long as it's possible for other folk to locate, and perhaps even visit, the island when we want them to.[8] This is duty as mandate; this is duty as tax.

Thrift is the apt schematic here. Thrift trades sparse and tactful forms, not mass-reproducible cerebral mementos. Thrift is good example but not *an* example. Thrift is sensible. Thrift carves up.

The critic as gesture is as diligent as a miser.

When constriction is applied to the wordage permitted by thrift, transubstantiation occurs: we are no longer shuffling marks on a page, on a screen, we are creating new beings.[9] The role constriction plays is that of the joyful enforcer (not of the tyrannical polemic), acting with contextual knowledge and candor.[10]

Consistency shares a little more than half of its letters with constriction. This is clearly an alphabetic coincidence but an apt one, for consistency and constriction cannot be disaggregated. The two are mutually dependent at a technical level because insistent application and physical manipulation of both is required for new limber analytical topologies.[11] Together, constriction and consistency make a pair of muscular thighs: our heads are happy clenched between these very thighs.

This desire for anonymity is a useful proviso against solely interpretive reading. Reading is essential to both the actual act of producing critical writing and the intellectual world in which it bounces. There is much we must try *not* to remember. There is much we must attempt to dis-author. In wishing anonymity in reading, we are also wishing it in writing. Resistance through anonymity is not a relegation of responsibility, rather anonymity creates commodious possibilities for others' works and, in this way, anonymity permits our writing to exceed us, to exceed our own, limited, often class-based ambitions: to *assemble*.[12]

It is entirely possible that multiple voices chance on the same formal solution; this is agreeable if it occurs through happenstance, because then it demonstrates the right to assemble at one's own will, the right to party.[13]

However, there is no prize for the best fancy-dress costume. We must not, on *any* account, hide behind those syntactic masks others want to rent us. Not masks. Forget masks. Great big fucking gilt mirrors. Understanding our teeming methodologies as stroboscopic, we may apprehend only small moments, only our own small moments, not a linear historical discursive.[14]

We are always the stranger.

1 Audre Lorde, *Sister Outsider: Essays and Speeches* (New York: Crossing Press, 1984), 110.

2 Vilém Flusser, *Gestures* (Minneapolis: University of Minnesota Press, 2014), 56.

3 Giorgio Agamben, *What Is an Apparatus?* (Stanford, CA: Stanford University Press, 2009), 10.

4 G.W.F. Hegel, *Phenomenology of Spirit* (Oxford: Oxford University Press, 1977), 116.

5 Ludwig Wittgenstein, *Philosophical Investigations* (Oxford: Basil Blackwell, 1963), 167.

6 Simone Weil, *Gravity and Grace* (Abingdon on Thames: Routledge, 2002), 84.

7 bell hooks, *Remembered Rapture: The Writer at Work* (London: The Women's Press, 1999), 42.

8 Flannery O'Connor, *Mystery and Manners* (London: Faber & Faber, 2014), 53.

9 Sister Corita, *Footnotes and Headlines* (New York: Herder and Herder, 1967), 44–45.

10 Henri Bergson, *Laughter: An Essay on the Meaning of the Comic* (Copenhagen: Green Integer Books, 1999), 29.

11 Lisa Robertson, *Nilling* (Toronto: Bookthug, 2012), 12.

12 Judith Butler, *Notes Toward a Performative Theory of Assembly* (Cambridge, MA: Harvard University Press, 2015), 68.

13 Emma Goldman, *Living My Life* (New York: Knopf, 1934), 56.

14 Gilles Deleuze, "Hélène Cixous or Stroboscopic Writing," *Le Monde*, August 11, 1972.

In Communion: Art/Writing and the Fictocritical

Sarah Gory

> There is no art which is not an act of sublimated resistance.
> — Hélène Cixous

> *This text was written where I live and work, on the sovereign land and waters of the Wurundjeri and Boonwurrung people of the Kulin Nation. I pay my respects to their Elders, past, present, and emerging. I acknowledge that I am an uninvited guest on this land that was never ceded.*

In "A Defense of Art in Troubled Times," Teju Cole writes:

> In response to the alarm of seismic change, we are pressured not only to rethink fundamentals, but to exile from ourselves whatever is not deemed fundamental and immediate [...] What is lost is whatever we were hoping to save from the disaster, what we were hoping would outlast the fire. One of the key spaces requiring our vigilance and defense is art, and specifically the consolations particular to art.[1]

Throughout the first COVID-19 lockdown, I was working on an art magazine presciently themed "care." All of the pieces in the magazine were written before "pandemic" became a part of our everyday vocabulary. Yet I cannot help but retroactively read into these texts what was never, *could never*, have been intended in the first instance. Writing about the Hong Kong democracy protests, Yang Yeung reminds us that "to walk through the main roads, small alleys, places or neighbourhoods that a mass protest has touched is to negotiate tilted grounds. What used to be the flatness of the everyday [...] now acquires a different shape."[2] I map these words against the changes wrought in my hometown — the lack of cars and the sudden call of birds, masked faces, police surrounding the homes of the families my children go to school with, play with, learn with. Tilted grounds for tilted times. A form of radical care — for ourselves, for each other, for the cities we create and the ecologies we are destroying, for art, for practice — is needed, now as much as ever.

In a year that began with fire and is now mired in plague, the space that art and its dialogue hold in society remain essential, and essential to interrogate. Art as confrontation, art as consolation — or, perhaps, both at the same time.

A bridge, of sorts

I resist writing about mothering for so long, but it leaks out — an apt metaphor (leaking breasts, leaking babies, leaking ideas, leaking time, leaking boundaries, leaking, leaking in defiance of all who want to contain us).

> Lactating breasts, when they are taken outside the home, are capable of disrupting the borders of morality, discretion, taste and politics; in short, breasts are capable of transforming legislation, citizenship and cities themselves.[3]

I've just finished reading Rivka Galchen's *Little Labours* (2016) about the time a puma moves into her apartment. She writes: "I didn't want to write about the puma. Mostly because I had never been interested in babies, or in mothers; in fact those subjects had seemed *perfectly* not interesting."[4] I cringe while I read this. I, too, didn't want to write about babies, or mothers. For the longest time, I didn't want to read about them, either. Perhaps I'd internalized a measure of our cultural disdain for mothering as a subject of *serious literature*. Perhaps it was just that the motherhood writing I could see (and so assumed was what motherhood writing was, *could be*) "had become constrained, made predictable, by certain memoirist tropes, vocabularies, intensities."[5] Perhaps neither, probably both.

Despite my reluctance, writing motherhood seems to be a "literary bridge that I must inevitably cross."[6]

And yet in the way of the rhizome — "ceaselessly establish[ing] connections between semiotic chains, organisations of powers, and circumstance"[7] — this text which began as one thing is now another. A text about mothering is now a text about art writing which turns out to be fitting, in this new age of pandemic, where the things that I do variously — mothering, writing, art writing — are increasingly things that I do simultaneously.

Case in point: as I sit here writing this text about writing about art, my five-year-old has crawled into my lap and is now sounding out the words that I am *t y p i n g*.

Yellow, like sunlight

The children are a brew of emotions that find an outlet in their fists and cries, and so we talk about our feelings as colors. His frustration is *sharp red*, he tells me; later it has faded. She hugs me, warm after a bath, and tells me that everything is *bright pink*. When we fall over dancing through the park and he scrapes the skin off his shin but we still have to walk all the way back home, he tells me that with each step he is feeling *paler and paler yellow*. We stop to hug, to hold hands, and I think that maybe pain can be a secret opening for the light, like childbirth; the color of sunlight and egg yolk and "lemons from our backyard tree warmed by the sun."[8]

Yellow is an impossible color, undefinable. Take Charlotte Perkins Gilman's *The Yellow Wallpaper* (1892) and we have "a smouldering, unclean yellow,"[9] one that stands for sickness, bile, toxicity, decay. Yellow is also brilliant, golden, a giver of life à la Richard Le Gallienne: the sun sets upon a pot of yellow chrysanthemums and "sets them ablaze."[10]

Goya's *The Drowning Dog* (1820–23), a painting described by Spanish artist Antonio Saura as "the most beautiful in the world,"[11] hangs in the Museo Nacional del Prado in Madrid. The lower third of the painting is a dark mass out of which peers a dog, its body obscured so that only its face is visible. This dog and its presence here are wholly ambiguous. Is it sinking into the murk below or emerging into the expanse above? Is it "half-buried or unearthed [...] is it being inhumed or exhumed?"[12] Perhaps both, perhaps neither. Perhaps it is simply suspended in the space between. What is clear is that the dog is looking upwards, upwards into a sky that is yellow. The kind of unholy yellow that floods the sky before a storm, a "motionless yellow [...] everything dirty and saffron."[13] But saffron, it should be noted, is also the color that Buddhist monks dye their robes — a holy color.

Another Spanish artist, Rafael Canogar, once described Goya's Dog as a "visual poem," a communion of forms that brings to mind feminist philosopher Hélène Cixous's assertion that art and writing are "inseparable halves [...] non-simultaneous twins."[14]

Criticism in the expanded field

> Criticism is itself an art form, and like all art forms it must evolve or atrophy and die.[15]

When we say "art writing," what do we mean, exactly? Are we textually rendering art or is it art, textually rendered? Do we mean writing-about-art, in the vein of traditional art criticism—detached, theoretical? Or do we mean art-as-writing whereby even "criticism is itself an art?"[16] Or do we mean what these days is known as "criticism in the expanded field,"[17] a broad genre that expands Oscar Wilde's "critic as artist" to encompass the critical, the creative, and the literary in relation to, and as, art? Personally, I like the idea of something else, of writing and art in conversation, texts "written more *to* the work than about it."[18] The seeking of a common language. A communion, of sorts.

In *Art Monthly* in 2015, art critic Gilda Williams declared "art speak" as no longer the gold standard. Instead, she argued, art writing is now "producing texts that run parallel to or within art."[19] And yet, while it is certainly a contemporary trend (in Western discourse at least), this approach is hardly new. Since the nineteenth century, the idea of art writing *as a part of practice*, rather than as ancillary to or parasitic of practice, has been expounded by the likes of Baudelaire to Oscar Wilde. As Wilde declared in the dialogical text *The Critic as Artist*, art criticism could be "both creative and independent."[20] But, coming back to Williams's assertion, in the context of the twentieth century, wherein an academic style of "art criticism has become so synonymous with 'criticality',"[21] the recent turn toward "criticism in the expanded field" does represent a fracturing, a broadening. This turn, of course, has been preempted by conversations dating back to the 1960s, with seminal texts like Joseph Kosuth's "Art After Philosophy" (1969) and Rosalind Krauss's "Sculpture in the Expanded Field" (1979), among others, as well as by social and cultural changes in Western society at large.

And yet even *within* this increasingly expansive understanding of art writing, the creative-literary/critical-theoretical binary is largely maintained.[22] Creative-critical writing is said to write parallel to art, using the visual as a point of departure and often utilizing existing literary forms. Conversely, critical-theoretical art writing, even in the case of its less traditional forms, draws more from academic conventions and tends to contextualize art within art history, as opposed to other social, cultural, or political contexts.

A form of synesthesia

Which is all to say that art writing, like most writing (like most thought, like most discourse), still exists within "trajectories of received knowledges"[23] — the distance of critic, the affect of the poet. Which is also to say, writing is not just writing. Writing is loaded and coded, built on what came before, steeped in history; "the paradox of literary composition is that [...] it is literature that tells us how to make literature."[24] Which is to say, "there is such a thing as *marked* writing."[25]

So, if our writing is to "transform social and cultural structures,"[26] to write outside of (beyond, between) the trajectories of received knowledges — and why shouldn't it? — then we must refuse the limitations of those selfsame structures. It is not enough simply to write, we need to find a way to do so without the constraints of traditional (read: patriarchal, colonial) forms of knowledge production. It needs to be "a *new, insurgent* writing."[27] After all, "the master's tools will never dismantle the master's house."[28]

What happens then, to knowledge and to art, when we attempt to find a new trajectory, when we let the experiential and the theory "rub up against each other?"[29] When the experiential is filtered (mediated, read) through theory and theory is filtered (mediated, read) through the specific, the located? This text is accordingly interested in form itself as a *way of knowing*, whereby "style is important in artwriting, for we cannot entirely extract an artwriter's argument from the text in which it is presented."[30]

I've just finished reading Elena Ferrante's Neopolitan Novels and I'll quote (decidedly out of context) what the defiant, beautiful Lina calls dissolving boundaries: a "sticky, jumbled reality" in which "a tactile emotion would melt into a visual one, a visual one would melt into an olfactory one."[31] If we embrace art as in writing as in art writing as in art as a form of synesthesia thus described, then the precision of definition ceases to be so relevant. If we need a form, then, to write art-as-writing-as-art we need a symbiotic approach, one that already exists in the complex interactions of the rhizome "connecting any point to any other."[32]

Some would call that form: fictocriticism.

Expanding the fictocritical

> We must invent a name for those 'critical' interventions which belong to literature while deforming its limits.[33]

I've been immersed in fictocriticism for months now — reading it, reading writing about it, writing it, writing about writing about it — and yet here I am laboring over a few short paragraphs explaining *what it is* (or, more precisely, what it can do). I think the problem lies in trying to pin down a genre that doesn't want to be pinned down. And so, because it was through Cixous that I first encountered the potential of the fictocritical to "open up spaces of debate rather than to close them down with assertions,"[34] let's start here:

> A traveler in unexplored places; she does not refuse, she approaches, not to do away with the *space between*, but to see it, to experience what she is not, what she is, what she can be.[35]

Writing that collapses the creative and the critical into a single text is called many things and, increasingly, it is called fictocriticism. As a practice, fictocriticism has competing origin narratives, attributed variously to 1970s French feminist discourse or postmodernist writing. Whatever its origins, Cixous's blend of the poetic, theoretical, and critical is regularly acknowledged as both a forerunner to, and an exemplar of, contemporary fictocriticism — both in form and in her deliberate attempts to use that form as a means of textual disruption.

So, what *is* fictocriticism? According to Deleuze, meaning (*knowing*) is found in the connections *between* rather than the atomization of things (people, objects, ideas); knowledge comprises multiplicities, interactions, a horizontal map. Drawing on the concept of the rhizome, Stephen Muecke offers us this: where criticism uses concepts and fiction uses percepts, fictocriticism writes in the *space between* the two.[36]

As a term that has come to encompass "creative-critical writing more broadly,"[37] the conventions of fictocriticism are not fixed rules so much as inclusive practices that elide any "particular set of stylistic features."[38] Nonetheless, in Kerr and Nettelbeck's characterization of fictocriticism as a "hybridized writing that moves between the poles of fiction ('invention'/

'speculation') and criticism ('deduction'/'explication'), of subjectivity ('interiority') and objectivity ('exteriority')," we find a loose set of conventions.[39] As a form more interested in discursive knowledge production than the display of an end result, it embraces process and formal fluidity. It is also inherently non-hierarchical, interested not in "textual authority" so much as "textual collusion."[40] In other words: the dialogical (a communion, of sorts).

An act of defiance

Maggie Nelson asks of pregnancy: "how can an experience so profoundly strange and wild and transformative also symbolize or enact the ultimate conformity?"[41]

The same could be said of motherhood.

In truth, I was never ambivalent about mothering so much as I feared the conformity that motherhood represented for someone like me (cis, heterosexual, middle-class, educated). Conformity has always felt like a kind of violence, a capitulation to a world that is endemically unjust. Perhaps, then, this *writing about motherhood stuff* is a retrospective justification for choosing to conform. Or, perhaps, it is aspiration, a means of locating the radical *within* the performance of mothering (which is to say, within the writing about mothering). A Marxist framework would say that the way we act in the world constructs the world—hence, radicality as aspiration.

Practitioners of the fictocritical are not so much concerned with offering a precise definition of the term as they are with asking: "what can fictocriticism *do*?"[42]

For Heather Kerr, fictocriticism doesn't just inhabit the space between, it does so critically by making "visible what is necessarily effaced" by traditional academic structures.[43] Indeed, leading fictocritical writers contend that fictocriticism has a "radical flavour"[44] whereby its practice can be read as a disruption of traditional forms of knowledge production. As Gibbs writes, fictocriticism is "a meta-discourse in which the strategies of the telling are part of the point of the tale."[45] Which is to say, self-reflexivity is inherent within the form. Accordingly, fictocriticism rejects the dominant "science-rhetoric model"[46] of knowledge production and is thus able to "surprise the paternalistic voices of theory"[47] by upending their claims to universality. Which is also to say that fictocriticism "serves explicitly feminist agendas of locating the writer, whether they be male or female: of documenting and contesting the fiction of the disembodied scholar"[48] by replacing it with an embodied subject.

So, if fictocriticism is an "act of defiance"[49] — if "transgression is the name of the game"[50] — then perhaps it is defined not merely by stylistic conventions, but also by their utilization *for the purposes of* "textual resistance."[51] Insomuch as radicality can (paradoxically) be a convention, perhaps that is what fictocriticism affords us.

In which the personal is always political

> Amanda and Levka had met in a curatorial program in Sweden. Over drinks, they talked about the unspoken rules of the art world. "Any successful work of contemporary art must be subversive," Levka declared.[52]

Seth and I huddle together in the cold outside, streetlight silhouettes, the ember of our shared cigarette a star against the moonless sky. I'm explaining fictocriticism as both form and concept — its embrace of multiplicities, its specificity, its rejection of hierarchies, its nonconformity — and he asks me if the naming is then not inherently recursive. He is right, of course, because once a thing is named it becomes an existing form of knowledge, a structure begins to emerge.

And therein lies the risk for the fictocritical practitioner. Not simply the risk of "exclusion from the critical literature,"[53] but the risk that the *very act of naming* dilutes the radical potential of the form itself. The act of defining imposes boundaries on a form that in its very genesis is trying to break free of such limitations — indeed, embedded in the etymology of "definition" is a boundary, "the very word definition has 'ending' (*finis*) within it."[54] And as the term "fictocritical" comes to account for more and more — particularly when applied to creative writing that is subjective and reflexive but not necessarily critical — then it comes to *signify* less and less. Which is to note the paradox: if fictocriticism is to retain its relevance as a referential term it needs to adhere to certain conventions, and yet in adhering to conventions it risks the outsider status that affords it the ability to be a radical intervention. The question thus becomes how (or whether) we can we codify "a *systemic* conceptualisation of fictocriticism that can hope to capture its various historical strands as well as possible forms to come without stifling its subversive potential."[55]

Perhaps an answer lies in a refusal of the general in favor of an adherence to the located, the specific: a "precise intervention into a specific situation, fictocriticism is not iterable, surprise being of the essence, and no two impasses in writing or debate are ever exactly the same."[56]

For Cixous, language wielded outside of the patriarchy, the institution, is transformative: it "does not contain, it carries; it does not hold back, it makes possible."[57] Perhaps, then, what the fictoritical can afford us in the context of art writing is a textual form — a mode of discourse — that privileges *specificity* over generality in which the radicality (the subversiveness) is inherent rather than didactic and the personal is always political.

Formal symbiosis / sublimated resistance

> There's a very receptive, highly informed audience in the art world. It's as if all the intelligence has migrated there. There's no longer an identifiable "counterculture," but there is an art world.[58]

I like this quote, as I like most of Kraus's writing, although I'm not sure that no counterculture but the art world exists (perhaps I'm tripping over the 1970s throwback term "counterculture"). But when I think back to every radical or activist or alternative community I've been a part of — living in squats in the early 2000s, protests on frontlines around the world, underground festivals, feminist reading groups — art-making, in one way or another, has been deeply embedded in the fabric of those communities. Which is to say: "all expression is always indirectly political,"[59] it's just a matter of form; a question of communion.

If we understand art as subject rather than object, then writing becomes *a part of* rather than ancillary to practice, and the fictocritical becomes a method for self-reflexivity within the space of making. It subverts the traditional relationship between modes of art criticism, politics, and privilege by leveling the playing field (knowledge as rhizome); it becomes a "way of dehierachizing — everything."[60] It is little wonder, then, that the form has been embraced by marginalized writers (women, artists of color) who have been excluded by the institutions that have retained a hegemony over traditional (read: patriarchal, colonial) forms of writing.

If we take as true Cixous's assertion that "there is no art which is not an act of sublimated resistance,"[61] then perhaps it is the radicality inherent in the fictocritical that marks it as symbiotic; "form and function reciprocal and intertwined."[62] If form needs to mirror subject in order to embody it, then perhaps the fictoritical offers a textual rendering that speaks the same language as art.

A conversation of forms. A communion, of sorts.

Talking in tautologies

> The aim is not to rediscover the eternal or the universal, but to find the conditions under which something new is produced (*creativeness*).[63]

I go with my mom to Melbourne's Heide Museum of Modern Art. It's an unseasonably cool summer day, the kids' first week back at school. I'm supposed to be writing a review of an installation in the project space there, but we spend most of our time in *Terminus* (2019), Jess Johnson and Simon Ward's immersive, candy-colored exhibition. The first room we enter has a series of hanging quilts, a collaboration between the artist and her mother. My mom, incidentally, is both artist and quilt-maker. Johnson's part-Gothic, part-sci-fi humanoid creatures in their Baroque, Op art constructions, are uncanny, alluring. In a subversion of writing-about-art they are a form of art-about-writing:

> The text is almost always the starting point. Whatever amorphous vibe the words give off determines the imagery that comes. The phrases are often rhythmic and I choose them because they get stuck in my head like thought-worms.[64]

The drawcard of the show is Ward's immersive virtual reality rendering of Johnson's worlds. *Imagine watching this if you were high!*, Mom says to me, laughing, while we wait for our turn at the next headset in the small room off to the side. A grey-haired man sits on the wooden stool next to us; he's waiting for his son. My mom strikes up conversation with him. *You wouldn't want to come here and see that stoned!*, he exclaims. Mom elbows me, smiling; a communion, of sorts. I take my turn, experiencing a kind of vertigo as sexless bodies fall, limbs tumbling, out the end of a tunnel into a shapeless abyss. It's my first virtual reality experience so I cannot say whether the medium lends itself to the imagery or the imagery lends itself to the medium. Most likely it's someplace in between. Johnson described the feeling of seeing her intricate, dreamlike drawings animated as "like experiencing something that had already existed."[65] A kind of multiverse tautology, where the art that is made is already that art that has been made, whereby all art already exists.

I'm reminded here of Borges's universe, "which others call the Library" and that exists *ab aeterno*,[66] and in its very formation (no beginning or end: an endless becoming) requires a kind of *belief* in the conditions under which it exists (a belief in *language*, in *text*). "To speak is to fall into tautology."[67] Which is to say: everything is (already) known. And I'm also reminded of Joseph Kosuth writing in "Art After Philosophy" that "it is nearly impossible to discuss art in general terms without talking in tautologies."[68]

Toward new ways of knowing

Language dislodges like rocks in a landslide.[69]

Perhaps though, it is in the tautology, *in* the talking about, the writing about, that we can discover the specificity that constitutes not new knowledge per se but, more presciently, new *ways of knowing*. Because in the end "no two impasses in writing or debate are ever exactly the same."[70] And so it is precisely in the repetition that we can "move from citation [...] to recitation — the performance of repetition, a repetition of repetition in order not to reproduce identity, but to try instead to engender new differences."[71]

Eve Kosofsky Sedgwick asks: "What does knowledge do — the pursuit of it, the having and exposing of it, the receiving again of knowledge of what one already knows?"[72] It's less about amassing knowledge as it is exploring *ways of knowing*, "not to mention doing or being."[73] Knowledge as rhizomic, as multiplicities; an embodied knowledge in which the pursuit of (the writing of, the making of) *becomes* the knowledge. Art as practice rather than product. Sedgwick also talks about the gulf between knowing and realizing, the former an intellectual understanding and the latter an embodied one that demands a kind of repetition, a kind of performativity:

> The apparent tautology of learning what you already know does not seem to constitute a paradox, nor an impasse, nor a scandal. It is not even a problem. If anything, it is a deliberate and defining practice.[74]

Language is "an incomplete instrument of expression"[75] — of course it is, that much we can agree on. And yet we write because of a conviction, deeply held or not, that "the inexpressible is contained — inexpressibly! — in the expressed."[76] What if both statements can be true simultaneously? Thus understood, art writing is not explication so much as it is conversation, one where text and art speak to one another in communion. One translates the other in an endless circle. Which is to say, the discovery of something new, or at least something meaningful, need not be a destination (a thing to own) but an ongoing practice.

It is in this practice, this *space between* knowing and realizing (between the theory and the story; the critical and the creative) that the fictocritical lies. An opening of language within the space of making, a "performance of repetition in order, ultimately, to do something differently, to undo something, to make a difference."[77] A bringing of the textual and the extratextual together toward locating the specificity in the tautology of art-speak, whereby each utterance "embod[ies] different readings and ways of coming to knowledge."[78] New *ways of knowing*.

This little patch of yellow

The year before last, I arrived at Melbourne gallery The Substation under a midday sun to see artist Steven Rhall's *Defunctionalised Autonomous Objects* (2018) the day before it closed (the art of being perpetually just-in-time). The exhibition featured no work titles, no room sheets, no material lists. It was a blurring of boundaries, what Rosie Isaac called "exhibition as artwork."[79] I sat to catch my breath in the cool, sitting on the floor in front of a black air dancer, the kind they have in car display yards. It felt like a kind of temporal overlapping from the outer edges of Howard Arkley–esque suburbia to this inner-city gallery, the one drenched in bleached sunlight, the other shrouded in shadows. Two eyes of yellow were staring back at me,

I remember that. Sometime later, we borrowed one of the works that appeared in the exhibition, a photograph of words — a list of materials in the manner of an image caption — tattooed on the back of the legs of the artist (text *in* art, rendered *as* art), dissolving the boundary between artist (subject) and object. I don't remember the details of the exhibition anymore, but I do remember the mirrors, the peepholes, the immersive "exhibition as artwork" sensation. I do remember being stared at by those yellow eyes. *Defunctionalised Autonomous Objects* refused us the option of detachment. There was no subject/object — the exhibition was an exercise in the dialogical.

> At the moment when I say "I do not paint," I say something which is true but which I could also alter by saying that if I paint, I do so otherwise.[80]

I've never seen a Vermeer in real life, but I have read Proust's *The Captive* (1923) where he evokes Vermeer through the eyes of his author-character, Bergotte. Bergotte is dying and he goes to see *View of Delft* in which he notices "the precious substance of the tiny patch of yellow wall."[81] This tiny patch of yellow wall is an opening, a becoming, a sense of the sublime. "That's how I ought to have written," thinks Bergotte, so as to have made "language precious in itself, like this little patch of yellow wall."[82] Bergotte didn't want to write *about* the patch of yellow wall but to write *within* it, to evoke textually what Vermeer evoked visually. Art and writing "as non-simultaneous twins."[83]

When Hélène Cixous writes that she reads artworks as "painted books"[84] she is suggesting what we already know: that *all* art speaks a common language.

Art/writing: in communion.

1 Teju Cole, "A Defense of Art in Troubled Times," *Art/Basel*, 2018, https://www.artbasel.com/news/a-defense-of-art-in-troubled-times.

2 Yang Yeung, "Care and Political Dissent: The Story of Hong Kong-Based Artists Stephanie Sin and Suifong Yim," *un Magazine*, vol. 14, no. 1 (May 2020), http://unprojects.org.au/magazine/issues/issue-14-1/.

3 Alison Bartlett, "Dear Regina: Formative Conversations About Feminist Writing," *FemTAP: A Journal of Feminist Theory and Practice*, vol. 1 (2006): 66–67.

4 Rivka Galchen, *Little Labours* (London: 4th Estate, 2016), 13–14.

5 Maria Tumarkin, "Against Motherhood Memoirs," in *Dangerous Ideas About Mothers*, ed. Camilla Nelson and Rachel Robertson (Perth: UWA Publishing, 2018), 183.

6 Maria Tumarkin, *Otherland: A Journey With My Daughter* (Sydney: Vintage, 2010), 4.
7 Gilles Deleuze and Félix Guattari, *A Thousand Plateaus: Capitalism and Schizophrenia* (Minneapolis: University of Minnesota Press, 1987), 7.
8 Quinn Eades, *All The Beginnings: A Queer Autobiography of the Body* (North Melbourne: Tantanoola, 2015), 210.
9 Charlotte Perkins Gilman, *The Yellow Wallpaper*, first pub. 1892 (New York: Virago, 1981), 13.
10 Richard Le Gallienne, *Prose Fancies* (*Second Series*), first pub. 1896, Project Gutenberg, 2004, http://www.gutenberg.org/files/14103/14103-h/14103-h.htm.
11 Antonio Saura cited in Marta Segarra, "Hélène Cixous's Other Animal: The Half-Sunken Dog," *New Literary History*, vol. 37, no. 1 (Winter 2006): 119.
12 Hélène Cixous, *Poetry in Painting: Writings on Contemporary Art and Aesthetics*, ed. Marta Segarra and Joana Masó (Edinburgh: Edinburgh University Press, 2012), 11.
13 Ibid., 10.
14 Ibid., 2.
15 Joyce Carol Oates, "Confronting Head On the Face of the Afflicted," *The New York Times*, February 19, 1995, https://www.nytimes.com/1995/02/19/arts/confronting-head-on-the-face-of-the-afflicted.html.
16 Oscar Wilde, "The Critic as Artist," Corpus of Electronic Texts Edition, 1891, https://celt.ucc.ie/published/E800003-007/text001.html, 153.
17 Laura Edbrook and Susannah Thompson, "Editorial," *Journal of Writing in Creative Practice*, vol. 10, no. 1 (2017): 4.
18 Chris Kraus, *Social Practices* (Los Angeles: Semiotext(e), 2018), 9.
19 Gilda Williams, "Write On," *Art Monthly*, vol. 384 (March 2015): 11.
20 Wilde, "The Critic as Artist," 153.
21 Susannah Thompson, "The Dress of Thought: Form and Style in Contemporary Art Writing," *Journal of Writing in Creative Practice*, vol. 10, no. 1 (2017): 104.
22 Ibid., 102.
23 Danuta Raine, "Essaying the Self: Ethnicity, Identity and the Fictocritical Essay," *TEXT Journal*, special issue no. 5 (2009), http://www.textjournal.com.au/speciss/issue5/raine.htm.
24 Jane Smiley, "Can Mothers Think," in *The True Subject: Writers on Life and Craft*, ed. Kurt Brown (Minneapolis: Graywolf Press, 1993), 10.
25 Hélène Cixous, "The Laugh of the Medusa," trans. Keith Cohen and Paula Cohen, *Signs*, vol. 1, no. 4 (Summer 1976): 879.
26 Ibid.
27 Ibid., 880.
28 Audre Lorde, *The Master's Tools Will Never Dismantle The Master's House* (London: Penguin, 1979).
29 Eades, *All The Beginnings*, 31.
30 David Carrier, *Principles of Art History Writing* (Pennsylvania: The Pennsylvania State University Press, 1991), 5.
31 Elena Ferrante, *The Story of the Lost Child*, trans. Ann Goldstein (Melbourne: Text Publishing, 2014), 176.
32 Deleuze and Guattari, *A Thousand Plateaus*, 12.
33 Jacques Derrida cited in Stephen Muecke, "The Fall: Fictocritical Writing," *Parallax*, vol. 8, no. 4 (2002): 125.
34 Anna Gibbs, "Fictocriticism, Affect, Mimesis: Engendering Differences," *TEXT Journal*, vol. 9, no. 1 (2005), http://www.textjournal.com.au/april05/gibbs.htm.
35 Cixous, "The Laugh of the Medusa," 886.
36 Muecke, *The Fall*.
37 Helen Flavell, "Who Killed Jeanne Randolph? King, Muecke or 'ficto-criticism'," *Outskirts*, vol. 20 (2009), http://www.outskirts.arts.uwa.edu.au/volumes/volume-20/flavell.

38 Anne Brewster, "Fictocriticism: Pedagogy and Practice," in *Crossing Lines: Formations of Australian Culture*, ed. Caroline Guerin, Philip Butterss, and Amanda Nettelbeck (Adelaide: Proceedings for the Association for the Study of Australian Literature Conference, 1996), 29.

39 Heather Kerr and Amanda Nettelbeck, *The Space Between: Australian Women Writing Fictocriticism* (Nedlands: University of Western Australia Press, 1998), 3–4.

40 Carl Rhodes, "Writing Organization/ Romancing Fictocriticism," *Culture and Organization*, vol. 21, no. 4 (2014), https://www.tandfonline.com/doi/full/10.1080/14759551.2014.882923.

41 Maggie Nelson, *The Argonauts* (Minneapolis: Graywolf Press, 2015), 82.

42 Stephen Muecke, "Introduction: What is Fictocriticism," in Stephen Muecke, *The Mother's Day Protest and Other Fictocritical Essays* (London: Rowman & Littlefield International, 2016), xi.

43 Heather Kerr, "Fictocriticism, The 'Doubtful Category' and 'The Space Between'," *Journal of the Association for the Study of Australian Literature* (1996): 95.

44 Flavell, "Who Killed Jeanne Randolph?," 2009.

45 Anna Gibbs, "Bodies of Words: Feminism and Fictocriticism – Explanation and Demonstration," *TEXT Journal*, vol. 1, no. 2 (1997), http://www.textjournal.com.au/oct97/gibbs.htm.

46 Ross Watkins and Nigel Krauth, "Radicalising the Scholarly Paper: New Forms for the Traditional Journal Article," *TEXT Journal*, vol. 20, no. 1 (2016), http://www.textjournal.com.au/april16/watkins&krauth.htm.

47 Gibbs, "Fictocriticism, Affect, Mimesis."

48 Bartlett, "Dear Regina," 17.

49 Gibbs, "Fictocriticism, Affect, Mimesis."

50 Rhodes, "Writing Organization/ Romancing Fictocriticism."

51 Gerrit Haas, *Fictocritical Strategies: Subverting Textual Practices of Meaning, Other, and Self-Formation* (New York: Transcript Verlag), 12.

52 Kraus, *Social Practices*, 179.

53 Flavell, "Who Killed Jeanne Randolph?"

54 Robert Nelson, "Towards the Perfect Ending," in *Robert Owen: A Book of Encounters*, ed. Angela Connor (Melbourne: Perimeter Editions, 2020), 142.

55 Haas, *Fictocritical Strategies*, 12.

56 Gibbs, "Bodies of Words."

57 Cixous, "The Laugh of the Medusa," 889.

58 Kraus, *Social Practices*, 170.

59 Hélène Cixous and Mireille Calle-Gruber, *Hélène Cixous Rootprints: Memory and Life Writing* (London: Routledge, 1994), 6.

60 Ibid., 10.

61 Cixous, *Poetry in Painting*, 7.

62 Thompson, "The Dress of Thought," 112.

63 Gilles Deleuze and Claire Parnet, *Dialogues*, trans. Hugh Tomlinson and Barbara Habberjam (New York: Columbia University Press, 1987), vii.

64 Jess Johnson cited in Chloe Mandryk, "Jess Johnson: Hex Nemesis," *Art Almanac*, May 31, 2017, https://www.art-almanac.com.au/jess-johnson-hex-nemesis/.

65 Jess Johnson cited in Suzanne Fraser, "Terminus: Jess Johnson and Simon Ward," *un Extended*, September 27, 2018, http://unprojects.org.au/un-extended/reviews/terminus/.

66 Jorge Luis Borges, *Jorge Luis Borges: Collected Fictions*, trans. Andrew Hurley, first pub. 1941 (New York: Penguin Books, 1998), 112.

67 Ibid., 117.

68 Joseph Kosuth, "Art After Philosophy," *UbuWeb: Papers*, 1969, http://www.ubu.com/papers/kosuth_philosophy.html.

69 Kraus, *Social Practices*, 22.

70 Gibbs, "Bodies of Words."

71 Gibbs, "Fictocriticism, Affect, Mimesis."

72 Eve Kokofsky Sedgwick, *Touching Feeling: Affect, Pedagogy, Performativity* (Durham, NC: Duke University Press, 2003), 124.

73 Maggie Nelson, "Finishing Touches," *LA Review of Books*, January 13, 2012, https://lareviewofbooks.org/article/finishing-touches/.

74 Sedgwick, *Touching Feeling*, 166–167.

75 Wilde, "The Critic as Artist," 102.

76 Nelson, *The Argonauts*, 3.

77 Gibbs, "Fictocriticism, Affect, Mimesis."

78 Edbrook and Thompson, "Editorial," 4.

79 Rosie Isaac, "Review: Defunctionalised Autonomous Objects," *un Extended*, December 18, 2018, http://unprojects.org.au/un-extended/reviews/defunctionalised-autonomous-objects/.

80 Cixous, *Poetry in Painting*, 7.

81 Marcel Proust, *Remembrance of Things Past: Volume 2*, trans. C. K. Scott Moncrieff and Stephen Hudson, first pub. 1913 (London: Wordworth Editions, 2006), 600.

82 Ibid.

83 Cixous, *Poetry in Painting*, 2.

84 Ibid., 12.

Ascending/Descending *Sonic Shadows*: Prologue and Tactile Reading Notes

Fayen d'Evie & Lizzie Boon

Prologue

I want to point out that if we literally took about two steps... you'd be running into the old Botta staircase, which no longer exists... it was literally right behind us.[1]

I remember those stairs, I didn't quite register that they were all gone.[2]

This coauthored text is both script and transcript, a circulatory writing process oriented through blindness and crafted through an embrace of syncopated time. Through the scripting and transcription of this text, writing and publishing is filtered through disability justice and vibrational poetics, blundering toward the development of an ethics of sensorial translation. Too often, disability is approached by the art world as an inconvenience to be evaded, or a legal protocol tangential to creative practice. Inverting this logic, renowned disability theorist Tobin Siebers refers to disability as "not a physical or mental defect, but a cultural and minority identity [...] capable of effecting social change."[3] This text is offered as a provocation, arguing that embracing and critically rethinking access can expand the perceptual space of publication.

Artist and writer Fayen d'Evie advocates for the radical potential of blindness to expand the critical and perceptual horizons of artistic and curatorial thinking. Invitations to write for print publications present a political and ethical dilemma for her project, risking reinforcing the exclusion of blind audiences and readers from the ocularcentric art world. By positioning this text as both script and transcript of a parallel audio work, the coauthors offer an experimental response to d'Evie's conundrum. By taking accountability for the creation of an audio version of the text, the coauthors resist and protest the persistent marginalization of blind audiences. Simultaneously, we exploit the print invitation to embed an invitation to Deaf readers to engage with a sensorial transcription of the sound works. This text is thus a proposition and a clarion call for radical publishing access.

The drafting of this text will script an audio track, one element in a sequence of ekphrastic reverberations that relocate the echoes of an encounter with *Sonic Shadows* (2010), a site-specific installation by Bill Fontana.

> *Right now, we're at a quiet moment, but I've been surprised at how much the very directional sound will... reflect off the surfaces down here.*[4]

> *We're standing underneath* Sonic Shadows... *On the same bridge is a large Calder hanging sculpture that is looming above us... From my vantage point, it looks like dinosaur bones.*[5]

Sonic Shadows debuted at the San Francisco Museum of Modern Art (SFMOMA) in November, 2010. Live signals were fed from remote accelerometers to eight loudspeakers and four ultrasonic emitters mounted on mechanical arms on SFMOMA's fifth-floor oculus bridge, so that directional sound bounced around the atrium void. Most of the accelerometers had been fixed to pipes in the museum boiler room, to relay real-time fluctuations in flows of water in pipes of varying size and shape. A few accelerometers had been installed on the steel truss oculus bridge, to react dynamically to the resonant vibrations of visitors' footsteps. *Sonic Shadows* thus sampled and layered the active movements of visitors, as well as processes that are normally concealed from public view but which undergird the working museum.

> *Yeah, there's the constant of this air conditioning... but then a softer sound... from* Sonic Shadows... *It sounds like something skating across a surface. Like, sliding across a surface, and it's very directional. It goes from here to here, here to here. And then I heard a car horn outside.*[6]

The softest sound I could hear, sort of a murmuring that I assumed was human voices, but far enough away that it didn't seem that they were in any kind of proximity.[7]

Yeah, I also heard that humming... then there were peaks from the street. Somebody honking, the traffic. I heard some doors opening and closing, and then I also heard the sound sculpture as the next layer... and I could not go below that.[8]

Among those who visited the inaugural installation of *Sonic Shadows* was blind architect Chris Downey, who shared his impressions in an essay published on the museum website: "Stepping into the SFMOMA atrium, we were greeted by strange sounds of dripping water, metallic pings, and intermittent clicks. Just as we thought we might recognize a sound, it vanished. Sometimes it seemed to travel right past, while others seemed to swerve somewhere near [...] Most interesting to those of us without sight was the way the ultrasonic beams bouncing off the walls demonstrated the shape of the architecture we could not see."[9]

I thought about the Fontana piece and these skating sounds, and how they almost sound like... if you could imagine what the sound of like a flying insect would be... because they do have this sense of movement to them, and so to me... takes on like something living...[10]

I think I've heard... three registers of sound... air moving, the kind of rotation of sound moving from above, and then... the sounds behind what seemed like a wall, almost sounded like a TV... I was struck by the sound in relation to the space, sounds being inside the room and outside the room.[11]

In July 2017, *Sonic Shadows* was reinstalled at SFMOMA for the museum's first large-scale group exhibition exploring sound in contemporary art. Co-curated by Rudolf Frieling and Tanya Zimbardo, the exhibition, *Soundtracks*, promised perceptual opportunities for discovering the museum's recently expanded architecture. The new extension was not a subtle intervention. It dwarfed the original building, nearly tripling gallery space and transforming SFMOMA into the largest museum of modern art in the United States.

Four days after the opening of *Soundtracks*, on July 19, 2017 — a Wednesday, the day in the week that the museum is closed to the public — Fayen d'Evie led a small, invited group of SFMOMA staff and guests in an ascending encounter with *Sonic Shadows.* The group included: then-Director of Collections, Jill Sterrett; then-Director of the Artist Initiative, Robin Clark; Assistant Director of Education and Public Practice, Megan Brian; Associate Media Conservator, Martina Haidvogl; Assistant Curator of Media Arts, Tanya Zimbardo; and photographer Don Ross. Among the guests were Chris Downey, local curator Devon Bella, and Georgina Kleege, a literary and disability studies professor from University of California, Berkeley. Kleege had been a close co-conspirator with d'Evie on a succession of artist-curatorial projects oriented through blindness.[12]

> *Elevator: Going up.*[13]
>
> *Let's gather… along this glass wall… we'll do exactly the same listening exercise… a couple of minutes of tuning into the sounds and their different shape and intensity from the loudest to softest…*[14]

D'Evie's ascending score for the encounter with *Sonic Shadows* drew on echolocation exercises to train attention toward the quietest sounds. She gathered the group in the museum atrium and invited each person to listen for the loudest sound, to tune into its shape and intensity, and then put that sound aside, and listen for the next loudest, and tune into its shape and intensity, and then put it aside, and so on, and so on, until they were finally listening for the quietest sound of all. After each listening meditation, d'Evie passed around an audio recorder and invited each person to describe the sounds that they had heard. This process was repeated over five levels, rising from the atrium to the fifth-floor oculus bridge, so that the audio recordings would cumulate as a collective description of the ascending encounter.

Excerpts from the polyphonic description have been collaged into a series of audio tracks that have been published on *Re-Locating Echoes*, a hybrid virtual archive, exhibition space, and publication platform under development by d'Evie and sound artist Bryan Phillips.

> *Well, the obvious sound for me is the sound coming from the bridge,* Sonic Shadows. *The very mechanical sound. Then tried to put that aside and then I heard a knock on the door, put that aside, and then heard someone whistling.*[15]

> *I think that there's a quality of the sound that feels more fleshed out from up here... There's this kind of rowing and fading almost ringing, or sort of bell-like resonance.*[16]

The audio-descriptive sound work revealed that the expansion of SFMOMA's architecture, and the mechanics supporting the functioning of the new building, had vastly changed a listener's experience of Fontana's *Sonic Shadows* in 2017, as compared with its inaugural installation in 2010. In the wake of the perceptual displacements exposed by the ascending score, the curatorial team asked Fontana if a new title or year ought to have been attributed to the 2017 reinstallation. Fontana insisted on staying with the original, leading Zimbardo to conclude that *Sonic Shadows* "was much more open of a score than we had imagined."[17]

Speaking at a conference in 2007, Jill Sterrett proposed that "shepherding contemporary installations into the future—the complex negotiation between [...] a work's initial appearance and its extended life—distils down to mediating its variability."[18] Building on Sterrett's comments on incompleteness and intermittence as characterizing reinstallation, Tina Fiske has proposed literary translation as a method for conservators to consider the play between prolonged periods of absence and sporadic, iterative presence: "how might looking at translation ethics direct the conservator to recognise and avoid effacing difference, not least where it is generated by the periods of absence that arguably underwrite installations and certainly punctuate their iterations?"[19]

> *Up here the swoosh-skating insect-like sound becomes more a part of like a forest sound, because there's many more sounds contributing to it, so it's much more dense and complex...*[20]

> *There was that more consistent clicking sound that would go by, somewhat of a tinny, metallic clicking sound, which is pretty prevalent, then the occasional drip sound behind it...*[21]

If we consider Fontana's *Sonic Shadows* as the point of origin for a series of ekphrastic echoes, then d'Evie's ascending score offers a secondary reverberation. The audio-descriptive work *Ascending Sonic Shadows* can be approached as a tertiary reverberation to Fontana's *Sonic Shadows*, engendering new meaning while pointing to the displacements (difference) involved in any translation (reinstallation).[22] The audio track scripted within this text attends to a further reverberation: an artist book by d'Evie and printmaker Trent Walter, which experiments with translating the kinesthetics of the processual encounter and the sensorial process of the listening meditations into a tactile publication.

> *That humming sound, or that ongoing kind of unbreakable sound that's recurring became more prominent ... almost distracting from the other sounds. The kind of skating, moving sounds were there, but this humming became more impenetrable.*[23]

> *When we first arrived on this level and all sort of lined up on a row in the overlook, I felt that the sound piece had become ... immersive in a way that was welcome. It had a weird kind of ritual tribunal feeling to me as we were all kind of perched and leaning forward...*[24]

The materiality of the book took shape incrementally at Walter's print studio Negative Press, where Lizzie Boon works as an archivist and curatorial assistant. A few years earlier, during undergraduate studies in art history and curatorial practice, Boon had initiated a series of writing and publishing experiments, with d'Evie as mentor. This progressively branched into a collaborative professional relationship founded on complementary inquiries into the performative and expanded potentials of published space. Simultaneously, at Negative Press, Boon was immersed in a deepening exploration of print practices and archival handling. The incidental collision of Boon, d'Evie, and Walter, working in one space, unfolded a congruous opportunity for conversation, feedback, and experimentation.

From the mezzanine office above the print workshop, Boon would overhear bursts of chatter as d'Evie and Walter debated how printed imagery feels, or how visual instability could open new modes of reading, even for ocularnormative audiences.

As d'Evie and Walter calibrated and recalibrated their thinking and their material approach, Boon took note of the slow accumulation of print spreads and structural form. Over time, her arms-length spectatorship of the project dissolved. The artists sought Boon out for close readings of experimental page spreads, and progressively implicated her in conversations around tactility, erasure, and kinesthetic reading.

A certain intimacy is ushered in while archiving an artist's body of work. The archivist, absorbed in close visual analysis, oral history, documentation, categorization, sequencing, and indexing, carefully and slowly configures material and immaterial structures that may preserve and articulate the memory of the work. It is pertinent to propose the act of archivist as the haptic "be-holder." In her work, d'Evie has reclaimed the etymological root of "beholding" as "to guard, to preserve, to maintain, to take care," which in practice implies "close attention, by thoroughly regarding, handling [and] holding."[25] It might be understood that the archivist's intimate knowledge of the nuances of an artist's work are acquired through thorough be-holding.

[*Layered audio of the interior space of the print studio.*]

Tactile reading notes

[*Layered audio of the interior space of the print studio.*]

I'm noticing how beautiful it is right here in the sun. The sun is falling on my arms, I'm also noticing that what goes on below is not occupying my attention anymore... that we are so much more in the physical sphere of peace.[26]

[*Layered audio of handling materials within the print studio.*]

Negative Press is a printmaking studio in a light industrial zone in Brunswick, Victoria, Wurundjeri Country. It occupies a space in the middle of a strip of warehouses, with disparate neighbors: a bitcoin mining business, a brewery, a mechanic, a burrito maker. Behind a roller door, Trent Walter has been building a dynamic and collaborative environment for the printing and publishing of prints and artist books of contemporary artists, mostly Australian. Recent projects include *Screenprints, Woodblocks & Unique Relief Prints* (2019) by John Nixon, and a ten-color screenprinted pamphlet *Female Orgasm: A Codex of Sorts, After Ursula K. Le Guin* (2018–19) by Emily Floyd in collaboration with graphic design collective Experimental Jetset.

Over the past two years, d'Evie and Walter have worked together to develop an edition of thirty artist books, titled *Ascending/Descending Sonic Shadows* (2019). The book builds on an earlier collaboration between the pair, exploring tactility and hallucination as ways of thinking and reading prints, and mnemonic devices for recalling and sharing stories of private encounters with artworks. *Ascending/Descending Sonic Shadows* continues this intangible archival impulse, recalling and sharing the story of a specific encounter in July 2017 with Fontana's installation *Sonic Shadows* at SFMOMA.

> *There's a kind of anticipation as we ascend each level. The sounds from the work seem more prominent or I guess more relatable in some way than they did earlier.*[27]

> *I'm struck by the rise and fall of this humming sound that also has a kind of small ringing sound in the middle of it. I miss the skating-rattley sound. That's gone away now.*[28]

Each book is section-sewn, forty-four pages, with a four-page braille colophon. The page spreads alternate between debossed and printed spreads. The debossed spreads were made by translating photographic documentation into a succession of screenprint films, which were used to expose photopolymer plates that were then relief printed, creating tactile indentations. The technical term for this process is blind embossing. The source photographic images ascend in vantage point, beginning at the ground floor of the atrium and moving progressively closer to the ultra-directional speakers fixed on the oculus bridge. The printed pages are monotone, in a color called Concentrated Blue. While the debossed pages ascend, the interspersed printed pages reverse the sequence, descending from the oculus bridge to the atrium floor. The succession of debossed and printed pages meets in the middle, crosses over, and each set then continues its path of ascent or descent. The book can be read from front to back, or back to front, or can be embraced as a continuous circulatory reader, perpetually climbing, whereby each time the destination is reached, the pathway opens to climb higher.

Certain things are turning on, turning off, adjusting...[29]

I felt that up here the sounds were a little bit flatter, which I thought was interesting because we're actually much closer... on the third floor, because of the architecture of the building, we're sort of below an entire bell that would collect the sound and feed it to us... Here we're much closer, so we only hear bits and pieces of it, we don't get the full collection of it at once.[30]

The bell-sounding sound was... sort of seductive and it made me not want to continue down to put it aside and listen to other sounds, because it was really mesmerizing and inviting and it felt meditative and so I really felt like wanting to hold onto it...[31]

The first debossed image that a reader encounters at the front of the book is also the last image the reader encounters in its print rendering at the rear of the book. In this first/last image, the mechanical form of the bridge strikes across the photographic frame, its mass interrupted by Alexander Calder's skeletal hanging sculpture, which cascades into the rounded expanse of the atrium.

We're going to go up the stairs. Is that right? Then you go up and across the bridge... It can sustain our weight, right?[32]

From here it sounds much more watery to me. It's splashing, and splishing, and floating, and less metallic than I remembered, and more immersive...[33]

When reading the debossed image via touch, searching fingertips sense shifting forms and textures. The atrium ceiling is configured by a sharp round ridge, while the Calder sculpture is a cluster of lines and dips fitting the soft pads of the reader's palm. A smooth intermission is felt as the reader's fingertips pass across the negative space until they again find rhythm, tracing along the linear patterning of the oculus bridge. The subsequent pages continue to narrate architectural interiors, whether situating the reader more directly in the light-filtered ceiling space of the atrium, or in more intimate proximity with Fontana's mechanical pan-tilt arms as from the perspective of the oculus bridge. With each image, fingertips trace, stroke, trail, and creep, as the reader's hands tighten or expand across the surface of the indented paper.

> *It's really lush when you're up here... It's really immersive. The skating, trickling sounds, almost sound like vigorously played violins. Then I also noticed you can hear the sounds of the mechanical arms that are moving the speakers around, they have their own hum and so they're not only transmitting sounds through cords, but their own sound.*[34]

> *I was occupied... revising my prior descriptions of the sounds... the one that I was thinking of as a rattly noise now is more of a whooshy, liquid noise...*[35]

The screenprinting films that mediated the translation from photograph to print form were created with dot sizes ranging from thirty-five to ten lines per inch. By contrast, the standard for commercial books is 150 lines per inch. The comparatively large dot sizes of the films used in *Ascending/Descending Sonic Shadows* introduce pixelation of the source imagery. Visually, the affect is disruption at close range and, with certain combinations of dot size and image, hallucinatory shimmering. Following Roland Barthes's notion of the photograph as a shared hallucination, an epistemology of hallucination displaces the evidentiary status of photographic documentation. An image can instead be engaged with as a conversational frame for the sharing of descriptive memories, counter-memories, imaginative fictions, and speculations.

> [*Layered audio from print studio of pages flipping, fingertips reading pages.*]

Still, whether debossed or printed, each printed image registers marks that resolve into a representation of *Sonic Shadows* as installed in 2017, and distinct from its debut in 2010, before the expansive renovation of SFMOMA so radically changed the architectural space. *Ascending/Descending Sonic Shadows* can thus be approached as an archival proposition to conserve a kinesthetic memory of a specific experience of Fontana's work. Conservation here is not the elusive quest to maintain an object in its original form, but a more nebulous quest to carry forwards memories of ephemeral moments through corollaries, translations, redescriptions.

> *At first I thought someone was humming in the distance, and then it was like, "No, this is too consistent." But... the tone would*

> *change, and it was really interesting because it was subtle... and I was feeling it in the rail, but I was also feeling it in my cane...*[36]

> *Up here I feel like I'm in the centre of the sounds and they're circling around me.*[37]

The screenprinting process modestly impresses texture and form, inviting tactile interaction. The larger dot sizes emboss sweeping and fuller form, with broader smooth respite in the negative space. As the dot sizes get smaller, so too do the intricacies within the texture, calling for closer attention to the tiny shifts in shape across each spread. As the pages yield to one another, a tactile meta-rhythm is established. The debossed forms articulate more clearly. The printed pages invite a tactile encounter too, but through very subtle material shifts in ink across a page, and through the imprint of the leading and following pages.

> *The sound from up here occupied a more imaginary space. Almost as if they took on some kind of animal nature. I don't know if it's the same sound in every speaker, but this one where I've been meditating for a while has these kind of wobbly animal or human gentle creature-like sounds.*[38]

What tactile reading allows for is ambiguity. It not only enables a slowing down, but also invites liberation from the authority of immediate visual feedback. Through a process of repetitive touch, the reader deciphers sensory language: rough and woolly grain, rounded linear ridge, softer refined groove. The reader finds patterns, alters intensity and pace, and, in time, accesses deeper tactile details in the pages.

> *It's so hot from the sun coming through... my heartbeat is really heavy, and so this is the first level where my internal sounds are mixing in with the* Sonic Shadows... *in a slightly fight-or-flight way.*[39]

> *Aside from the heat, I... noticed more of the droplet water-type sounds.*[40]

> *The wateriness that somebody mentioned was something that I remembered historically in the work, and I wasn't hearing it so clearly until we got right to the bridge. Then it came back.*[41]

The translation of the embodied encounter with *Sonic Shadows* is not only through the sequence of printed imagery, but also through the action of tactile reading. The ascending score at SFMOMA trained listening toward the quietest sounds. As Jill Sterrett noted during a handling of test spreads for the publication, the subtle nature of the blind embossing requires fingers to search attentively for the quietest mark, a correlative sensory translation of the listening score. Through tactile engagement with the printed artist book, a reader may train their sensorial inquiry toward quieter and quieter moments of discovery in the tactile field.

> *The exercise of listening to the piece on multiple levels and isolating experiences in each space… became kind of a cumulative or anticipatory experience…*[42]

As a performative possibility, the book invites erasure. Tactile engagement with the pages of the book demands a spatialized, repetitive, motion-based investigation, triggering a slow erasure of the textures and gesture of forms. Academic Erica Fretwell wrote: "in the world of touch, to read is to erase."[43] The threat of degradation here is not vexed, it is ancillary to the performative embodiment of touch. Erasure implies duration. In the Bergsonian sense, duration is a coexistence of past and present, a constant continuation. Through a kind of durational reflexivity, *Ascending/Descending Sonic Shadows* offers a portal for conservation of embodied memory through kinesthetic transference. Erasure through touch becomes a material vocabulary that carries a choreographic translation of the ascending encounter, mirroring the ephemeral perceptual experience. Touch is a double-sensation that Fretwell succinctly classifies as agent and recipient. She asserts: "touch [as] a sense and a story — specifically, a story of a self that is radically coextensive with and other than itself."[44] In a conservational framework, erasure is flipped on its head, made generative rather than degenerative.

> *The thing was the boiler room got remodelled and they could not find the original sounds anymore…, there's new pipes now and the water flows differently in them. That's why the work is so much more dynamic now… For me coming from conservation it's so interesting how it's not just the pipes themselves that we*

> *would have needed to conserve, but it's even the water inside them, and how the water inside the pipe moves...*[45]

As a series of reverberations, Fontana's *Sonic Shadows*, d'Evie's kinesthetic score, the polyphonic audio-description, the edition of artist books, the reader's performative tactile encounter with the pages of a book, and this scripted text, enact back and forth, back and forth, back and forth. Rebecca Schneider's writing on the archival remains of performance points to "citational performance" as a call to action that can be "resonant in the varied and reverberant cross-temporal spaces where an echo might encounter response."[46] She asks: "can we account not only for the way differing media cite and incite each other but for the ways that the meaning of one form takes place in the response of another?"[47] Troubling citational linearity, Schneider dwells on conversations that take place inter-temporally, invoking future-past lags, time drags, deferrals, repetition, reoccurrence. She asks: "when we habitually read documents as evidence and evidence as indication of a past supposedly gone by, do we overlook the liveness of temporal deferral, the real time of our complicities?"[48]

Here, we directly address you who are listening to this audio text or reading the printed transcript.

How are you complicit?

Will the echoes of *Sonic Shadows* attenuate here, or, in some manner, reverberate on?

> [*Fade in recordings from the interior of the print workshop, and the action of tactile reading.*]

> *I was mostly reflecting on the direction that sound can happen, whether you emit it towards an artwork, or the artwork emits it towards you.*[49]

> [*Fade out recordings from the interior of the print workshop, and the action of tactile reading.*]

Appendix

Lizzie Boon, "Ascending/Descending *Sonic Shadows*: Tactile Reading Notes," November 4, 2019

Explicit invitation of **the cover**: Tight, then broad. Automatic left-to-right movement before settling into the curves.

The hand is inquisitive of what is behind, beneath, within the cut circles. Visual observation: ability to read is disjointed.

The reading of the **braille colophon**: Return to a left-to-right motion. Even with limited ability to understand braille there is an embodied comprehension by the hand to touch closer, more intricately, and to be led by sensation.

Blank page: Closer touch. There is a small string of vertical dots impressed near the center of the page. Visual observation: small patches of residue are concentrated on the right hand of the page from the preceding braille. I presume this will alter and expand over time.

First debossed spread: Almost smooth at first touch. The fingertips find the reverse of the vertical dots on the left-hand spread. Both hands engage — a flat stroke with the palm and then a more intricate inquiry with both index fingers. Searching for moments of difference among the broad soft texture across the majority of the spread.

First printed spread: Both hands edge up the gutter and on finding the top they splay outwards in both directions. Meeting the outside edges, they weave in toward the center again. Gradually moving slower, subtle finger palm-size smoothness is discovered in incremental patches. Visual observation: referential to the cover.

Debossed spread two: Both hands placed on the page at random. Beginning to feel more comfortable releasing the structure of left-to-right reading and becoming less bound by the structure of the paper. Subtle in texture, I become more attuned to the shifts from the soft coarseness to the smoother sectioning. It is as though my fingers search for this smoothness not as respite, but rather as exploration for image-making in my head through the sensations. Prominently debossed. A series of vertical lines on the left-hand page, intercepted by some diagonal fractures across each.

Printed spread two: Both hands begin on the left-hand side of the spread. There is a spot in the top corner that my right hand lingers on for some time. I cannot figure the form. Moving to the right-hand side, moments of difference are more apparent. Circling the fingertips of both hands in the top right-hand corner, there is a strong indent that my fingers find. It sweeps on the slightest curve and off the page's edge.

Debossed spread three: Overall texture more definite, too strong to describe as rough, but rougher than the previous debossing. Moving from the top middle of the spread, splaying wider as the texture underneath indicates a string of lines on a curvature. I draw an amateur drawing of the sun in my head, likening that drawing to the pattern underneath my fingers, the rays of that sun drawing. The form dissipates as I move down the page. Intermittent smooth patches reveal themselves; my right index finger finds stillness in what feels like a groove made for my finger to perfectly fit into at the bottom of the right spread.

Printed spread three: Following a blanket search of the page, my hands are immediately summoned to the right-hand spread, notably configuring a form likened to an upside-down "L" in one spot and then with a wider expanse underneath. I assume it is a depiction of the mechanical tilt arm. The overall texture is looser, with more space in between.

Debossed spread four: The left-hand page is explored first; the dot size of the texture is noticeably bigger. It causes the form to feel increasingly pronounced. I am getting feedback of difference that is more immediate with a broad swiping action of the spread. My fingers draw squiggly lines down the pages, finding a wide sweeping form with smoother curves across the bottom third of the page. Visual observation: small patches of dots that accumulate to make a bunch of curved vertical lines creating an abundance of movement across the spread.

Printed spread four: Tactilely clearer. Movement is not patterned in a particular way. Visual observation: strong structures with diagonal rectangles taking up the majority of the spread.

Debossed spread five: Moving from top left to top right, distinct diagonal lines are found. Engaging with each individually, I trail down to their end points, where most take me to the edge of the page. Toward the bottom half of the page, I find wider sections that are smooth. Experimenting with each finger individually, I identify the individual dot size more easily. Perhaps a close attention has developed along with a slightly larger dot size. Particular focus is on my pinkie fingers. Brushing back and forward near the bottom of the spread like playing a xylophone, the structure of the dots acts like different keys.

Printed spread five: Some heavy texture top left (left-hand page) and bottom right (right-hand page). My hands creep slower with the printed pages, the points of difference feel deeply embedded.

Debossed spread six: Between both hands, three textures can be identified — smooth, tight, and sharp (bottom left in particular). Wider dots that are simpler to find patterns within (moving in diagonals). No longer constructing images with touch, but rather through sensation, uncovers patterning and deeper intricate shifts in the paper. Syncopated rhythms. I fixate on two small smooth dots oriented vertically. Visual observation: the tilt arm shift is clear.

Printed spread six: I take a break. I have been receiving substantial tactile feedback and am curious what will happen if my fingers settle while I rest, and then I return. Will I enter with the same state of tactile depth?

Debossed spread seven: My hands take a few minutes to reacquaint with the page, but I find myself attuned to the feeling under fingertip. Experimenting with my full hands across the page. This uncovers more obvious tactile feedback, especially with the smaller dot size. Through a slow full-hand encounter with the page I receive greater embodied tactile vibrations, whereas the fingertip touching is required for investigating micro areas of the page. Body more implicit in the reading. Visual observation: the print page before has bled through, overlaying image into the debossing.

Printed page seven: Strong tactile qualities on the right-hand page. A curving form from top to bottom where it dissipates by the bottom edge of the page. Visual observation: this spread is distinctly different on each page, and the broader sections of smoothness are obvious in the printing.

Debossed spread eight: The most explicit tactile experience, only taking a few moments to detect the points of difference in the page. Spending thirty seconds, I am able to establish a pattern in the page for my hands to follow. Finding the mirroring patterning of the debossing, the form of the atrium wall. Going over again, my hands enact a swaying movement in unison. Visual observation: striking, complementing the tactile encounter with this spread.

1 Voiced by Jill Sterrett in the collective audio-descriptive work "Ascending *Sonic Shadows*: Re-calling an Encounter with *Sonic Shadows* (2010) by Bill Fontana," July 19, 2017, https://relocatingechoes.space/sonic-shadows.

2 Voiced by Georgina Kleege, ibid.

3 Tobin Siebers, *Disability Theory* (Ann Arbor: University of Michigan Press, 2008), 4.

4 Voiced by Tanya Zimbardo, "Ascending *Sonic Shadows*."

5 Voiced by Martina Haidvogl, ibid.

6 Voiced by Georgina Kleege, ibid.

7 Voiced by Tanya Zimbardo, ibid.

8 Voiced by Martina Haidvogl, ibid.

9 Chris Downey, "On Bill Fontana's *Sonic Shadows*," *Open Space*, July 11, 2011, https://www.sfmoma.org/publication/soundtracks/bill-fontana/#chris-downey-on-sonic-shadows.

10 Voiced by Megan Brian, "Ascending *Sonic Shadows*."

11 Voiced by Devon Bella, ibid.

12 The *Sonic Shadows* encounter was the first experiment in what would evolve into an incremental research project for d'Evie and Kleege, collaborating with SFMOMA staff to explore ways that blindness could introduce new approaches to sensing, documenting, archiving, and recalling ephemeral encounters with artworks. For more context on this research project, see: Fayen d'Evie, "Re-describing the Periphery," 2019, https://www.sfmoma.org/read/redescribing-the-periphery/.

13 Voiced by coded electronic announcement in SFMOMA elevator, July 19, 2017.

14 Voiced by Fayen d'Evie, "Ascending *Sonic Shadows*."

15 Voiced by Don Ross, ibid.

16 Voiced by Tanya Zimbardo, ibid.

17 Tanya Zimbardo in conversation with Fayen d'Evie at SFMOMA, February 11, 2019.

18 Jill Sterrett, "Artists' Installations and the Museum," in video recording of conference *Shifting Practices, Shifting Roles*, Tate, March 22, 2007, https://www.tate.org.uk/context-comment/video/shifting-practice-shifting-roles.

19 Tina Fiske, "*White Walls*: Installations, Absence, Iteration and Difference," in *Conservation: Principles, Dilemmas and Uncomfortable Truths*, ed. Alison Bracker and Alison Richmond (Oxford: Elsevier Ltd. in association with the Victoria and Albert Museum, London), 237.

20 Voiced by Megan Brian, "Ascending *Sonic Shadows*."

21 Voiced by Chris Downey, ibid.

22 Tanya Zimbardo in conversation with Fayen d'Evie, February 12, 2018.

23 Voiced by Devon Bella, "Ascending *Sonic Shadows*."

24 Voiced by Robin Clark, ibid.

25 Fayen d'Evie, "Orienting through Blindness: Blundering, Be-holding and Wayfinding as Artistic and Curatorial Methods," *Performance Paradigm* 13, (2017): 43.

26 Voiced by Robin Clark, "Ascending *Sonic Shadows*."

27 Ibid.

28 Voiced by Georgina Kleege, "Ascending *Sonic Shadows*."

29 Voiced by Chris Downey, ibid.

30 Voiced by Martina Haidvogl, ibid.

31 Voiced by Megan Brian, ibid.

32 Voiced by Fayen d'Evie, ibid.

33 Voiced by Robin Clark, ibid.

34 Voiced by Megan Brian, ibid.

35 Voiced by Georgina Kleege, ibid.

36 Voiced by Chris Downey, ibid.

37 Voiced by Martina Haidvogl, ibid.

38 Voiced by Devon Bella, ibid.

39 Voiced by Fayen d'Evie, ibid.

40 Voiced by Don Ross, ibid.

41 Voiced by Jill Sterrett, ibid.

42 Voiced by Robin Clark, ibid.

43 Erica Fretwell, "Stillness is a Move: Helen Keller and the Kinaesthetics of Autobiography," *American Literary History* 25, no. 3 (2013): 569.

44 Ibid.

45 Voiced by Martina Haidvogl, "Ascending *Sonic Shadows*."

46 Rebecca Schneider, *Performing Remains* (Oxon: Routledge, 2011), 194.

47 Ibid., 168.

48 Ibid., 142.

49 Voiced by Robin Clark, "Ascending *Sonic Shadows*."

How to Decolonize the Art World: Three Scenarios

Maddee Clark

I started working as an editor of *un Magazine* in 2018 with my collaborator, artist Neika Lehman (Trawlwoolway). *un Magazine* is an independent print- and web-based art writing publication based in Narrm (Melbourne), Australia.[1] Neika and I were the first Blak editors of the magazine,[2] hired in an identified position for a one-year tenure.[3] We came to the role with a shared desire to interrogate how our local art world used the word "decolonization," and the broader aestheticization of anti-racism and decolonization in curatorship and art.

Yorta Yorta curator and editor Kimberley Moulton, whom Neika and I both look up to in our practices, has noted:

> Slowly, more Indigenous curators and artists are having agency within these spaces to drive an Indigenous curatorial methodology that isn't embedded in ethnographic systems of classifying or commercial driven conceptions of what Aboriginal art should look like.[4]

This slow collective struggle by Blak arts practitioners to develop First Nations–centered practices has happened alongside a sustained questioning of the values of the mainstream arts world in relation to First Nations peoples. Keeping this in mind, I want to explore some of the discussions being had within the Australian art world in response to neoliberalism, conservative attacks on arts funding, and the increasing collectivization of Aboriginal arts workers within the industry. I explore some of my experiences as a Blak arts worker and editor, including the editorship of *un Magazine* and our chosen theme of "decolonization" as an aesthetic. I provide some reflections on this, as well as exploring the misuses of the term decolonization in the art world. I also reflect on an extended occupation of artist-run initiative West Space in inner-city Narrm by Blak arts collective this mob in 2018 as another example — similar to our "first ever" Blak editorship at *un Magazine* — of an action designed to prod at the operation of white privilege in arts spaces.

The 20th Biennale of Sydney

During the 2016 Biennale of Sydney, I took part in a "Futuring the Arts" workshop in an independent arts space in Gadigal Country, inner-west Sydney. The Biennale, which has run since 1973, has a reputation as the biggest and most influential contemporary arts event in Australia. The twentieth iteration was titled *The Future Is Already Here, It's Just Not Evenly Distributed*. The group of creatives running the space took on "futuring" as a community response to the arts funding cuts that had recently taken place under the (conservative) then–Abbott Government. Futuring was used as a mode to reimagine the survival of the arts in response to forms of artistic repression, offering a framework centered around possibility that demanded creative responses from participants. Aside from myself, the workshop was attended by a small community of non-Indigenous creatives attached to various universities and arts colleges. Initially, participants were instructed to reassess the future of an art world without its usual modes of funding, institutional support, and cultural status. This was a "future" world in which art had been stripped of what it had come to mean for these workers: university and public support, an allowance of physical and cultural space, influence, assured financial backing, and class status. This structured and collaborative practice of "futuring" seemed to provide a useful way into discussing the funding problem facing this arts community, a problem that would potentially require a radical rethinking of traditional modes of generating cultural dialogue and its familiar identities — gallery spaces, curators, classrooms, and academic spaces. The category of "artist" and its attendant cultural position and status were under critical reinterpretation. Participants were being asked to understand art in a way that could adapt to a world in which institutions and government no longer defined or funded it, to imagine a future in which this institutional dissolving had already taken place. Grappling with this, the participants attempted to articulate a vision of the arts industry "after" capitalism, to think without the limitations of our current situation, using the future as a tool.

The ensuing discussion brought up a few issues for me. One key issue is the dual positioning of art as simultaneously a vehicle for political criticism and indictment, *and* as a space of political complicity and complacency. The 2014 Biennale of Sydney, two years prior to my engagement with this event, was subject to a boycott on the grounds of its significant financial links to Transfield, the company contracted to operate the Australian Government detention center on Manus Island. Artists who pulled their work from the 2014 event stated that they saw their participation "as an active link in a chain of associations that leads to the abuse of human rights. For us, this is undeniable and indefensible."[5] They also noted of the Biennale that "there will be no movement on their involvement in this issue ... the financial agreements are too important to re-negotiate."[6] Utopian theorist Fredric Jameson argues that in capitalist modernity there arises an assumed separation between art and culture, and the social world (I like to call this the art/life distinction). This, he argues, "inaugurates culture as a realm in its own right and defines it as such," bringing into question the potential for art to be critical, subversive, and effective.[7] As such, art's very distance (or perceived distance) from its broader social context "allows it to function as a critique and indictment" while also "doom[ing] its interventions to ineffectuality and relegat[ing] art and culture to a frivolous, trivialized space in which such intersections are neutralized in advance."[8] For Jameson, it is questionable whether art is "necessarily reappropriated and co-opted by the social system of which it is a part."[9]

While Transfield ceased to be a sponsor of the Biennale following the 2014 boycott, making the action an apparent political success, the paradox of political criticism/complicity still hovers over public art discourse. In some circles, artists who did not want to pull their work from the 2014 Biennale might have been defended on the grounds that, as artists, they should not have to deny themselves wages nor bother themselves with political concerns. But this only furthers the attempt to create a distinction between cultural and social realms — an example which reads almost exactly as Jameson writes. The contemporary position of art in the public sphere, even when it explicitly critiques particular social norms or patterns of violence, is as an uncomfortable enabler and benefactor of state and neoliberal regimes of terror, such as the offshore detention industry. Its chains of support and funding, as in the example of the 2014 Biennale of Sydney, place art in opposition to its assumed ability to mobilize political criticism.

An arts community that is accustomed to the prestige of institutional legitimacy, elite audiences, and public funding may see a decline in the state of the arts in neoliberal societies as a kind of crisis moment. However, while art is often considered in capitalist, postcolonial societies to be the exclusive territory of the elite — universities, institutions, the upper classes — non-white peoples have long produced arts and knowledges not funded by, nor necessarily generated for the consumption of, an elite and moneyed class. In fact, Aboriginal arts are still considered in many ways to be outside the scope of real art, and of modern art. In *Living Texts*, Palyku scholars Ambelin and Blaze Kwaymullina, with Lauren Butterly, put forward a broadened scope for understanding Indigenous textuality and cultural production outside of presumed disciplinary and epistemic frames. Their thinking illuminates the ambivalent and confused power relations between Indigenous and non-Indigenous forms of art, communities of practice, and their modes of production. They reference Indigenous thinker David Mowaljarlai on the conceptualization and institutionalization of art in an Aboriginal context:

> Someone told me just recently that "rock art is dead." If "Art" was dead, that would not matter to we Aborigines. We have never thought of our rock-paintings as "Art." To us they are IMAGES. IMAGES with ENERGIES that keep us ALIVE — EVERY PERSON, EVERYTHING WE STAND ON, ARE MADE FROM, EAT AND LIVE ON.[10]

The crisis represented by government-led arts funding cuts is related to a breaking down of meaning in art, and art's assumed cultural location. Throughout the "Futuring the Arts" workshop, we were asked various iterations of the following questions: if art is decontextualized from gallery, curator, arts college, corporate benefactors, and other culturally embedded capitalist structures, what is it? Can anyone become an artist, without having to pass through the walls and borders which support the very notions of art? Don't these mechanisms allow for a kind of quality control? What will happen to the "quality" of the arts if this is allowed to happen? Following this, Kwaymullina et al. conclude from Mowaljarlai's teaching that "Aboriginal stories, however expressed or embodied, hold power, spirit and agency."[11] Problematizing the context of the Western property law, publications, and industry norms in which these products exist, Kwaymullina et al. assert the need for new means of looking at Indigenous cultural production. What becomes clear through their analysis is that Indigenous forms of cultural production are not afforded status in the arts and publishing industries. And yet they have always existed and functioned as forms of communication, as expressions of Indigenous lifeworlds and spirituality, well before their meanings began to be co-opted into conventional descriptions of "art." What is clear in the context of the history of cultural production in Australia is that the assumption of a supportive public and institutional life for artists in a setting such as the Biennale of Sydney is situated within a particularly white, moneyed, and educated arts elite. The lack of consideration for "deinstitutionalized" forms of art in the "Futuring the Arts" conversation went unquestioned.

The workshop itself began with an exercise: participants were asked to introduce themselves as if it were twenty years in the future. As an icebreaker activity, this was also revealing. Participants were asked to provide a vision of both themselves and their future environment. The future setting, they were told, had no limits; they could create any setting they desired, rather than limiting themselves to what was considered reasonable or possible in the current climate. Some participants described futures in which society had regressed to an idealized, pre–Industrial Revolution, pre-capitalist reality; there was no plastic, no money, no machinery. Sydney was pictured by some participants as a community garden and, in these future visions, permaculture practice had become widespread. In some futures, cars had been eradicated and everyone used bikes. One or two participants even mentioned that, in their futures, they and their children spoke Gadigal language. However, no one described a future that included Aboriginal people. Nor were there any iterations verbalized that included organized Aboriginal governance, sovereignty, or even treaty between Indigenous and non-Indigenous people. Blak presence was completely erased from the future as told by the workshop.

Editing "The Decolonial Issue"

The appropriation of Blak aesthetics, lifeways, and languages without proper engagement with Blak people's presence within the art world includes, for Neika and I, the use of decolonization as a visual rhetoric and a theoretical signifier. Arts organizations and institutions utilize "decolonization" as a buzzword without interrogating their deeply held values, and without developing sincere relationships with First Nations people. It was clear to Neika and I when we took the editorial position at *un Magazine* in early 2018 that "decolonization" was being used by the local arts scene as modelling anti-colonial virtue without properly interrogating the origins of colonial wealth, or the material conditions of the art world itself. Our discussion of this in *un Magazine* 12.1, "The Unbearable Hotness of Decolonisation," wasn't intended to be a criticism of any one person, or even of a wholly articulated art movement — and it wasn't even solely confined to art. We saw traces of a particular discourse on decolonization everywhere — on social media, in fashion, and in the academy. We also did not exempt ourselves from the critique. Partially, the issue was intended to make us probe our own intellectual, artistic, and writing practices. We reflected on our own habits of using such phrases as "x artist is *decolonizing* representation." And having heard statements like "x artist has single-handedly decolonized the Melbourne art world," we reacted with dismay every time we came across the term in local visual art discourse. We became obsessed with the tendency of our white artist friends to adorn themselves with decolonial and anti-racist branding — stickers, T-shirts, tote bags, hashtags. One tote bag designed for sale as merch for Queensland First Nations artist Tracey Moffatt's show at the Venice Biennale in 2017 featured the block lettering "INDIGENOUS RIGHTS" and "REFUGEE RIGHTS" on alternate sides, so wearers could rotate depending on their mood.

The flippancy of this gesture seemed like an intentional remark on the aestheticization and branding of social movements, an artistic performance into which the buyer was co-opted. A white art-world friend bragged about how they were singled out by ticket inspectors on the train for wearing a DECOLONISE NOW T-shirt — public racialization as a badge of honor that can be purchased. An exhibition curated in early 2018 for Plimsoll Gallery in Palawa Country, Hobart, Tasmania, by a white curator claimed to be generating a "decolonial geographic" presented through a critique of landscape painting. No Indigenous nations, decolonial movements, or even individual thinkers from Australia were referred to. In this case, the "decolonial" spirit was assumed to be a product of artistic critique. Critique itself — the possession of an ability to critique, to know — is often seen as generative of a so-called decolonial standpoint in the art world. This example presented, to us, an image of decolonial theory in the art world as profoundly depoliticized, disconnected, and superficial. Dr Alex Wilson from the Opaskwayak Cree Nation in Manitoba, Canada, has expressed similar sentiments:

> It feels like the term has become a catchphrase. I see decolonization stickers on people's computers and there's an irony in that — a sign that our movement has been branded.[12]

Our mood board for *un Magazine* 12.1 included two memes from our favorite Indigenous Instagram accounts. The first uses the moment when Regina George, played by Rachel McAdams in the film *Mean Girls*, calls Cady Heron pretty. When Cady responds "thanks," Regina George quickly moves to interrogate her. "So, you agree? You think you're really pretty?" In this version, "pretty" is replaced by "decolonized." "So, you agree? You think you're really decolonized?" The second meme, which we published alongside our editorial in the issue, was shared by many of our mutual Instagram friends on Invasion Day 2018.[13] The image is a popular template referring to moral panic campaigns about teen sexting, asking: "Is your child texting about decolonization?" Taking the place of the original text — "So you agree? You think you're really pretty?" and "Is your child texting about sex?" — decolonization is produced as, alternately, a kind of unforgiveable vanity, or a secretive, alarmist moral crisis. It is also, through memeification, brought into conversation with the familiar visual and cultural rhetorical devices that make up the social media world. Memes intrigued us as a form of circulated information, presenting complex issues for conceptualizing intellectual property and moral rights. They evade the logics of branding, authorship, and capital while simultaneously reaffirming these through the assertion of informal moral rights in the use of watermarking and crediting — and they have a normalizing, affirming effect.

In one of the articles in the issue, white settler critic Kate Leah Rendell explores the influence of the most destructive and socially irresponsible companies on facilitating community arts in Australia. Through specific examples, she demonstrates how the art world can perform decolonial intent while also existing fully within, and remaining dependent upon, colonial modes of production. On the participation of extractive resource industries in supporting Indigenous arts in the Northern Territory, Rendell writes: "the wielding of local power [...] ensures questions of 'ethics' remain precarious and each individual is in some way connected or implicated":

> One of the prompting questions for this edition of *un Magazine* was "How do we develop practices that bring us into encounters with place?" With [Jacky] Green's work in mind, I would extend this to ask, when brought into these encounters with place, how do we ensure we do not look away from the implications? Green's work *Yee-haw, Money Trucks* [2017] depicts six figures each riding a large yellow mining truck cutting across country. In the accompanying text he writes, "Just like the cowboys scream Yee-haw at the rodeo I imagine the miners riding their trucks across our country screaming, 'Yee-haw, I'm rich, Fuck you!'" It is a clear and uncompromising indictment of the colonising greed explicit in the continued expansion of the McArthur River Mine in Borroloola. Yet, faced with this work I was also left wondering about the rest of us—perhaps not as euphoric as the miners on their trucks yet nevertheless implicated as beneficiaries of the material consequences of the mine.[14]

Seen in this way, the coloniality of the art world depends upon often disingenuous expressions of decoloniality and performances of *awareness*. *Knowing better* and *not being racist* is a form of capital one buys and sells in the hyper-intellectualized and globally conscious art world—something one achieves through the consumption of diverse arts and culture and education.

Becoming immersed in the art world of Narrm through our role with *un Magazine* was a surreal experience for Neika and I. Paradoxically, the production of the issue on decolonization drove more offers of partnership on projects with a decolonial thematic our way. As Filipino-Australian writer, curator, and artist Andy Butler noted in a recent article, "we're at an interesting time when the sorts of artistic institutions that have driven people to collectivize are now scrambling to work with them."[15] Months after our first issue was published, at an exhibition opening, the white head of an artist-run initiative approached us with a demand that we both join her board. She told us she wanted to decolonize her organization. We were puzzled. She hugged us, and we left. Later, we received a request from her to attend an event she was running. This event proposed that we would be seated in a circle, on the floor, to "decolonize" the space by complicating the usual expectations of a panel discussion.

The ways that bodies are organized, the ways we're expected to be in dialogue, are certainly part of a decolonial effort and value system. As curators, educators, and facilitators in Blak spaces, we've experienced more egalitarian and principled ways of organizing our events in safe and autonomous settings. For example, at the BLK Schools discussion, as part of independent programming space Testing Ground's *Black Tourmaline* program, organizer Aisha Trambas, an artist and poet, eliminated the panel structure completely to help us leave the institutional attributions of expert status at the door, in recognition of the types of often-unrecognized knowledge held by all participants.[16] However, there is a difference between this type of attentiveness to the way an event is structured, and demanding an extractive and non-relational utilization of Aboriginal presence to perform the decolonial values of an institution. Quandamooka scholar Aileen Moreton-Robinson recounts the following incident in her work *Talkin' up to the White Woman* (2000):

> Being asked by a university (with one day's notice) to be part of a welcoming committee to meet a white feminist professor at the International airport at 5.30am. The professor had been invited to receive an honorary doctorate from the university, but she threatened not to come to Australia unless she was met and welcomed by Indigenous women. This seemingly noble but colonial gesture by the professor was soon eroded by her questioning us on what we were going to do at the Sydney Olympics about the denial of Indigenous rights in this country.[17]

The "welcome to country" by Aboriginal women is here positioned as a performance of both the anti-colonial and feminist values of the white woman. The colonial gesture is in the demanding of the labor, time, and intellectual energy of the Aboriginal women involved. The incident forms part of Moreton-Robinson's relationship with white feminism as one of extraction, entitlement, and overall use of Aboriginality as a utility to perform a white woman's politics. The art world makes similar use of Aboriginal people for unpaid labor, time, and intellectual contributions, all the while using their presence and labor as emblematic of the "decolonial" values of an organization.

While the concept of decolonization is utilized across the contexts of social organizing, media, academia, and the arts, it's worth understanding what notions of decolonization are being theorized by Indigenous thinkers. Unangan critical race theory scholar Eve Tuck's article "Decolonization Is Not a Metaphor," which provided part of the inspiration for *un Magazine* 12.1, notes that decolonization has been hyper-abstracted to account for professional practices, knowledge practices, and cultural and aesthetic processes. They define decolonization in opposition to this pattern, noting that "decolonization brings about the repatriation of Indigenous land and life; it is not a metaphor for other things we want to do to improve our societies and schools."[18] The presumption of a separation between art and life (maybe better stated as a separation between mind and body, or culture and lands) is again brought into play here. Two critical decolonial theorists, Ngũgĩ wa Thiong'o and Frantz Fanon, who have both influenced my thinking, have noted the importance of decolonizing the mind in the former European colonies. Their writing is done with the recognition that nations who may have achieved a type of material, economic, and political decolonization still carry colonial baggage in their written, linguistic, and visual cultures. A quote attributed to Fanon states compellingly: "imperialism leaves behind germs of rot which we must clinically detect and remove from our land but from our minds as well." This implies a necessary process of cleansing and self-purification, bringing into uncomfortable light the individual and spiritual implications of decolonial work, and the attention to micro detail required. In the case of Australian arts culture, the visual or surface-level components of the arts world perform politics in a way that places absolute faith in them to act on our behalf. Wilson writes on this tendency to overlook land-based solutions in favor of surface-level cultural expressions, and points to problems with the term "decolonization," noting that:

> I avoid using it because I do not think we (or our struggles) should be defined by colonization. I am Nehinuw (Cree) and our people, like all Indigenous peoples or people of any culture, have a worldview that, over time, has not changed in some aspects and has changed significantly in other

> aspects [...] If we describe ourselves as "decolonizers," it implies that colonization is what defines us, but my people were Cree before the colonizers arrived. While we have been impacted by colonization, our Cree identity and worldview have survived and have persisted. I rarely use the term decolonization because it gives colonization power. It also assumes that we do not change as Indigenous people, and we have always been changing [...] What's visible is far less important or substantial than the 90% of the iceberg that is beneath the surface of the water [...] Many Indigenous people recognize that decolonization requires repairing that damage and restoring the relationships between our visible and material culture and the deep knowledge, value systems, philosophies, cosmologies and other invisible aspects of our cultures. I do not think you can do that without land-based knowledge.[19]

For Wilson, decolonization as a descriptor functions as a form of entrapment, positioning Indigenous practice through its resistance to colonialism, rather than as a form of autonomous life. The ways in which decolonial theory is currently utilized are, in Wilson's view, overly attentive to colonialism, continually locating Indigenous nations in the position of struggle and leaving little room for other readings. She notes that her own reasoning for not using the term — though it is useful and valuable as a descriptor for action — is because it defines Indigenous lives and practices primarily through their relationship to colonialism. Her commentary on the branding of decoloniality expresses a further suspicion toward the logic of branding itself: if a social movement is branded, accessible, and marketable, it should be carefully scrutinized.

The occupation of West Space by this mob

At the start of NAIDOC week 2019,[20] West Space gave over its entire gallery as a studio and exhibition space to this mob for about six weeks. this mob is an open collective of Aboriginal and Torres Strait Islander artists and community. There is no hierarchy or formal organization, and the membership of the collective is not exclusive. Previously, this mob had used other gallery spaces — such as Schoolhouse Studios — as closed studios for shows in development and to facilitate community building and intergenerational mentorship. Aboriginal artists often engage in such practices as a means of disrupting ideas of viewership and production. Taungurung artist Kate ten Buuren, who started the collective, wrote the following on the importance of this mob's collective actions in generating a critical, mutually beneficial, and non-competitive First Nations support structure in the arts:

> The opportunity to sit down with more established Blak artists, in a way that fosters your growth as an artist, is an invaluable experience that isn't provided in mainstream education settings or the workplace, and for young mob it can seem really inaccessible. this mob believes mentorship is a really important part of our learning: to spend time with our Elders, learn the right protocols, and seek advice that will help our practice as a collective.[21]

From the launch party for *un Magazine* 12.1, held at the Footscray Community Arts Centre,[22] I have a vivid memory of Wemba Wemba and Yorta Yorta artist and academic Paola Balla shooing away attendees who were trying to peer into the development space for the forthcoming *Blak to the Future* exhibition. This was despite the fact that the space was walled-off, displaying a sign that read: "keep out — show in development." That area was established as a safe, protected space for the development of emerging Blak artistic and curatorial talent, but visitors still attempted to peek inside, as if the construction of a wall and a sign asking people to stay away might be an interactive exhibit in itself.

this mob's West Space occupation was unique in that it did not focus on a curatorial outcome. Andy Butler notes that in this arts climate, in which the logic of "neoliberalism, precarity and constant production is one that is felt acutely," the use of the space by this mob to build community around arts practice rather than exhibit work subverted not only the logics of capital and production, but also "the way artists are meant to interface with the public."[23] Further subverting the norms of the relationship between the gallery and the artist-as-contractor, this mob drafted a contract, which West Space were given to sign, detailing how the relationship between the gallery and the collective was to be conducted. The document outlines some instructive principles for arts practice. West Space is named in the document as "the Accomplice." Among the clauses, the Accomplice is asked to prioritize the rights of Aboriginal Elders, children, and disabled people to access the gallery and experience art, and they are instructed to demonstrate proper protocol in making the space welcoming. They are asked to pay rent to Traditional Owners via the local Wurundjeri Land Council and the Boon Wurrung Foundation, and to "commit to ongoing support of First Nations artists in their programming. this mob refuse to be a tick in your diversity box and encourage you to pay attention to the artists we bring into the space." These two clauses are vital for arts workers to pay attention to, especially so in a climate where, increasingly, organizations are bringing Indigenous workers into their programming to fill empty spaces in ways that serve the needs of the organization, and do not establish ongoing benefit to the Blak arts community at large. Paying respect to Traditional Owners in the form of rent also ensures that the needs of the local Traditional Owners are prioritized, alongside the benefits gained by those artists who are Indigenous but not necessarily of the land they're living and working on. Another clause states that the Accomplice must agree to "limit the amount of bureaucratic processes where possible," and "respect our processes of making and presenting work," in recognition of the fact that Indigenous art-making processes are often devalued, and bureaucratic processes often function as exclusionary and gatekeeping practices. Finally, the contract ends with an agreement that "the Accomplice respects our sovereign right to Indigenous governance, our right to self-determine, and commits to sharing power in a way that uplifts, empowers and enables this mob and broader community to more confidently operate in the arts world."

What if our agreements were binding?

I am writing this article in 2020, in the midst of the COVID-19 pandemic. As with the 2016 crisis generated by funding cuts to the arts in Australia, artists and writers are currently facing doubts about their work security on a large scale. There have been many crisis moments in the arts in the past year alone, many "threats" and many moments where the death of the arts altogether, in its current form, has been foreshadowed.

Yet, it is the very institutionalization of the arts, as Butler has noted, that provoked the necessary collectivization of artists who are routinely excluded from spaces marked white (he notes that an "inside joke among artists of colour in the past has been to call it [West Space] 'White Space'").[24] How these art institutions might start earnestly paying their dues remains to be seen, but the questions have now been asked. The imperatives of bureaucracy and funding have driven Indigenous collectives into situations where we need to make self-determined agreements with our partners in the art world to keep our work going, and to trust that they will make those agreements in good faith. But we all want to know what happens after the "First Nations special issue," the temporary reoccupation, or the very special exhibition guest. These episodic guest spots have become the normalized mode through which Blak writers, curators, and artists contribute their critical labors. Given the immense contribution of our writers and critics to the field, consideration must be given to ways to reshape arts discourse in line with the learnings we take from these crises. We want to know what happens after the moment of interruption, and before regular programming resumes — if it ever does.

1 Narrm is a Woiwurrung language name used for Melbourne, alongside Birraranga, which is attributed to the Boonwurrung. Both are commonly used in reference to the greater Melbourne area.

2 "Destiny Deacon developed the term 'Blak' as part of a symbolic but potent strategy of reclaiming colonialist language to create means of self-definition and expression." Hetti Perkins and Claire Williamson cited in Kate L. Munro, "Why 'Blak' not Black?: Artist Destiny Deacon and the origins of this word," *NITV*, June 29, 2020, https://www.sbs.com.au/nitv/article/2020/05/07/why-blak-not-black-artist-destiny-deacon-and-origins-word-1. The term "Blak" is specific to Australian Indigenous collective self-understanding, used interchangeably with other respectful terms like "Aboriginal" and "First Nations"; when referring to global Indigeneities, I will use either "Indigenous" or nation-specific names.

3 Identified positions, under Australian employment frameworks, are positions that, often for the purposes of affirmative action, are to be filled by employees with a particular attribute, for example Aboriginality, disability, or gender.

4 Kimberley Moulton, "Collecting My Thoughts: Authenticity, the Museum and Representation," *Indigenous Story*, n.d., https://indigenousstory.com.au/works/128/collecting-my-thoughts-authenticity-the-museum-and-representation/.

5 Cited in Nicole Hasham, "Asylum Seeker Protest: Five Artists Pull Out of Sydney Biennale," *Sydney Morning Herald*, February 26, 2014, https://www.smh.com.au/entertainment/art-and-design/asylum-seeker-protest-five-artists-pull-out-of-sydney-biennale-20140226-33hbd.html.

6 Ibid.

7 Fredric Jameson, *Archaeologies of the Future: The Desire Called Utopia and Other Science Fictions* (London: Verso, 2005), xv.

8 Ibid.

9 Ibid.

10 David Mowaljarlai cited in Ambelin Kwaymullina, Blaze Kwaymullina, and Lauren Butterly, "Living Texts: A Perspective on Published Sources, Indigenous Research Methodologies and Indigenous Worldviews," *International Journal of Critical Indigenous Studies*, vol. 6, no. 1 (2013): 5.

11 Ibid.

12 Alex Wilson and Marie Laing, "Queering Indigenous Education," in *Indigenous and Decolonizing Studies in Education: Mapping the Long View*, ed. Linda Tuhiwai Smith, Eve Tuck, and K. Wayne Yang (New York: Routledge, 2018), 136.

13 The name given by Aboriginal people to January 26, the original date of the landing of British ships on Aboriginal lands in 1788, and the date of the Australian national day. Invasion Day is considered by Aboriginal people to be a day of mourning, signifying the beginning of invasion.

14 Kate Leah Rendell, "An Unsettled Settler Response to *Open Cut*," *un Magazine* vol. 14, issue 1, ed. Maddee Clark and Neika Lehman (May 2018), http://unprojects.org.au/magazine/issues/issue-12-1/an-unsettled-settler-response-to-open-cut/.

15 Andy Butler, "this mob at West Space," *The Saturday Paper*, August 10–16, 2019, https://www.thesaturdaypaper.com.au/2019/08/10/this-mob-west-space/15653592008590.

16 See: https://blacktourmaline.studio/program/2019/6/8/blk-schools.

17 Aileen Moreton-Robinson, *Talkin' Up to the White Woman: Indigenous Women and Feminism* (Brisbane: University of Queensland Press, 2002), xvii.

18 Eve Tuck and K. Wayne Yang, "Decolonization Is Not a Metaphor," *Decolonization: Indigeneity, Education and Society*, vol. 1, no. 1 (2012): 1.

19 Wilson and Laing, "Queering Indigenous Education," 135, 136.

20 NAIDOC (National Aboriginal and Islander Day Observance Committee) is a week-long national celebration of Aboriginal and Torres Strait Islander history and community. It has roots in the 1938 protest against the Australian sesquicentenary by Aboriginal community members in Sydney.

21 Kate ten Buuren in Maddee Clark, "Connection and Resistance," *Art Guide Australia*, July 13, 2018, https://artguide.com.au/connection-and-resistance.

22 Footscray Community Arts Centre is an important site of community arts programs and Indigenous cultural activity in Narrm's inner west. To date, it has been the host of three iterations of the *Blak to the Future* exhibition, which is a collective project between emerging Indigenous curators and mentors.

23 Butler, "this mob at West Space."

24 Ibid.

Anyone with a Link Can Edit

Sara Kaaman, Jessica Gysel & Katja Mater (Editors, *Girls Like Us*)

The self-conscious collective
Create new document.

> I wished that woman would write and proclaim this unique empire so that other women, other unacknowledged sovereigns, might exclaim: I, too, overflow; my desires have invented new desires, my body knows unheard-of songs. Time and again I, too, have felt so full of luminous torrents that I could burst — burst with forms much more beautiful than those which are put up in frames and sold for a stinking fortune. And I, too, said nothing, showed nothing; I didn't open my mouth, I didn't repaint my half of the world. I was ashamed. I was afraid, and I swallowed my shame and my fear. I said to myself: You are mad! What's the meaning of these waves, these floods, these outbursts? And why don't you write? Write! Writing is for you, you are for you; your body is yours, take it.[1]
> — Hélène Cixous, 1976

It's 2020. We write. She, they, them, he writes. All bodies write. We write through fiber-optic cables under oceans, waves encapsulating our outbursts of words and desires. We write through the 4G and 5G towers hovering over natural and urban landscapes. We write as a feminist publishing collective that runs on electricity and Wi-Fi. We exist in the physical realm; one can find our printed pages in bedrooms and bookstores around the world. But we also live in the shared online documents of to-do lists, collected notes, names, ideas, financial calculations. Spreadsheets and folders. *Girls Like Us* rides the metaphors[2] of digital interfaces,[3] carrying us across, standing in for connection.

And yet, we try playing by different temporalities. We appear in print when the feeling is right (when the deadlines are stretched). Almost all work and time is donated. We are makers of our own time. Our shared documents live in a constant state of flux.

As you know, we have a soft spot for collectives, collaborations, friendships and support structures. People doing things with other people: loving, working, organizing, living. These strategies for surviving together form an underlying thread throughout all our issues.[4]

At this moment, we ask ourselves: what does it mean to work together? What does it mean to work together as a collective? What does it mean to work together as a feminist collective? What does it mean to work together as a queer feminist collective? What does it mean to work together as a queer feminist collective on digital platforms? What does it mean to work together as a queer feminist collective on digital platforms built on surveillance-capitalist business models? What does it mean to write together?

Writing collectively is so much more than writing collectively. It's researching the past and exploring the archives. It's reading together, more often aloud than silent. Experimenting with fonts, formats, photographs, filters, fantasy, frontlines, f-words, focus, feminisms… Rethinking the future while digging into the past. Walking the paths that have been carved out ages ago, and taking different exits. Pausing in between to rethink. Constantly reframing and reshaping. Rewriting the past, present, and future. Formulating new ways of living together, eating together, loving together. It's about giving voices to others, or making other voices heard. It's about different geographies, different time zones, different backgrounds, upbringings, cultures.

It's a collection of collectivities. A collection of interviews, Q&As, essays, love letters, diaries, archives, travel journals, biographies, autobiographies. A collection of lives, lifestyles, life stories, life speculations, lives lived, and lives unlived. Hidden life, underground life, life under the radar. Herstories, forgotten, never told, never surfaced.

It's collectivities. Plural. As in many: plural pronouns, off the gender spectrum. A collective is making errors, failures, taking risks, and welcoming going down with them. A collective is about the process as much as the end result. The collective is reinventing itself, always. It's learning by doing, setting borders, and time and time again reshaping them, crossing them, marking and unmarking them.

It's about text (and texting). Quotes. Fiction. Autofiction. Speculative writing. Sci-fi. Dystopias and imaginary worlds. It's about images. Dream-state projections. Free-flowing, undefined experiments. Inhaling, exhaling, taking a break. And starting all over again.

It's remembering that the impersonal is apolitical. Putting an asterisk next to the small and forgotten. In the margin. The labor of daily tasks and routines. The labor of unpaid labor. The putting in your face of things you never thought about. Opening perspectives, showing unseen worlds.

Double tap. Hold. Pinch to zoom.

Painstakingly someone(s) (hello, hi, hej) has written these words, shoulders hunched over machines of loving grace. Yet another someone has edited these words, a third has designed the layout of this page, a fourth has proofread, a fifth has received the digital file for printing, a sixth has prepared the plates for printing, a seventh has operated the printing press, an eighth has folded, a ninth has bound and trimmed, a tenth has packed these books into boxes for shipping, an eleventh has transported the boxes, a twelfth has received the shipment and unpacked the boxes, a thirteenth and countless more have helped the book reach its readers. All these hands and minds at work, careful, caring. Physical labor, and hands that made it possible for these words to reach your eyes.

> Our hands are tools; they transform thought into action, shape our reality, connect us to the world and all the beings that are part of it. An extension of our hearts, they can bring the ones we love closer, and keep at a distance those we distrust. Their sophisticated anatomy enables both the use of brute force and the most delicate of gestures.
> They feed us, defend us, but also hold a lot of stress. [...]
> Hacking with Care is a collective composed of hackers-activists, caregivers, artists, sociologists and friends.
> It represents the merging of our visions and practices of hacking, activism and care. To us, hacking and care are not defined solely by their techniques or tools (whether these be hands or machines) but by what visions of a world, what ways of living, our actions support. In computer and telecom technology, the "handshake" is the process by which two devices establish a connection before they start to communicate.[5]

The paper collectives

Open recent document.

Collective friction, slowness, arguments, dreams, and documents miraculously materialize into a printed magazine. Because we want to be held, carried around, shared with friends, spilled coffee on, slept on, forgotten, discarded, or saved. Because we are bodies, we want to meet the physical bodies of our readers. The magazine is a reason to gather. We write futures together.

We want a future outside of straight time. A future in which all our friends and lovers and their lovers are coming over for dinner around a table we built together. We want a future that is fair, fun, furry, fabulous, fierce, free, and not fucked up. We want futures. A future in which we have dismantled the harsh economic systems that govern our lives and loves. We want a future of cohabitation and self-governance. A future that sees and acknowledges emotional labour. We want a future that understands the reality of being broke, of being evicted, of being talked down to, of being ignored. We want a future that embraces weakness, where we come together, where we can lean on each other and stand strong.[6]

We write in the company of all the feminist publication projects that have come before. Pile after pile of aged, yellowing magazines, pamphlets, fanzines. Brittle paper that tears easily. Materials matter; the spaces of the page as a place to gather or a Great Escape, the sound of pages turning softly or eagerly, hungry readers. Physical relics to touch. Digital (PDF) relics to save. Peeking back into the past has been a constant navigational tool. A history of feminist publishing efforts — material witnesses to past lives and struggles. Publishing creates publics, creates spaces. A spread is an opening into other possible worlds.

We try to make space to come together and meet. Leave the digital screen to meet IRL, AFK. With the editorial team, with our collaborators, with potential editors, with students, with other independent publishers, with peers and non-peers. To walk the talk, to do what we preach in the form of brainstorms, workshops, summer schools, book fairs, and physical magazine making.

On February 27, 1977, Charlotte Bunch gave a talk titled "Feminist Publishing: An Antiquated Form?" Her notes for the talk, published in the third issue of *HERESIES* magazine, read:

> What is the specific importance of feminist publishing/ writing?

> --If words the written word is important, then it's important where, why, and how to do it. I'm not talking about IND. (sic) morality or duty of why a particular person publishes where that debate has polarized too easily and often denies ind. Complexities -- I mean the underlying basic issue of why feminist publishing is vital to feminist writing + to women's power
> And why it should be supported as crucial to our future.
> [...]
> Now there are over 200 feminist newspapers, magazines, presses and publishers
> and another 30-40 women's bookstores. All of that material from mimeo (sic) to finely published books is the feminist press.
> [...]
> No, the feminist media isn't just a stopgap
> --it isn't just ind. (sic) choices about where to publish, which can involve various issues
> --it is our future, as an institution and as the well-spring of our words and thought and action.
> It is our looking back and going forward in the written word.[7]

The legacy of queer and feminist publishing is being traced and played with through projects like Loraine Furter's *Speaking Volumes* research, the online workshop *Liberation in Print* by Common Interest, Danielle Aubert, Delphine Bedel, *Just for the Record*, *The GenderFail Archive Project* by Be Oakley, Nat Pyper, *MsHeresies* by Rietlanden Women's Office, *Queer.Archive.Work* founded by Paul Soulellis, the book *Liberation in Print* by Agatha Beins. Many efforts are being made to open up a fragmented history; this list is too short, hereby acknowledging all of its omissions.

But a part of feminist practice has been to, simultaneously, write your own feminist history. In *The New Woman's Survival Catalog* (Berkeley Publishing Company, 1973), itself a milestone in the history of Euro-American feminist publishing, one chapter is dedicated solely to listing and presenting feminist publications, publishers, and printers in the US at the time (there were many!). In *Rolling Our Own: Women as Printers, Publishers and Distributors* (Minority Press, 1981), the editors (Eileen Cadman, Gail Chester and Agnes Pivot) map another lively landscape of Euro-American feminist publishing. Through interviews with writers and publishers in the UK and US, they talk through collective writing, publishing, pamphlets, illustration, typesetting, printing, distribution, and "sexism in the radical book trade," and they share a directory of women's liberation newsletters, magazines, and journals.

HERESIES was one of the hundreds of feminist magazines that Charlotte Bunch mentioned, published out of New York with the subtitle *A Feminist Publication on Art and Politics.* Every issue was a collage, carefully edited by a different editorial collective. Its statement of intent, repeated in all issues, reads:

> HERESIES is an idea-oriented journal devoted to the examination of art and politics from a feminist perspective. We believe that what is commonly called art can have a political impact, and that in the making of art and of all cultural artifacts our identities as women play a role. We hope that HERESIES will stimulate dialogue around radical political and aesthetic theory, encourage the writing of the history of femina sapiens, and generate new creative energies among women. It will be a place where diversity can be articulated.
>
> [...]
>
> HERESIES will try to be accountable to and in touch with the international feminist community. An open evaluation meeting will be held after the appearance of each issue. Topics for issues will be announced well in advance in order to collect material from many sources.[8]

The outcome of a collective is always limited (and expanded) via its members. A collection of experiences never complete, always questioning, evaluating, growing. Sharp critique and loving praise can exist within the same voice, within the same word. Accountability is a practice.

The secret is the place and moment where knowledge appears and disappears, shows or fades in its relationship to power. Secrets become a way to distribute and circulate different stories, schemes or memories. Maybe the utopia we're searching for has been here all along and would reveal itself if only we understood how to look.[9]

The interfacial collectives

Last modified May 3, 2020.

Girls Like Us have always been a collective *across*, more often sharing digital spaces than physical. Twenty-five thousand, seven hundred and eighty emails later. One hundred and twenty-four gigabytes of archives scattered across hard drives and clouds.[10] *Girls Like Us* writes all its editorials collectively in shared documents hosted on cloud service platforms. We have agreed to the terms and conditions that give our data over to the corporations that host us. We (the queers, the feminists, the publishers, the activists, the archivists, the artists, the everyones) gather on platforms everywhere. We share knowledges on and with the platforms. Convenience trumps criticality.

A message, a heart, a GIF. Surveillance capitalism is smooth, well-camouflaged, well-designed, comes with so much ease and so many benefits, and it feels (oxytocin) good. Even the word *platform* is designed, and it does well in covering up a business model of extraction. The "platform" is potentially neutral ground, a space where the owner of the platform doesn't necessarily harvest intimate details of its performers. A platform is *a raised level surface on which people or things can stand. A raised floor or stage used by public speakers or performers so that they can be seen by their audience.*

Framed as inescapable, indescribable, uncontrollable and essential, economies are everywhere. Oppressive and enabling, lucrative and undervalued, there are economies that trade our emotional labour, desires, love, fertility, time, minds, queerness, politics, and clicks. There are economies that we can control and that control us, and those that we can subvert to serve our collectives.[11]

We meet in interfaces: designed "drives," "folders," and "documents" contingent on a stable internet connection. We submit to the interfaces. As users, we are the pillow queens and powerless bottoms of digital capitalism. Through the interfaces, writing pushes itself into our lives, into our bodies. Go to the bathroom; bring your phone. Text your friends. Text your lovers. Email a collaborator. Go to bed. Draft an email. Sleep mode.

In the essay "Black Gooey Universe," American Artist critiques the genesis and development of the Graphical User Interface (GUI/gooey) — that smooth, designed, responsive surface, the only part of our devices that we actually see.

By simplifying the programming process to one method and

abstracting it further through clickable icons and images, a limitation was placed on transgressive or nuanced possibilities available in early devices. [...] *In the computers we interact with most often at this moment (our smartphones), this interface has been further reduced by superimposing the map of correspondence of the mouse and cursor onto the virtual display itself. With this reduction comes a lack of mobility on behalf of the user (only being in one program at a time, never really closing, opening or "seeing" files), which reflects a pattern of making the mechanic apparatus invisible and thus easier to consume from and pour oneself into.*[12]

Secrets can be both beautiful and terrifying. There are times when it takes enormous amounts of courage to bring light to the shadows. At other times the world of coded messages is a necessary safe haven. A secret can be a private space for self-creation — or a shared site of pleasure.[13]

We know — "everyone knows" — that the well-designed front ends of commercial digital platforms are cover-ups for the surveillance, extraction, and commodification of social relations. This awareness is omnipresent, and refreshing (y)our memory feels naïve. But willfully we still ask: how can we reach beyond the singular, individual subject, how can we be more than one, in the digital interface? How can we clear the haze of self-promotion and commodification that influences so much of our online lives? How can we find ways to enact care, carefulness, collectivity, on (or off) the streamlined platforms? Many people are gathering! Touching each other's profiles, touching each other's hearts. Reaching out and into each other's lives. How can we access the true potential of collectivities in digital spaces? And how can they be radical? In a speculative proposal titled "QueerOS: A User's Manual," Fiona Barnett et al. write:

> QueerOS diverges from the digital network culture, widely accepted today, in which Terms of Service and License Agreements are quietly updated by corporations in order to limit users' rights to their own data, where agreements are to be scrolled past and clicked through, and consent is not taken seriously. QueerOS demands that consensual agreements are the means by which we build new architectures of possibility and make our dreams of abundance real.
> By agreeing to the QueerOS Terms of Service the user binds themselves in a relational network of queer kinship with and between people and systems, bodies and objects, one

> and another. [...] The interface marks the site at which human-machine interaction is situated. For most users, the interface is the only means of engaging with a given operating system, as all possible actions are mediated by the predetermined interactions built into the system. The interface is therefore a site of control, of restriction; it is a black box that accepts limited input to produce limited output, the workings of which remain hidden. [...] A more productive interface would be expansive, proliferating the relationality allowed for by the inter-face, its inter-activity, its nature as that which is between or among, that which binds together, mutually or reciprocally. Far from the extractive impulse of contemporary systems that mine and surveil, it is an act of consent and mutual transformation.[14]

Hide this program, close all your tabs.
Scroll-back-to: when an *interface* was the surface of touch between two persons' skin.[15]

Future collectives
Create new shared folder.
A couple of months into a global pandemic, dependence on communication via connected screens is bigger than ever. Never before have we spent so much time with interfaces and so little time with faces.[16] Post-virus infection, in March 2020, Paul B. Preciado writes:

> Between the fever and the anxiety, I thought to myself that the parameters of organized social behavior had changed forever and could no longer be modified. I felt that with such conviction that it pierced my chest, even as my breathing became easier. Everything will forever retain the new shape that things had taken. From now on, we would have access to ever more excessive forms of digital consumption, but our bodies, our physical organisms, would be deprived of all contact and of all vitality. The mutation would manifest as a crystallization of organic life, as a digitization of work and consumption and as a dematerialization of desire.[17]

This hallucinatory divination is not yet reality. And the tech-pessimism performed in this text can be countered with more nuance, without falling into tech-optimism. Graphic designer, artist, and educator Paul Soulellis does so in his 2017 talk "Performing the Feed":

> I approach network culture through the lens of experimental publishing and publishing as artistic practice, and I see that lens shifting dramatically right now, as algorithmic media and the network become more and more entangled. *Making public* is expanding into a new array of gestures and performative conditions that need to be examined and theorized, perhaps as a new paradigm.[18]

Soulellis defines the (old) publishing paradigm as revolving around "a fixed container in time and space — a carved stone, a poster, the book object, the printed page." As opposed to this: "In the new publishing paradigm, the container is open and fluid, maybe non-existent. Authorship is certainly no longer fixed — voice might be disguised, unrecognizable, or non-human."[19] For sure, digitality holds its own potential for play and radicality.

In a World WITh Too many choIcES and Too lITTlE TImE To ExplorE, play IS an ExcEllEnT STraTEgy. oBJEcTS, rolES, BodIES, SETTIngS — anyThIng can BE TranSFormEd In play. playIng acroSS TImE, SpacE, archITEcTUrE, BEdS, hoUSES, lIVES, papErS. SUddEnly, a chaIr IS a planE IS a STory IS an anImal IS an aVaTar IS a nEW rEalITy. rEThInKIng ThE procESS oF maKIng mUSIc. pUShIng dEadlInES, crEaTIng momEnTS To ExpErImEnT. or playIng on a KEyBoard aS a Way To EScapE War. maKIng Up WorldS, FIlmIng ThEm. SUrFIng Warm and cold WaVES. playIng WITh IdEnTITIES. playIng En maSSE, lEarnIng From Each oThEr. playIng To BE FrEE.[20]

On the occasion of the twenty-fifth anniversary of "The Cyberfeminist Manifesto for the 21st Century," cyberfeminist VNS Matrix (collectively) write "A Tender Hex for the Anthropocene":

> she barks:
> are vandals sleeping in the software?
> terror-garbed, unreason bound,
> they seize and sound
> flipping wayward surveillance agents
> [corrupt, clinging like caterpillars]

into hyperdrive
a greedy storm builds
the sky is crashing into the sea,
        [...]
machines must be perverted, re-instrumentalised,
redeployed in the service of the birds unking the castles,
crown the swans
fly on our feet
towards a new nature[21]

As feminist writers, makers, publishers, we stay cautious when facing (and using) the seamlessness and ease delivered to us by large corporations. Could we learn from history that ease for some means someone else is paying a price? Can we stay with friction? Can we resist competition, and reach for collectivities? Can we burst the frames?

We stay in the margins.
We keep printing.
And we're looking for the digital margins.
Hold, touch. Release.
Fold. Wrinkle. Cut.

1 Hélène Cixous, "The Laugh of the Medusa," trans. Keith Cohen and Paula Cohen, *Signs*, vol. 1, no. 4 (Summer 1976): 876.

2 From the Ancient Greek μετά (metá: "with, across, after") and φέρω (phérō: "I bear, carry").

3 "People learn more quickly when an app's virtual objects and actions are metaphors for familiar experiences — whether rooted in the real or digital world. Metaphors work well in iOS because people physically interact with the screen. They move views out of the way to expose content beneath. They drag and swipe content. They toggle switches, move sliders, and scroll through picker values. They even flick through pages of books and magazines." From "Human Interface Guidelines," iOS Design Themes, Apple, accessed April 25, 2020, https://developer.apple.com/design/human-interface-guidelines/ios/overview/themes/.

4 "Editorial," *Girls Like Us*, issue #8: FAMILY, 2016, https://www.girlslikeusmagazine.com/issues/open/issue-8-family/.

5 Hacking with Care, "The Handshake: A Manual," *Girls Like Us*, issue #10: FUTURE, 2017, https://www.girlslikeusmagazine.com/issues/open/issue-10-future/.

6 "Editorial," *Girls Like Us*, issue #10: FUTURE.

7 Charlotte Bunch, "Feminist Publishing: An Antiquated Form?," *HERESIES: A Feminist Publication on Art and Politics*, vol. 1, no. 3 (Fall 1977): 24–25.

8 See: http://heresiesfilmproject.org/.

9 "Editorial," *Girls Like Us*, issue #6: SECRETS, 2014, https://www.girlslikeusmagazine.com/issues/open/6-secrets/.

10 "To users, the cloud seems almost formless, or transparent — always available, ever-changing, hanging in the air, on screens, in waves, appearing and disappearing, 'formless cyberspace' indeed.

Yet at the core of this informational ghost dance lies a rudimentary physical form — steel and concrete infrastructure. If the enormous, energy-slurping data factories are the cloud's true form, then these instances of the 'space of flows' recall the medieval castle, the treasure chest, and the military base." Metahaven, "Captives of the Cloud: Part II," *e-flux*, issue #38, October 2012, https://www.e-flux.com/journal/38/61219/captives-of-the-cloud-part-ii/.

11 "Editorial," *Girls Like Us*, issue #11: ECONOMY, 2018, https://www.girlslikeusmagazine.com/issues/open/issue-11-economy/.

12 American Artist, "Black Gooey Universe," *unbag*, 2018, https://unbag.net/end/black-gooey-universe.

13 "Editorial," *Girls Like Us*, issue #6: SECRETS.

14 Fiona Barnett, Zach Blas, Micha Cárdenas, Jacob Gaboury, Jessica Marie Johnson, and Margaret Rhee, "QueerOS: A User's Manual," in *Debates in the Digital Humanities 2016*, ed. Matthew K. Gold and Lauren F. Klein (Minneapolis: University of Minnesota Press, 2016), https://dhdebates.gc.cuny.edu/read/untitled/section/e246e073-9e27-4bb2-88b2-af1676cb4a94.

15 Sentence borrowed from Klara Utke Acs.

16 The original meaning of *interface* (from 1874) is "a plane surface regarded as the common boundary of two bodies." See: https://www.etymonline.com/word/interface#:~:text=interface%20(n.),%2B%20face%20(n.).

17 Paul B. Preciado, "THE LOSERS CONSPIRACY," *Artforum*, March 26, 2020, https://www.artforum.com/slant/the-losers-conspiracy-82586.

18 Paul Soulellis, "Performing the Feed," a talk delivered at *The Cybernetics Conference*, November 18, 2017, https://soulellis.com/writing/nov2017/.

19 Ibid.

20 "Editorial," *Girls Like Us*, issue #5: PLAY, 2014, https://www.girlslikeusmagazine.com/issues/open/5-play/.

21 VNS Matrix, "A Tender Hex for the Anthropocene," 2016, https://vnsmatrix.net/projects/a-tender-hex-for-the-anthropocene.

The Museum and the Trouble with Discourse

Megan Patty

In my time as an art museum publisher, I have seen many bookshelves — from a performance artist's loft in Brooklyn to a fashion designer's Paris atelier, an arts center on Melville Island to an architect's studio in Shibuya. It is always a window into an artist's world, and often the beginning of a conversation about books. In looking to these shelves, I am able to silently take note of what might drive artists in their practices, the theorists that they might reference — it is an instant audit of information, from spines and titles alone. This careful and quick scanning is able to jumpstart my interaction with them, silently moving through many steps of initial conversation to begin to understand how we might make a book together.

To take a survey of the bookshelves of any number of readers who may be interested in art would turn up a consistent result — a proportion of spines would herald the logo of an art museum somewhere in the world. Accordingly, if we were to take an audit of the annual volume of art writing published, art museums stand to be key figures in the production of art discourse. Today, there are fifty-five thousand museums worldwide in over two hundred countries, many of these museums with an imprint publishing art writing to various degrees of note. In reflecting on this over time, the sheer volume of these publications, bearing these logomarks, has confounded me.

Museum publishing outputs have been historically known as "catalogues," and they have been defined by this term since the late 1850s. These are typically the spines referenced on bookshelves and coffee tables, however they have traveled a long history to arrive where they are today. Museums were some of the first large producers of cultural content and of early forms of historical discourse, and so they hold a large part of the responsibility for the types of information and art writing that have shaped Western art discourse (in particular). In this way, taking a look back at museum publishing and tracking its development can tell us about particular types of institutional publishing and the ways its contributors have approached art writing.

Since the sixteenth century, collectors of heritage material — largely held in private natural history collections — produced lists or concordances that collated and published information on their holdings. These publishing outputs were for an audience mostly comprised of other collectors or scholars, and functioned to disseminate the existence and holdings of collections during a time when leisure travel was largely unaffordable and interested audiences were less able to view collections in person.[1] Following unrest in Western Europe in the 1700s, collections moved from royal or private holdings to nationally run museums. These collections were formalized with the intention of preserving, protecting, displaying, and communicating them to the public, in major centers around the world. Many of the art museums we are familiar with today were formed at this time, including the Musée du Louvre, Paris (1793); the Rijksmuseum, Amsterdam (1808); the Museo Nacional del Prado, Madrid (1819); and the National Gallery, London (1824). In 2019, the world's oldest art museum, the Louvre, remained the most visited with 9.6 million visitors — the potential reach of their publishing imprint, Musée du Louvre Editions, is therefore astonishing.

Many early publications from these museums tell a story of young institutions forming a relationship with their publics, as the very concept of a museum for the public was relatively new. The catalogues produced were crude by today's lavishly illustrated standards; they were typically indexed lists of items with little in the way of image reproductions or longform writing. These publications were concerned with telling the story of institutional development, and were envisaged as a primary communication tool for the early museum. In many cases, in the absence of labels or other didactic materials, they also took the form of a room brochure detailing an exhibition hang. In this way, in the early years of museums, the catalogue performed many useful functions: it could communicate the collections; it could include a list of holdings; it could celebrate emerging philanthropy; and it could even offer a mapping of an exhibition hang as a way to locate works of art when visiting the museum or as a reference afterwards. Art museums went along publishing these small publications of lists and information for some time — longform art writing and discourse during those years came from private scholars or public commentators in newsprints attached to exhibitions at the French salons and the Royal Academy in London. Here, the salons provided a key link in the development of the public sphere and of public interest in art and culture more broadly. It was through these salons in France that art found an audience in society at large, away from the royal court and broader than the aristocracy. The salons were an access point to art for many, and so it was in this historical context that written critique emerged, and a broader audience or public for art discourse and art writing was formed.

Later, in 1857, in an introductory address to the science and art department of the South Kensington Museum, London (whose art department went on to form the core of what is now known as the Victoria and Albert Museum), curator Sir John Charles Robinson explained the task of the catalogue, its function and purpose:

> Catalogues full and complete, and also judiciously abridged, should be prepared, accompanied by historical and descriptive essays, and illuminated by engravings; by these aids each section of the collection would be as it were a standing treatise; designed to allure and lead on the observer to the methodic study of the subject; and the most indifferent observer would perforce be taught something.[2]

These remarks from a key figure and curator in British museology are important, as Robinson immediately highlights the social function of the catalogue as the dissemination of knowledge beyond the museum to its publics. Robinson's words are an early recognition of the role of the museum in the production of art discourse, and of the burgeoning relationship between the museum and its publics — a recognition that its role communicating culture was as important as its role collecting and caring for objects, hence the note that resulting published texts should be "descriptive." Around this time, many museums had also formed in the United States, including the Metropolitan Museum of Art in New York (1870) and the Art Institute of Chicago (1879), alongside many smaller private collections becoming public museums across the country. The introduction to the General Catalogue for the Isabella Stewart Gardner Museum, an art museum in Boston, Massachusetts, in 1935 states:

> This catalogue is written primarily for the lay visitor to the Museum, and is an attempt to give, in very brief fashion, such information about all but the least noteworthy objects on exhibition as will answer the questions which visitors ask most frequently, and aid in some degree the layman's understanding and appreciation.

In this introduction, we see knowledge-sharing as intended for the general visitor — not the specialist or the scholar, but an audience that may, through their reading of the catalogue, become engaged with the museum and its collections. The role of these early publications was important for museums of many scales to develop an interest among their publics and to begin to foster this interest in order to expand the role of museums into education more broadly.

In their form, these early catalogues of lists and indexes were simple and discreet, printed using letterpress and black ink in a small, folded format. An 1873 example from the Metropolitan Museum of Art, New York, which was published when the museum was temporarily located in a townhouse on 14th Street, is eighteen pages, simply printed and folded. The catalogue lists the works in an exhibition of loans alongside the people who lent them, dividing the works into alphabetized rooms. In this way, it acts primarily as a record of the exhibition, the works, and the lenders, and as a wayfinding device for visitors unfamiliar with the museum's temporary home. Museum publishing at the time was disseminated to a small audience and relied on a museum director or curator who could invest in the preparation, printing, and lithography of the catalogue. Many early catalogues are non-illustrated or only partially illustrated in stone lithography, presumably due to the cost and availability of lithography at the time. Interestingly, some contained reproductions of the artists' signatures, perhaps to confirm the authenticity of the museum's holdings or simply for the interest of the reader.

The move from these simple publications to the type of museum publishing that we know today occurred in the late 1920s and 1930s, particularly in the United States where museums began producing more sophisticated publications that were intended for commercial sale. As a museum publisher and researcher, I have seen many examples of these titles from the 1930s and 1940s. Printing at the time remained expensive, however art writing seemed to be coming into some prominence,

with longform essays beginning to emerge and museum curators writing and being key contributors to this form of art discourse. Looking to a leading example of museum publishing, the Museum of Modern Art (MoMA), New York, tells an interesting story — its publishing activities set a benchmark for institutional publishing around the globe and formalized the discipline of museum publishing that continues today.

The publishing department at MoMA was founded in 1929, with a dedicated team to address the production of publications at each stage. In 1934, MoMA held an exhibition titled *The Making of a Museum Publication*, which was, according to the press release, a display of the "entire process, step by step, involved in the production of its publications, from authors' copy to finished book." This press release details the publishing ambitions of the museum, perhaps as a positioning statement to show the value of a publishing program to the broader public. The release also details the impetus behind the museum's investment into new longform scholarship, and the communication and dissemination of that scholarship to readers. For the burgeoning discipline of museum publishing and the new department, the exhibition was a strategic way to engage broadly and to highlight the value of publishing by making the process public. The closing statement lists the department's output at the time, some twenty-three publications over five years documenting the museum's exhibitions of its collections. Through this list, we see the strategy of the museum articulated, a focus on modern and contemporary practice that MoMA is still known for today: *Paintings by 19 Living Americans*, *Modern Architecture*, *Edward Hopper*, and *A Brief Survey of Modern Painting*. Such titles clearly set the museum apart from the program of its nearby counterpart, the Metropolitan Museum of Art, which was primarily concerned with publishing its much broader historical collections, aligned with its remit of collecting "5,000 years of art from across the globe," as opposed to MoMA's "modern art" mission.

MoMA is also a striking case more broadly. The formalization of both the publishing department and the role of publisher saw the appointment of Monroe Wheeler to Director of Publications in 1939. An important figure in the development of the discipline, Wheeler came from a fine art press in Paris, before working with MoMA as a library committee member for its 1934 publishing exhibit. Following this, he commenced formal engagement with the museum's publishing program (until 1967), and established the MoMA imprint as it is known today. A key contribution here was Wheeler's establishment of the imprint as influenced by trade fine art publishing, yet with a set of aims more closely aligned with the museum. From the correspondence held in the MoMA archives, we know that Wheeler worked closely with the museum's director and was a key figure in the exhibition committee, developing a deep understanding of the relationship between books and exhibitions, and of the potential role of publishing within a museum of modern art more broadly. Wheeler was also active in various art presses of the time, engaged in the field, and publishing commentary about museum publishing. Two 1946 articles published in museum periodicals, widely read by the profession at the time, capture his vision:

> Enlightened museum publishing calls for far-sighted planning. We still underrate the curiosity, the open-mindedness, the native aesthetic sensibility, and the educability of our people. The challenge to produce significant art books grows ever more formidable and challenging.[3]

This statement about the planning and the structure involved in a museum imprint might seem less enlightening today. However, for a discipline that was, at the time, trying to carve out a clear space next to curatorial and exhibition departments, it is quite interesting. It makes a statement around museum publishing being more than simply a reaction to exhibitions or collections, and it alludes to a clear understanding of the role that books play for a museum's publics.

Later, in 1964, an article in the *Auckland Star* newspaper reaffirmed MoMA's quality contributions to museum publishing, and also the imprint's value to art and design historical discourse and scholarship:

> The Museum has come to be regarded as the world centre for the field it deals in. Largely this is because of the publishing policy. For each of the special exhibitions that it mounts in a constant stream throughout the year, it produces a book (not merely a catalogue) to preserve what was of permanent value in the show. Often the book becomes the best thing available on its subject.[4]

The article goes on to state:

> In each of the fields in which the Museum is active — painting, sculpture, drawings and prints, architecture and design, photography, films, and art education — it has published outstanding books that make a lasting contribution to that field.[5]

Here, we see an understanding of the museum's role in publishing art writing and shaping art discourse. By the 1960s, museum imprints were well developed, publishing numerous volumes per year, and engaging with broad subject matter. Wheeler's own thoughts on who should be writing for the museum speak to a publisher already questioning the responsibility of the museum in providing deeply researched and well-written art writing. In 1946, he was questioning the role of the museum curator's own staff in producing such writings, alluding to the possible shortcomings of this model:

> At present we have neither the quantity nor the quality of the art writing we could use. The museum world needs more writers who can leaven the heaviness of scholarship, humanize the themes of art criticism and give them new readability. It may be strongly recommended to those in charge of museum organization to try to engage a skillful writer or two as such, writers who are able not only to contribute independent treatises in fields where they have authority, but to elicit from their more specialized and less literary colleagues the subject matter of other volumes, or at least to help them in their writing, which is a technique like any other, not at everyone's command.[6]

Wheeler's quote illustrates a shortcoming in art writing and art discourse still seen today in museum publishing and art publishing more broadly. In the years since 1946, there have of course been some gains to address the types of problems with art writing that Wheeler carefully points out. One such endeavor, to "leaven the heaviness of scholarship, and to humanise the themes of art criticism," has been undertaken since 1976 by *October*. Published by the MIT Press, the peer-reviewed journal continues to be a counterpoint to both museum or institutional publications and wider art criticism seen in platforms such as *Artforum* or

Art in America. Cofounder Rosalind Krauss, herself a writer in the field of art criticism, was frustrated by the current titles widely read in the United States (namely *Artforum*) for their lack of engagement with the critical social issues of the time. So, she collaborated with fellow writer Annette Michelson to begin the journal, which was interested in art and art writing as well as their social and political dimensions and the ways in which theory intersected with modern art discourse. The fact that two writers founded *October* is crucial to the ambition and the lineage of the publication, now numbering some 173 editions. The publication's writerly character is something long admired and often studied and invoked by other publications—the journal's issues are often responded to by other publications, conferences, papers, and exhibitions. They act as a starting point for both discussion and reflection; their commitment to publishing many longform articles on the same theme or event gives rise to a humanness in art criticism. A number of special issues tackle art-specific concerns, such as "Abstraction" (Winter 2013) and "Postwar Italian Art" (Spring 2008), as well as key social concerns impacting contemporary art discourse, such as "Occupy Wall Street" (Fall 2012) and "In what ways have artists, academics, and cultural institutions responded to the U.S.-led invasion and occupation of Iraq?" (Winter 2008). The contributors to *October* are art writers, academics, theorists, cultural critics, and often artists with a writing practice. A number of critical texts relating to the understanding of contemporary art and theory have been published in the journal, including vital texts by scholars such as Claire Bishop and Hal Foster, as well as Krauss and Michelson themselves. *October* has broadened the field of art writing for over forty years.

Yet one journal cannot, of course, address all of the problems with art writing, particularly regarding the representation of voices and topics. Who is more or less audible, and who in fact may be rendered mute? *October* largely deals with American art, large exhibitions and biennales, populist exhibitions, and other issues with broad appeal. Much is left out of this art writing and discourse—not least, many forms of non-Western art and many voices writing on art around the world. In his key 1997 treatise *After the End of Art*, critic and academic Arthur Danto illustrates his frustration with art writing and the discourses surrounding art at this time, including the legacy of MoMA and museums:

> Modernist critical practice was out of phase with what was happening in the art world itself in the late 60s and through the 1970s. It remained the basis for most critical practice, especially on the part of the curatoriat, and the art-history professoriat as well, to the degree that it descended to criticism. It became the language of the museum panel, the catalog essay, the article in the art periodical. It was a daunting paradigm, and it was the counterpart in discourse to the "broadening of taste" which reduced art of all cultures and times to its formalist skeleton, and thus, as I phrased it, transformed every museum into a Museum of Modern Art, whatever that museum's contents.[7]

This treatise from Danto illustrates an accelerating critique of institutions, which began in the 1960s and 1970s with artistic practices of institutional critique and became the topic of much contemporary art and discourse during the 1990s. Prevalent in academic and art journals, this critique often came from museums' own programming channels, which were beginning to unpack their many shortcomings, thus making them both part of the problem and part of the solution. We can clearly see how this is, in and of itself, a problem. These organized and institutional platforms for art writing had become stagnant, formulaic, and gentrified. This aside, in the 1960s another platform for art writing emerged, one that sat alongside museum publishing and also mainstream criticism and presses.

During the 1960s and 1970s, art practice and the art market was changing. The commodification of art was occurring in a pronounced way, particularly in New York, where artists began looking to the possibility of the book, rather than the institution, for exhibiting their work. The channel of the museum became a frustration, and increasingly so too did galleries. Museums were slow to reflect the many social and political concerns of the time, their lengthy planning and exhibition processes prohibitive to acquiring or exhibiting work quickly or responsively. And times were changing fast, with the public and the artistic community deeply engaged in various activist causes, including women's liberation, gay rights movements, and protests against the Vietnam War. Further, the economy in New York had stagnated, crime and police corruption were rampant, and many families moved away from the city during the 1970s, adding a further loss of tax revenue to the city's hip pocket. By 1975, New York had plunged into a fiscal crisis. The city was grimy, gallerists desperate, and the market unable to take risks exhibiting experimental work — such as conceptual art — that might not prove financially advantageous. Instead, the book became an exhibition space for artists and collectives, including the likes of Seth Siegelaub, Ed Ruscha, Kathy Acker, Carl Andre, Lawrence Weiner, Lucy Lippard, and Sol LeWitt. Often tied to the conceptual art and performance art movements, artists made small-run publications to explore the potential of the book. Their activities were largely self-organized in the form of publications, exhibitions, and periodicals, and culminated in the 1976 foundation of influential artist bookstore Printed Matter Inc., New York, by Lucy Lippard and Sol LeWitt, who had met at MoMA when Lippard was a research librarian and LeWitt worked the night desk. Printed Matter endures today as a critical platform for art publishing practices, and its activities create a community around books in the form of events, art book fairs, publications, editions, and reading groups.

It was from this concern with the possibility of the book — supported by bookstores such as Printed Matter, Boekie Woekie in Amsterdam (est. 1986), and others — that, from the early 1980s, a proliferation of independent art publishing and small imprints emerged. It was an area that challenged both institutional critique and existing forms of art writing and its structures.

In the 1980s, many independent art publishing houses were associated with celebrated graphic designers or artists, such as Lars Müller Publishers in Switzerland and Steidl in Germany, or gallerists, such as Koenig Books in Germany. In the late 1990s and 2000s, independent publishing gained a renewed momentum. Artists, editors, independent curators, and graphic designers were undertaking publishing activities to explore their own work and the work of their colleagues, as a space for exhibition-making, and to develop and share new discourses that were excluded from larger institutions. Prominent examples from this period include: Roma Publications (established in 1998 by Roger Willems and Mark Manders), Lukas & Sternberg (now Sternberg Press, established in 1999 by Caroline Schneider), Valiz (established in 2003 by Astrid Vorstermans), Onomatopee (established in 2006 by Freek Lomme and Remco van Bladel), Triple Canopy (established in 2007 by Caleb Waldorf et al.), and Badlands Unlimited (established in 2010 by Paul Chan). These imprints challenged existing models of art publishing, not only art writing.

With relative freedom, these imprints were and are able to explore writing from lesser-known authors. Without the pressure of a museum curator or A-list critic, a freedom emerges to publish voices who may be emerging, forgotten, or simply unpopular. This freedom also enables wide-ranging discourses and the publishing of academic writers in new realms. It throws down challenges to the discipline of art writing and to writers themselves to, as Wheeler reminded us earlier, "contribute independent treatises in fields where they have authority, but to elicit from their more specialised and less literary colleagues the subject matter of other volumes." By 2005, the proliferation of independent publishing led to the founding of Printed Matter's NY Art Book Fair by artist AA Bronson; by 2015, the number of independent exhibitors at the fair numbered over three hundred from thirty countries, with more than thirty-five thousand people attending the event.

Contemporary museum publishing can learn from independent art publishing and from critical discourse the likes of which is published in *October*. Wheeler's early critiques regarding writing and the museum have not yet been addressed. In my own practice as a museum publisher, I have witnessed some shifts in the ways in which art writing and the museum are entangled — and I clearly see the problems that persist. Since the modern museum's foundation, the art writing that surrounds it has largely been commissioned from directors and curators who were, for the most part, white male art historians with lengthy theses on European art. These voices figured heavily in museum imprints and trade publishers' catalogue raisonnés until very recently. (An element of this will seemingly always persist.) The dominance of such figures in museum discourse only began to shift in the mid-2000s, with slow changes in the types of writers and authors being commissioned by museum publishers to write about art. As Donna Haraway so aptly puts it:

> All readings are also mis-readings, re-readings, partial readings, imposed readings, and imagined readings of a text that is originally and finally never simply there. Just as the world is originally fallen apart, the text is always already enmeshed in contending practices and hopes.[8]

Some positive change has come from moves to decolonize the museum, which has enabled Indigenous and First Nations writers to be commissioned to write for museum publications. In a recent publication, *TIWI: Art & Artists* (2020), published by the National Gallery of Victoria (NGV), Melbourne, I had the opportunity to engage writers, scholars, artists, and cultural commentators from around Australia but also, and most importantly, writers from the Tiwi Islands, situated off the coast of the Northern Territory adjoining the Timor Sea, to write for this longform publication.[9] The recognition of cultural knowledge and the production of art by the Tiwi people is best represented and discussed by those who can write through embodied experience, but art history has not historically recognized this. In turn, publishing such writing shifts the perspective of the publication from one that could be colonial and anthropological to one that instead recognizes Tiwi culture as a living culture, a culture that has survived colonial oppressions and has regenerated, transformed, and influenced art making. It is one small example of a nod to change, long-needed and often overlooked.

This negotiation of territories between a museum and its imprint is one a museum publisher knows well. The further negotiation with writers to write about art for the museum when they may have neither written about art nor for the museum before is a careful balance, navigating what could be a mistrust in the museum to discuss the institution anew. At times, this negotiation is challenging, for various reasons, many of which are not obvious, such as the need to represent works of art in ways that feel as rich as their intention, working to layer opinions and voices in the museum's imprint to be closer to reflecting a contemporary readership. This speaks to a reconfiguration of the relationship the museum has with art writing. It is about doing, as well as meaningfully undoing. Commissioning an unexpected author, challenging an artist to rethink the communication or reception of their work by someone not in their current orbit. Giving a lesser-known writer a platform. Challenging a well-known author on their unacknowledged bias. These are small ways to begin to reshape art writing and discourse, in the hope that museum imprints continue to be seen on bookshelves, and that the art writing contained within these volumes is as vital as it is vibrant, with the inflection of many contributors across generations, geographies, and practices.

1 Sarah Anne Hughes, *Museum and Gallery Publishing: From Theory to Case Study* (London: Routledge, 2019).

2 John Charles Robinson, "On the Museum of Art (no.5)," from a series of introductory addresses to the science and art department, South Kensington Museum, December 14, 1857.

3 Monroe Wheeler, "The Art Museum and the Art Book Trade," *Museum News* 24, no. 2 (1946): [7]–8.

4 "Background to the Publications Department," *Auckland Star*, May 1964, Museum of Modern Art Archives, New York.

5 Ibid.

6 Monroe Wheeler, "The Museum as Publisher," *Art in America* 34, no. 4 (1946): 218.

7 Arthur C. Danto, *After the End of Art: Contemporary Art and the Pale of History* (Princeton, NJ: Princeton University Press, 1997).

8 Donna J. Haraway, *Simians, Cyborgs, and Women: The Reinvention of Nature* (Routledge, New York, 1991).

9 Judith Ryan, ed., *TIWI: Art & Artists* (Melbourne: National Gallery of Victoria, 2020).

Donald Judd's Writings

Flavin Judd, interviewed by Brad Haylock & Megan Patty

Donald Judd (1928–1994) was one of the most important artists of his generation. He helped to forge a new trajectory for American art in the twentieth century, not only as an artist but also as a theorist, and he was a steward of spaces for the sympathetic and continuing display of his own work and that of his contemporaries. Early in his career, from late 1959 until early 1965, Judd earned an income as a regular critic for *Arts Magazine*. His style as a writer is forthright and unapologetic. Judd is also known for his spaces, particularly 101 Spring Street, the cast-iron building in SoHo, New York, which he bought in 1968 and which served as a home and a studio for more than twenty years, as well as his properties in Marfa, a small ranching town in Texas in which Judd spent much time from the early 1970s onward. Perhaps most notable of Judd's Marfa properties is La Mansana de Chinati, also known as "the Block," a whole city block in downtown Marfa formerly used by the military. The old quartermaster's office became Judd's home on the site, and two former airplane hangars were converted to house his extensive library and studios for large works. In 1977, Judd set out the ideas for a foundation to preserve his work and that of others. His two children, Flavin and Rainer — respectively named after the artist's friends and contemporaries, Dan Flavin and Yvonne Rainer — today lead Judd Foundation. In this interview with Flavin Judd, we discuss the role of writing in Judd's career and its significance to his artistic and intellectual legacy.

BH/MP: The book *Donald Judd Writings*, which you coedited with Judd Foundation archivist Caitlin Murray, is an extraordinary and extensive collection of your father's writings.[1] It is a clear successor to those books of his writings that Judd edited in his own lifetime, most notably *Donald Judd: Complete Writings 1959–1975*, which was first published by the Press of the Nova

Scotia College of Art and Design in 1975 and reprinted by the Foundation in 2015.[2] More recently, you have coedited the book *Donald Judd Interviews*, which extends this tradition further.[3] In her foreword to the *Interviews* book, Rainer emphasizes the responsibility of the Foundation to steward not only Judd's physical works but also his intellectual legacy. Clearly the recent books are central to the latter aspect of the Foundation's work, but can you tell us more about how these books came about, and what you understand their significance to be now that they are actually circulating in the world?

FJ: It was recognized a long time ago that we needed to get a complete volume of Don's writings out. The small books he did during his lifetime (the Nova Scotia and Van Abbemuseum books, etc.) were incomplete.[4] The task was a large one, so it had to wait until various other projects, like the restoration of 101 Spring Street, were finished first. Then Caitlin Murray and I started collecting all of Don's writings and notes to figure out what we could include. I made the decision that the book should be one volume and should contain everything from the Judd Foundation Archives we could find that was more interesting than a grocery list.[5] We didn't leave much out. Obviously, Don is known for being an artist but that activity was not him and was not all he did, so the writings had to fill out the picture. The interviews were the same idea: everything we could find in one volume. This is actually an idea that Don had when he was alive but it was never done. I don't think you can understand somebody by reading 2,000 pages of their writing but you can understand some of what they were working on, and that's a start.

BH/MP: You also codesigned the *Writings* and *Interviews* books. Can you tell us about the thinking behind the design of these volumes? They could have followed the format of *Complete Writings 1959–1975*, for example, which is the height and width of US Letter and some three hundred pages in extent, but instead the recent books have a smaller page size and comprise more than a thousand pages each. Was the design of these led by a concern for pleasing proportions, or perhaps it is a matter of portability for the reader?

FJ: The idea was that the books would not be too expensive (there is no hard cover) and that they would fit in a pocket—

maybe not your back pocket, but a coat pocket. While I like the 1975 *Writings* book, I didn't think we had to abjectly copy it. It was not designed by Don or anything.[6]

BH/MP: Many artists also write, perhaps now more than ever, but Judd is surely exceptional as an artist who was also so influential as a critic of contemporary art. Should the figure of the artist-critic be more common, or is such polymathy particular to Judd (who, we should emphasize for readers, is also known for his architecture and furniture)? And a related question: Judd wrote that "an excellent artist has to know the work of older excellent artists as the person's own work is being formed," but can you offer specific insights into the significance of Judd's early work as a freelance critic to his own development as an artist?[7]

FJ: I don't think there are many "shoulds" in art but knowing more than less is one of them. It's clear reading his early reviews in the Nova Scotia book that he's working out his dissatisfactions while writing them. Don was not a very social guy so maybe he wouldn't have seen 15–30 shows per month if he wasn't writing the reviews. Writing makes you think in an order beyond looking. He was very unhappy with the activity of painting at the time but he didn't know where that activity should go to dispel his dissatisfaction. I think that by seeing the work of people like Lee Bontecou, Yayoi Kusama, John Chamberlain, and others he slowly figured it out. The dissatisfaction was a strong engine but it needs to push in a direction. The exploration of the works of others helped him find that direction, even if the works themselves that he was writing about had nothing to do with his later work. It's important to try to learn everywhere, from everybody, and writing criticism does that.

BH/MP: In Judd's notes and drafts, we occasionally see ∴, the mathematical symbol for "therefore." This idiosyncratic shorthand is surely a trace of the breadth of Judd's knowledge and thinking. Tellingly, you used the symbol as the title of your introduction to *Donald Judd Writings*. But the symbol doesn't appear in the final versions of any of his texts. At the back of the *Writings* book, you also included reproductions of a few pages of your father's drafts and notes — handwritten, or typewritten with handwritten corrections — which give us another insight into his writing process. Since you're so familiar with all of his writings, not only in their published form but also in their various states of development, can you tell us more about *how* your father wrote?

FJ: He studied logic (at Columbia during the time period when Susanne Langer lectured) and I think logic, which starts out simple enough — $A \neq B$, etc. — is one of the building blocks of his thinking.[8] It's not quite language, which has its own rules. It's the rules of thinking and it can apply to anything and that's what Don did. Many questions are not real questions but just non-questions posed in a meaningless way, if you look at the logic. This is not some elaborate Russell-style edifice but small logic that makes figuring things out possible — what we use every day.

BH/MP: The converted hangar at the Block in Marfa, which houses Judd's library of more than thirteen thousand books, is a magical place, but the public today can experience the space only from the edge of the room. Can you tell us what it was like to experience those spaces as part of your everyday life?

FJ: To me it was a normal house and the library was a normal library, only bigger. But then most people (the parents of other kids) didn't seem to read as much as Don. They seemed, on the whole, content with what they knew. It was clear though that books cost money and not everybody had thousands of dollars to spend on them. I felt the library was a luxury but a beautiful one. Don was a voracious collector of books and knowledge, and if you lived in Marfa pre-internet you needed a large library. When we were small, Rainer and I flipped back and forth between our spaces at home (the Block, etc.) and other people's houses we stayed at while Don was away, so we experienced both types of living. They both felt like home. Besides some of the more conservative local Texans, it was mainly New Yorkers, happy to live in glorified broom closets on the Upper East Side. I thought it was weird, secure as they were as to how people should live.

BH/MP: In the last essay in *Complete Writings 1959–1975*, "Imperialism, Nationalism and Regionalism," Judd delivers a scathing analysis of nationalism through the ages, and laments its persistence. Religion had become tepid, he argued, and already by 1975 nationalism was squarely "the real religion."[9] His words resonate today as we see new strains of nationalism simmering around the world. Judd was not a scholar of politics in a conventional sense, but he was evidently unafraid to engage in political debate, and his strong moral foundation is clear in most of his other writings too. What would Judd say about the role of the artist and that of the critic in the face of manifold crises in this third decade of the twenty-first century?

FJ: I think he would stand by his earlier writings. For Don, it was important to think about everything you could and to take as little as possible for granted. That meant investigation of the political situation and pretty much any other situation. While he didn't think his art was directly political, he felt that all people had to be political just to protect their rights and the rights of others. The moral stance that is evident in the writings is also evident in the art. I think that he would wonder why more people have not done the same kind of foundational research and reassessment, because when you do that you tend to enmesh activities and theories together so that the actions come from a related, investigated set of concerns. If you discover that religion is simply a kind of therapy made of stories then you are not likely to become a priest.

It could be argued that the crises of the recent decades can be traced back to the austerity spending of Nixon and his Reaganesque offspring, so Don's writings of that era are perfectly timely. A country built on genocide should not surprise when its government does not represent the people governed.

BH/MP: Your father was outspoken in his disapproval of museums and galleries in general, and indeed of certain museums and galleries in particular. We're yet to see the kinds of changes he would have wanted, such as more spaces dedicated to the permanent display of work, but in the past quarter century we've seen a notable shift of a different type: museums and galleries now play a more active role in the production of artistic discourse. What would Judd have thought about this change in the ecosystem of art writing?

FJ: It should not be forgotten that Cardinal Scipione Borghese built his villa not to live in but to house his art collection. He did this to impress upon visitors and ambassadors his power and wealth. The art was a form of persuasion, the display of art had and has a purpose. "The production of artistic discourse" in this case is just marketing. The commercial art world is a way for the ultra-rich to ease their complicity in damaging the planet and the people on it by paying a writer $500 to write about their favorite artist, which makes it possible to launder the proceeds of their corporate shenanigans when they buy and collect said artist. As Don wrote:

> 20 April 1985: We are tokens of civilization for the primitiveness of the powerful.[10]

BH/MP: Following your recent books of your father's writings, what comes next for the Foundation in the communication of his intellectual legacy? Are there more writings yet to be discovered and published?

FJ: There are not more writings forthcoming, but there are more books.

1 Donald Judd, *Donald Judd Writings*, ed. Flavin Judd and Caitlin Murray (New York: Judd Foundation and David Zwirner Books, 2016).

2 Donald Judd, *Donald Judd: Complete Writings 1959–1975* (Halifax: The Press of the Nova Scotia College of Art and Design, 1975; reprinted New York: Judd Foundation, 2015).

3 Donald Judd, *Donald Judd Interviews*, ed. Flavin Judd and Caitlin Murray (New York: Judd Foundation and David Zwirner Books, 2019).

4 Donald Judd, *Complete Writings 1959–1975*; and *Complete Writings 1975–1986* (Eindhoven: Van Abbemuseum, 1987).

5 The Donald Judd Papers, which include Judd's writings, correspondence, drawings, and studio records are part of the Judd Foundation Archives in Marfa, Texas. *Donald Judd Writings* includes a selection of essays, notes, letters, and art criticism from 1958 to 1993. *Donald Judd: Complete Writings 1959–1975* includes most of Judd's art criticism from 1959 to 1975.

6 Judd designed the jacket for *Donald Judd Furniture: Retrospective* (Rotterdam: Museum Boijmans Van Beuningen, 1993).

7 Judd, *Writings*, 273.

8 Five books by Langer are part of Judd's library in Marfa, Texas.

9 Judd, "Imperialism, Nationalism and Regionalism," in *Complete Writings 1959–1975*, 220.

10 Judd, *Writings*, 415.

Publishing as Relay

Anna-Sophie Springer
& Caleb Waldorf

> There is no Platonic reality of texts. There are only physical objects such as books and computers, foci of attention, and codes that entrain attention and organize material operations.
> — N. Katherine Hayles, 2005

> Triggers for joy are almost always something others might share, at least potentially, even if we experience them alone.
> — Lynne Segal, 2017

Preface: Measuring the moment

A year has passed since we first got together to reflect on our respective publishing practices, to consider various aspects of contemporary media ecologies, and to analyze the emotional and theoretical landscapes that envelop our work. We examined the differences between publishing in print (more typical for K. Verlag, the publishing atelier for exhibitions in book form managed and directed by Anna-Sophie since 2011) and publishing online (mostly the case for Triple Canopy, a magazine cofounded by Caleb, who has been the creative director since 2007). We also discussed our concerns about the cultural responsibility and social conditions of independent publishing practices; already tainting our mood was a growing unease about the spread of disinformation and vitriol on social media and the general retreat of the Left in a world of fake news and *so-called* fake news.

While these concerns remain valid a year later, as this book was being prepared for print a series of world-changing events began to unfold. It is mid-2020 and we are somewhere in the middle of an unprecedented global pandemic as the United States — currently leading the world with more than two hundred thousand deaths from COVID-19, which have disproportionately harmed BIPOC communities — is in the thrall of one of the largest insurrections against systemic racism and white supremacy in its history. Meanwhile, solidarity protests for the Black Lives

Matter movement have spread across the globe, as have conspiracies about the novel coronavirus and (much smaller) protests over resultant public health measures. These events de-normalize both connections and dependencies, inequalities and privileges, leaving few aspects of life untouched. In a matter of a few months, reality itself has undergone a substantial, long-overdue reappraisal. In the shadow of this revaluation, some aspects of our work that felt more urgent last year seem to be of less consequence today, while concerns that were peripheral last summer have moved to the center of our attention.

One concern we share is that of a functional and ethical distribution system developed by and for small publishers. During a spring of lockdown and an eerily quiet summer, the world has witnessed massive disruptions to on-demand, just-in-time supply chains. These disruptions are occurring against a horizon of economic scarcity as a result of resource exploitation, habitat obliteration, and ongoing climate breakdown. In this confounding situation, the discussion of alternative production and distribution models is even more urgent. Thus, our respective views on the "distribution problem" have been sharpened while we continue grappling with a complex series of new questions related to global circulation, supply, and the attention fatigue and mental exhaustion that characterize the current moment.

Revealing the racialized dimensions of risk, this year has also amplified the tensions between the political and the personal, the public and private — thereby urgently reconfirming the inextricable ties connecting social, public, and individual health. During the core phases of 2020's lockdown, being in community suddenly meant practicing remoteness. Months of "physical distancing" have posed unique challenges to effective collective strategies of mutual aid and resistance. In Berlin, where we both live, one response to a diminished circulation of people and goods was the invention of "Gabenzaun," which saw residents tie plastic bags full of items such as juice, energy bars, cigarettes, and dog food to urban fences for unhoused people and their companion species. A season of extended quarantine, mass death, and the failure of many governments to protect their citizens against the pandemic amplified core emotional issues such as loneliness, depression, and anxiety, as well as negatively impacted general well-being.

Imagining and enacting alternative ways of being together in 2020 is also, of course, a high-tech story of the digitization of sociality—protests, teaching, exhibitions, birthdays, funerals, and dinner and dance parties alike have moved online via Zoom, Instagram, Twitter, Facebook, or any of a number of other web-based platforms. Attempting to adapt, editors at big and small publishers are trying to figure out in real time how to maintain their communities by navigating both the familiar and unfamiliar aspects of these digital platforms, which were previously treated primarily as sites for promotion rather than as places to share or experience content. Thus far, the results have been mixed; perhaps this new normal can open up spaces for different types of listening and conversation, but this is yet to be seen.

In a recent *London Review of Books* podcast, Paul Gilroy pointed out that the "viral nature" of the Black Lives Matter movement relies on new technologies to pass on, connect, and multiply content.[1] In the past, we felt skeptical about the long-term impact of social media campaigns and the temporary solidarity streams they engender. But, as a movement deeply informed by the intersectional scholarship and organizing of Angela Davis, Ruth Wilson Gilmore, and many others, combined with both an intuitive and highly strategic attention to the affordances of networked technologies, the Black Lives Matter movement is an important step toward an internationalist political discourse and a collective renewal of the world.

One fundamental quality of running a publishing atelier is being involved in the mediation between public discourse and private emotions. For us, this means being involved in claiming spaces, amplifying voices, and sustaining the relationships that make things happen and that keep ties to and with the world—a world that we understand as shaped by histories both of suffering and of collective joy, and that is manifold and pluralized by difference. It is for this more utopian spirit in a dystopian year that we now relay this conversation to you.

In conversation

CW: I'd like to start our conversation with a schema: publishing takes things from one place and transposes them into other spaces over a duration, and, in this process, it can trace as well as define new territories—some short-lived, some immutable. Publishing can also be understood as an act of making something accessible; forms and formats in publishing are vehicles to assist in movement, the making of space, and the development of associations through common access. This blueprint applies to more than what may conventionally be considered to fall under the category of the publication, but is nonetheless a useful departure point for our discussion. We both operate in a similar area, facilitating work that traverses genres and disciplines. There are artists that have been in your publications at K. Verlag that have appeared in Triple Canopy; you did a book launch at A Public Library, a project space I operated in Berlin;[2] and, as one could naturally suspect, we've had booths next to each other at the art book fair Miss Read, also in Berlin. For all these overlaps, though, there are differences between how we've operated in, reacted to, and tried to shape the field of publishing. While reductive, the primary distinction we could make is that my practice has typically been situated on the web, yours in print and exhibition contexts. It is, of course, more nuanced than that, and this distinction creates a false binary that we should discuss, but I think it is important to acknowledge from the outset that we embark on a line of thinking about publishing from different perspectives.

I'm too old to be a "digital native," so I have memories of a less connected world, but the majority of my adulthood, and the entirety of my artistic practice, has unfolded alongside the rapidly changing technical landscape of the last twenty years. In varying ways and modes of expression, this transformation has been the point of convergence, or the backdrop, that situates most of my work. Artists have long been engaged with evolving technical and social networks as areas of analysis, use, and contestation. This is true whether we look to early digital experiments in distribution frameworks, like THE THING;[3] to older explorations of circulation and form by George Maciunas and his many interlocutors in Fluxus; or to the nexus of political journals and the avant-garde art movements of the interwar period in Europe and beyond. I point this out only to suggest that my interest in this area, far from being a radical departure from the past, feels tied to a legacy of artists working in publication (not to mention collaborative forms). But, as intuitive as this is to me, I also get the sense that my perspective is somewhat isolated within contemporary publishing in the arts.

This has led, particularly in the last few years, to a feeling of remoteness from the broad publishing landscape we are embedded in. This unease primarily arises from a gap that I perceive between the ideal(ized) potential of publishing as a means to expand publics and communities, and the dominant forms and frameworks that are being deployed. This is probably best exemplified by the rise of the art book fair, in which a fairly consistent group of publishers gets together to trade their physical wares within a somewhat closed ecosystem, typically one supported by art institutions of varying sizes that, irrespective of their locations, tend to exist within the same cultural continuum. As someone whose publishing atelier is also navigating these spaces, and since you are likely more reliant on them to sustain your practice than I am, at least financially, could you describe how you address this in your overall practice?

AS: As a publisher, my focus on the book-as-exhibition is informed by legacies of the "dematerialization of the art object" from the 1970s, and attendant experiments with publishing that were motivated by desires for institutional independence, pluralizing narratives, and alternative modes of circulation.[4] Before cofounding K. Verlag, I apprenticed as an editor at Merve Verlag, the theory publisher from the old West Berlin well known for translating French theory into German. No doubt the spirit of freedom that characterized their publishing house was extremely exciting, but, at the same time, I was disappointed by the lack of women writers in their program. I was interested in *écriture feminine*, especially the work of Hélène Cixous, and Chris Kraus, who was both an exceptional writer and a role model for publishing. Before I left Merve, I was translating Mark von Schlegell's *Realometer* (2009), which introduced me to Ursula K. Le Guin, and Nina Power's *One Dimensional Woman* (2009), which was an opportunity to bring together my enthusiasm for theory and my desire for a more self-aware, feminist publishing project.[5]

So, there is always a certain scene that we exist in and that we are trying to change. One of the aims of my practice—especially through an ongoing creative dialogue with my partner/collaborator Etienne Turpin—has been to push the boundaries of how we do things, what we think and talk about, and with whom. Perhaps that's got something to do with also being a translator? Whatever the case, on a practical level, a factor I consider important in publishing is that of accessing and redistributing cultural and institutional resources and working creatively to open up more potential for change.

When working on something, among the team, we ask again and again: what can a book be? What is an exhibition?

An interesting fact is that the atelier's publications are not limited to English or German; bilingual combinations and even translations are also common. This helps to incline the books beyond the narrower art scene and toward a broad range of contexts regarding content, geography, and contributors—a mode of diversity I am proud of. It's just one way of trying to work otherwise—that is, of being open as well as precise, and interrogating the book as an infrastructure for different ecologies of attention, teasing out rhythms, relations, and adjacencies among variegated systems of knowing and sensing.

Making books in this way is very conceptual. At the same time, I love physical publications—they survive long periods of time and can surprise you in unexpected places. Even a closed book communicates on intimate levels, via touch, smell, volume, weight, look, wear, etc.[6] I do like that a book both archives thought and activates the mind *apart from* electronic devices and screens, without ever being a closed technology. Speaking to Aby Warburg's notion of the "good neighbor," books connect, expand, and layer the imagination across dimensions of space and time.

Thinking about all of this turns publishing into a philosophical problem.[7] But publishing is also a political act. At K., each project is a collective learning process and an unforgettable interpersonal experience. In a world increasingly dominated by corporate interests, small presses like ours can take on themes that larger institutions won't or don't have to. At the same time, ethical or responsible publishing isn't merely an "awareness" problem; it's too apparent everywhere how quickly we forget. Something I have learned from my work is that publishing facilitates social alliances and helps to build an infrastructure for an ongoing debate about what it means to inherit and coproduce the world we are living in. Philosopher and cultural theorist Peter Sloterdijk captures this sentiment so well:

> Nietzsche, who knew that writing is the power to transmit love not only to one's nearest and dearest, but also, through the next person encountered, into the unknown, distant, future life. Writing not only creates a telecommunicative bridge between known friends, who at the time of the transmission live in a geographical proximity to one another; but it sets in motion an unpredictable process. It shoots an arrow in the air, described in the words of old European alchemists as an *actio in distans*, with the

> objective of revealing an unknown friend and enticing him into the circle of friends. In fact, the reader who sits down to a thick book can approach it as an invitation to a gathering.[8]

This possibility for collective joy — to borrow a term from socialist critic Lynne Segal — is, for me, the "fantasy of the library," a space not exclusive to physical, printed publications, and which doesn't foreclose the possibility that the content may deal with difficult material or suffering.

CW: It is interesting that Sloterdijk highlights the "thick book" as the arrival point for this complex system of interconnectedness. It appears that he is actually describing the internet! Which, arguably, is a much more effective means to extend connections and cohesion beyond an overly local and "physical" context. Perhaps this is most clear on the political Right, as evidenced by the present volume of conspiracy theories and the rise of negative solidarity, "the weak bond orienting isolated and competitive individuals against those who are failing to work or bear their share of austerity."[9] This points to a long-standing conversation we've had regarding the "distribution problem," which is clearly not limited to whether something is composed of HTML or ink on paper, but rather how immaterial and material objects are operative in the world.

AS: The philosophical discourse that Sloterdijk is a part of is a few thousand years old. So, technically, that goes much further back than the printing press, the codex book, and the internet. In this sense, it's less a question of the object/medium as a solid thing than of which solidarities are relayed and thus effectively brought into existence. The early internet liberated people from the mainstream. In today's platform version, there are profound forces at play; data mining, misinformation, and public pressure make a toxic mix. As we are ever more reliant on digital connectivity, one question is: can we reclaim it (and ourselves) from the vulnerability to financialized capitalism, where the generation of profitable data has become key? A subsequent question entails the construction of that "we" in the previous sentence: how do we build alliances that are not defined by ostracization, inflexibility, and a polarized conformity? It seems that social media (as one type of internet) encourages a particularly narrow understanding of purity and complicity, currently provoking a lot of "failed conversations." While Facebook, for instance, co-opted the term "friend" early on, today the platform is characterized by deep animosity. Also concerned with the corroding effects of fragmentation in the fight against structural oppression, artist and theorist Alex Martinis Roe has eloquently defended the notion of solidarity-in-difference, relaying the practice of *affidamento* (entrustment), which was cultivated by the members of the Milan Women's Bookstore Collective as a form of mutual commitment founded on the affirmation of difference.[10] Things are complicated and there is a lot of work to be done. To start with, "difference" must be protected to include more ambiguity than binary moral judgments such as like/dislike or friend/enemy.[11]

Through its publications, K. Verlag aims to contribute to this process. The recent book edited by Dora García, *Love with Obstacles (Amor Rojo)* (2020), on Russian revolutionary and socialist feminist Alexandra Kollontai as a predecessor of intersectional feminism, is one example. Another is *Despite Dispossession* (2021), an "activity book" developed by a diverse research group hosted by the Academy of Visual Arts in Vienna, which confronts realities of dispossession and violent appropriation, offering artistic and collective strategies for hands-on epistemic interventions into affected sites and bodies.[12] But to pick up on your point about distribution: surrounding all of these projects, there is the issue of how the work goes on its journeys — how it is made available and accessible to "unknown friends," and via which ecosystems.

Conversations with other artistic publishers show that even if you've contracted a distributor, connectivity between presses and receivers can still be limited or inefficient. Available commercial platforms listing titles for booksellers, such as (in Germany) VLB, Koch Neff & Oetinger, and Amazon, all entail costs for publishers.[13] If you are a small publisher with precarious resources and limited staff, it's difficult to keep up with all the administrative demands.

In Germany, an "interest group of independent publishers" has existed since 1979. You have to be a member of the Börsenverein, the German book trade association, to be a part of it, which requires a set of fiscal conditions that not all artistic publishers are able to fulfill. In the international art publishing scene, we might do well to form a working group and collectively organize a tighter exchange network for our output with bookshops, libraries, collections, and inclined readers. And again, in today's increasingly anti-intellectual, anti-cultural, and anti-educational political climates, this output is worth so much! From this perspective, finding ways to stabilize the structural and economic position of artistic presses as refuges for diverse forms of thought and expression seems to be of great urgency, along with considering the social and ecological responsibilities embedded in our activities.

CW: I do wonder to what degree the "inclined readership" you mention would also need to be strengthened in order to sustainably improve circulation. Couldn't one of the underlying issues around circulation have more to do with the challenge of *engaging* readers within an overflowing, yet fractured, cultural and political landscape? This question feels like an extremely urgent issue. The rapid acceleration of the overall media sphere and network ecology, and how they drive a hunger for immediacy, has clearly impacted the field we operate in. Speaking anecdotally, I get the sense that the intellectual "trends" of the past, even those of five or ten years ago, tended to evolve over years, not weeks or months. There is also the real and urgent need to utilize communicative spaces to draw attention to oppression and to mobilize resistance and mutual aid. This makes it challenging to engender the type of attention required from the perspective of the contributor, publisher, and reader, toward a more sustained kind of engagement — one in which the publication can be an anchor for resistance, one that perhaps exists in a very different temporality.

AS: You are speaking about cultural literacy, and I believe that's an essential point. It does seem that algorithmic acceleration has reduced schools of thought (knowledge) into themes (information), and that themes have gradually deteriorated into memes (mere relics of information). We are just beginning to understand the tremendous neurological effects this rapid process has on our minds and overall well-being.[14] At the same time, particularly in the context of the climate crisis, we are faced with another type of increasing acceleration that we don't know how to cope with: the unexpected speed with which models predicting climate change are currently overhauled by the scientific measurements of actual weather patterns, leading to increasingly dire forecasts.[15]

Traditional publishing frameworks take a long time, especially if peer review processes are involved, and data can be out-of-date by the time it is published. Nevertheless, quick social media posts and news feeds, on the other end of the spectrum, cannot capture the complexity and extent of the many serious issues at stake. What seems needed in a time of such volatile, existential pull is a new collective practice of presence and attention. It is by facing this challenge that the work of alternative publishers can make an important intervention toward a sensitive and actionable conversation.[16]

However, I completely share your concern for actual readers. The notion of presence and attention also emphasizes the value of sustained space and times of uninterrupted focus, generating a mental buffer to the mind-frazzling acceleration that you brought up. There is a computer scientist and productivity scholar, Cal Newport, who publishes best-selling books about what he calls "deep work," giving advice on how to *think* enough to produce meaningful work by disconnecting from the internet and drawing a decisive boundary around digital distraction.[17] It always depends on the context, and exceptions prove the rule, but, in my own experience, I usually get a good sense of calm and reflection as soon as I switch off the Wi-Fi — even if only for an hour at a time. And while my own writerliness is conditioned through fingertips touching a keyboard, my inner dialogue with a published author tends to feel more animated if I read their words on paper, pen in hand, rather than on screen. How many others feel that way, I don't know. But, being a publisher means facilitating between public discourse and private mentalities and emotions, and nourishing these connections is a contribution to society we make with our work.

CW: In the earliest days of Triple Canopy in 2007, one of the first concepts that we developed consensus around was the desire to "slow down the internet." At the time, this idea was enacted by taking an unusual approach to the interface and layout in the web browser. Subsequently, around 2013, when discussing what the future of our platform would be, and in recognition of the shifts in technology and our relationship to the screen, I made the joke that our new mantra should be to "slow down the world."[18] This idea manifested itself through a reconfiguration of our editorial program and platform, shifting from the idea that we were an online magazine to "a magazine whose hub is online."

This meant embracing the idea that different formats — whether an event, online project, exhibition, book, or something else — all had their own characteristics and affordances, and that they needed to be probed in tandem with the concepts and themes addressed in the issues we published, developed over long durations in collaboration with our contributors. That isn't some groundbreaking idea, obviously, since an event to launch a book or magazine isn't particularly novel. Rather, I was interested in recentering those tertiary forms of production and attempting to assess them along the same lines as other forms.[19]

But, in my experience, navigating the complex logistics of collaborative publishing, irrespective of medium, feels like an intractable challenge. It also isn't a particularly sexy conversation topic, though many of us spend time lamenting these issues in private settings. More importantly, as you noted earlier, publishers across many scales (because these challenges aren't limited to small publishing houses) spend a great deal of time attempting to learn, create, and manage systems and processes that are administrative in nature. (Often to the dismay of my collaborators over the years, I can be preoccupied with trying to get these organizational arrangements as refined as possible.) From my perspective, this aspect of the work is an integral "material" substrate, and when not functioning well it creates many barriers. Distribution — the ability to get a work in front of a reader — is clearly the most conspicuous component of these more general infrastructural issues.

One dimension that can propagate this dynamic is the underlying economics of independent publishing, which can typically be characterized as non-profit, at least in Western Europe and the United States. (Even if not officially non-profit, it is effectively so, since no one is making money.) It is a model that relies upon funding and support from grants and institutions, more so than sales. Even a cursory look into that system will show a restricted economic network and perhaps, by extension, cultural and political networks that are also narrow. In short, institutions fund publishers to make products; publishers make those products; those products are made visible within the institutional contexts in which they are funded, though often not circulated widely outside of them; rinse and repeat. This is an overly simplified and crude portrayal of the situation — and pessimistic! — but the truth in it points to what is valued. Specifically, this setup tends not to support publishing infrastructures, which impacts distribution — not to mention working conditions for collaboration and production. Ideally, infrastructural support would allow distribution to expand into communities that aren't already part of the previously mentioned institutional circuits. Maybe something like a "general" public? I also think this extends to the question of engagement, but drawing a direct line here is challenging.

AS: The steady pressure to present an effortless public image is also an effect of social media. Even if it makes us uncomfortable, we can subvert this by discussing more complicated, usually hidden structural questions. In my case, learning the "business" of running the press has taken much longer than developing creative expertise, although both are rooted in experimentation. As long as distribution and sales are in a niche, the issue of profit/non-profit is a constant problem. Structurally, however, when there are grants for publishing they are usually for projects, not subsidies for infrastructure or maintenance, which I understand is also an issue in the field of software development. So, essentially, the atelier survives by offering services such as in-depth consultation/conceptualization, copy-editing, design, project management, etc. I think a lot of people, even avid readers, would be surprised by the time and effort it takes to fully realize a publication. And, after splitting sales revenue across distributors, retailers, and shipping companies, "making money" from the books themselves is mostly an illusion, just like you said.

The systemic precarity is obvious. Many ideas and positions materialize at the margins of the cultural economy. And yet, for the sake of an open, pluralistic society, an intensified debate about the structural position of cultural production is urgent. As part of a large support fund to ameliorate the economic impacts of the coronavirus pandemic, the German Ministry of Culture has actually issued a one-off grant specifically for publishers and booksellers. But, once again, publishers can request a production grant — that is, they can funnel the money to contractors in the framework of a new project — but they cannot use the money to invest in general maintenance. We're better off than many, but we are also currently seeing how bureaucracy and working conditions usually don't match up.

So, your comment reminds me of the ways in which art institutions have begun to discuss "hospitality."[20] How people are hosted and cared for in the context of events integrally coproduces the affective credibility of public gestures. Appropriating the publishing context as a platform for artistic or curatorial investigations of book/exhibition modes also extends into thinking through precarity, accountability, and the structural and administrative ways in which publishing is realized. Confronting distribution, payment structures, and consignment systems is a part of that.[21] At the same time, it requires deconstructing the alleged power of independent publishers as *perceived* gatekeepers. It's a daily struggle to keep going. We'd do well to focus on improving all-round conditions rather than competing with each other by viciously recirculating our traumas and existential anxieties.

CW: I think we should return for a moment to your comment regarding the current political climate with its "increasingly anti-intellectual, anti-cultural, and anti-educational" characteristics. This political climate (both on the Right and the Left) has been facilitated a great deal by contemporary social media platforms, whose adverse physiological and psychological effects have been well documented. These platforms — Twitter, Facebook, Instagram, to name just a few — are more about fleeing in-depth encounters than engaging in ways that demand intimacy and empathy, which I think we both consider as means to effect social and cultural change. That being said, they *can* be used productively in mobilizing people for something like the Black Lives Matter movement, whether by, in this case, making visible the widespread oppression and murder of Black people in the United States, or more tactically by functioning to build mutual aid and solidarity networks in times of struggle. But those moments, unfortunately, tend to be fleeting — although this may be more of a personal outlook, since I feel like I've been in this cycle a number of times before.

Something that comes to mind is the Electronic Disturbance Theater, founded by Ricardo Dominguez, which, in the late 1990s, invented a form of electronic civil disobedience:

> Acting in the tradition of non-violent direct action and civil disobedience, proponents of Electronic Civil Disobedience are borrowing the tactics of trespass and blockade from these earlier social movements and are applying them to the Internet. A typical civil disobedience tactic has been for a group of people to physically blockade, with their bodies,

> the entranceways of an opponent's office or building or to physically occupy an opponent's office — to have a sit-in. Electronic Civil Disobedience, as a form of mass decentered electronic direct action, utilizes virtual blockades and virtual sit-ins. Unlike the participant in a traditional civil disobedience action, an ECD actor can participate in virtual blockades and sit-ins from home, from work, from the university, or from other points of access to the Net. Further, the ECD actor can act against an opponent that is hundreds if not thousands of miles away. The Electronic Disturbance Theater, primarily through its Flood Net device, is promoting ways to engage in global, mass, collective and simultaneous Electronic Civil Disobedience and direct action.[22]

The Flood Net system refreshed the targeted web page over and over again so that when many people joined a virtual sit-in, it was like a semi-legal DDoS (distributed denial of service) attack. I studied with Dominguez, participating in a number of sit-ins in the mid-2000s, and what I found compelling about this conceptual and activist artwork was that it engaged in the material substrate of the network, using it as a means to create a "collective weapon of presence."[23] In short, while it was a clear method for magnifying political struggles and creating forms of mutual aid (by taking down target websites), it didn't do this by signing on to Twitter and appending a hashtag to a tweet. It worked within the fabric of the internet itself, updating and reconfiguring historical forms of resistance in response to different structures of power, and redeploying them within a performative schema.

A "provocative" claim I presented in a lecture a number of years ago may be relevant here: the Iranian Green Movement of 2009 seemed to be punctured, at least in terms of international solidarity, by the death of Michael Jackson. In short, on Twitter the trending #iranelection was replaced with #RIPMJ. This is, of course, not the reason the uprising ended — that would be the state violence of the Iranian regime led by Mahmoud Ahmadinejad — but my simple observation at the time, which I think is still applicable, is that these corporate platforms should be approached cautiously and with vigilance.

AS: Of course, and I'd like to add another example. The manuscript of the incredible, award-winning book *No Friend But the Mountains* (2018), by Kurdish-Iranian poet and journalist Behrouz Boochani (with English translation by Omid Tofighian), was written and edited on a mobile phone using WhatsApp while Boochani was imprisoned (in contravention of international law) as an asylum seeker, for more than four years, in Manus Island Regional Processing Centre, a detention center administered by the Australian Government.[24] This mobile application made it possible to get the book out of Manus, which is important, however it was also necessary to have a publisher willing to publish and distribute the book. The risks to the publisher are incomparable to those faced by Boochani, yet it is important to consider the process as a sequence or series of events involving more than one platform.

Apart from this example, the cultural and neurological toxicity of social media increasingly worries me. I doubt that these monopoly technologies can be effectively used to produce the kinds of change we need right now. At the same time, with the Black Lives Matter movement in particular, there are ways that activists are harnessing these platforms to redirect attention to urgent struggles and to call people out to the streets. Yet there are also myriad examples of how, within the "post-truth" and "fake news" milieu, social media enables certain actors or groups (including but not limited to nation-states, of course) to undermine or eliminate democratic values, debate, opinion, and free speech. When social media facilitates digital hate campaigns, you can observe tactics of defamation and intimidation. This ultimately leads to often-invisible real-world suffering and psychological distress, as well as the silencing of those attempting to convene the difficult conversations we urgently need to cultivate. Otherwise, the outcome is further fragmentation and polarization, often to the point of violent social exclusion, scapegoating, and interminable enmity. Even when it doesn't go this far, I find it troubling to witness complex narratives reduced to a binary decision of like or dislike, not to mention the superficial yet depressing forms of attention seeking that often promote such plebiscitary reductions.

One voice I appreciate in the context of call-out culture is American author and activist adrienne maree brown, especially her writing on transformational justice.[25] Richard Seymour's analysis in *The Twittering Machine* (2019) is also excellent in this respect because he compares, in convincing detail, the social media user to the *gambling* addict (as opposed to drug addiction, which for Seymour is caught up in a different logic). Regarding the *writing* that we practice on these platforms, he insists on the difference between interacting with people in real life and interacting via a machine or platform:

> The machine benefits from the "network effect": the more people write to it, the more benefits it can offer, until it becomes a disadvantage not to be part of it. Part of what? The world's first ever public, live, collective, open-ended writing project. A virtual laboratory. An addiction machine, which deploys crude techniques of manipulation redolent of the "Skinner Box" created by behaviourist B. F. Skinner to control the behaviour of pigeons and rats with rewards and punishments. We are "users," much as cocaine addicts are "users."[26]
>
> What is the incentive to engage in writing like this for hours each day? In a form of mass casualisation, writers no longer expect to be paid or given employment contracts. What do the platforms offer us, in lieu of a wage? What gets us hooked? Approval, attention, retweets, shares and likes.[27]

Writing per se might not always be wage-driven, but, given this increasingly toxic social and political climate, defending frameworks of respectful collaboration and critical, open debate is essential. Again, perhaps it is worthwhile to reflect on the qualitative difference between the meaning of the writerly "friend" in the earlier quote above, and the social media machine. Although real-life relations are usually less categorical — if we think about them conceptually — they have to do with generosity and inspired, genuine connection, while the social media network, Seymour would argue, is founded on the exploitative structure of an abusive relationship. Scandals are also, essentially, a way for companies to make money. In turbulent times like these, it seems crucial to nurture ways of writing and reading that hold open such a space — K. Verlag is committed to doing that.

Witnessing how the conditions of a democratic, equitable society are undermined by neoliberal and increasingly proto-fascist austerity systems makes it even more important to create minor spaces that can play host to a more positive future — an ideal "world of many worlds" for both humans and other-than-humans. With the *intercalations: paginated exhibition* series, which was commissioned by the Haus der Kulturen der Welt's Anthropocene Project, we contributed to this ideal. The fifth volume, *Decapitated Economies* (2021), gathers reflections on surviving and flourishing in the ruins of traditional regimes of power and political economy. Among others, Chilean artist Elisa Balmaceda and Spanish ecofeminist Yayo Herrero López assay notions of the "sacrificial" and the "sacred" against the background of nature's cyclical rhythms, in a conversation borne of the recent political protests in Chile and the canceled COP25 Climate Summit. Steve Rowell and Priyanka Basu have a harrowing photo essay about the agricultural chemical fallout along the Mississippi River, and philosopher Nina Power contributes an essay on the psychological dimensions of contemporary politics, with a focus on the polarized emotions of love and hate as political forces.

CW: When collaborating with editors, writers, and artists on the production of "texts," I tend to come at the collaboration from the perspective of the reader. While this perspective is always present within written and visual traditions, it feels like sometimes this viewpoint gets lost. For my part, a central way to address this has been through the conceptualization, design, and development of new publishing systems. These systems attempt to work backwards from form and framework — which is where the reader encounters the "text" — to the act of writing and editing, with the aim of reconfiguring the sensibilities of both the writer and the reader. Sometimes they successfully achieve this, sometimes perhaps they do not.

These experimental frameworks can draw attention to the characteristics of contemporaneous reading environments, and simultaneously draw a connection to older forms. The elements that a "text" is composed of, from the paragraph to other structural divisions and devices used in organizing a publication — a codex, a magazine, a tweet — are not natural.[28] These systems can be defined as "physical and cognitive architectures," as Bonnie Mak does in her transdisciplinary study *How the Page Matters* (2011).[29] The degree to which these elements condition thought, whether positively or negatively, is highly situational, which is to say that it is greatly affected by the time and place of the writing/reading of a "text."

Clearly, the divergence between the screen and the printed object is more obvious than in the case of digital publications.

With the latter, the site of conception, production, and reading is synchronic. But unless you are self-publishing a blog, there is still a high degree of dissimilitude between where a work is typically conceived, written, and edited (document editing software, email, etc.), and the format in which that work is encountered by a reader. This is especially true with the work we've done at Triple Canopy, which has involved making four different "content presentation frameworks," all of which lay out text and media in a horizontally scrolling environment. As noted previously, this was an attempt to "slow down the internet" by providing a reading environment distinct from the endless scroll.

AS: If we assume that a text must eventually be finished, as editors we are indeed extravagant readers, collaborative interlocutors, and generous enthusiasts. What you said also reminds me of my friend Geraldine Juárez's apt remark: "I search therefore I scroll."[30] Some years ago, web designers began to use the horizontal scroll, and it is interesting to learn more about the conceptual rationale behind this decision for Triple Canopy. A similar desire for defamiliarization was behind our decision to split *Fantasies of the Library* (2015) across the middle of the book and have content run only on verso and recto pages, respectively. Breaking the habitual left–right–left–right page flow of a codex-bound text disturbs the reader-viewer's relationship with reading itself. Denaturalizing our most familiar frameworks is absolutely necessary for cultural renewal.

CW: At Triple Canopy, we continue to use the horizontal scroll, at least in desktop environments, in our latest framework called b-ber, which was released in late 2019.[31] It is both a method and an application for producing publications in a variety of formats: EPUB 3, Mobi/KF8, a static website, PDF, or an XML file that can be imported into InDesign for print layouts. All of these formats are generated from a single source of plaintext files and other assets. b-ber also functions as a browser-based EPUB reader, which explains the name. Rather than put the onus of design on the author, my goal was to enable the correspondence between media to be considered from the inception of a work by all involved in the process. b-ber pushes us to understand the publication in terms of infinite existing and potential formats and systems for translating code, rather than as the realization of an ideal and unchanging experience. To put it another way, it would be impossible to fully account for all of the ways in which a reader might encounter a work, given the array of devices and pixel dimensions, operating systems, and software, not to mention the visual obstructions caused by dust and scratches on our screens.

The challenge for publishers is namely how to think across media and reduce the temptation to pit one format against another, recognizing that no individual channel can ever fully account for how we'd like our readers to encounter and experience what we are publishing. This feels to me like the definition of hospitality. But, given this reality, how can we envisage the many forms and formats, and the encounters they engender, in collaborative publishing in art and literature? How can we publish simultaneously across formats while maintaining the "integrity" of the work? And, importantly, how does the "work" need to change to maintain its integrity across formats?

AS: The folks at *Emergence Magazine*, a publication focusing on the role of the "story," do a fantastic job at relaying their content across multimedia formats, from online publishing of texts to audio recitals of the pieces by their authors, and from video clips to a gorgeous printed anthology encompassing three online issues.[32] Curiously, they explicitly say that the occasional print copy, which is also an experiment in translating online content to paper, is an invitation to *slow down*. All levels of *Emergence Magazine* emphasize sensual experience. While the online platform offers a multisensory, more-than-textual encounter through audio, and still and moving images, the print publication enhances a sense of touch and vision by employing a striking variety of papers and beautiful inks. During the coronavirus pandemic, when the bookshops asked K. to postpone our spring releases, we got inspired by *Emergence Magazine*'s work and modestly began to publish sound files with authors' voices. At the request of our authors, we also, for the first time, released two e-books. Both examples show how publishing as encounter, event, and experience is a matter of careful selection, refrain, and connection — whatever the sphere or medium — with agency both on the creating and the receiving ends.

CW: I recently came across a book I first read in the late 2000s, *My Mother Was a Computer: Digital Subject and Literary Texts* (2005) by N. Katherine Hayles. It was instrumental in helping me think through "publishing." I hadn't thought about this book in a long time and it should be "out of date" given the rapid changes in technology and digitization since it was originally published. Yet, skimming the chapter I recalled most vividly, "Translating Media," I came across the following passage, part of which opened our conversation:

> The debates about encoding assume implicitly that there is some textual essence that can be transported from print to digital media. Even the anti-realist position assumes an essence, although now it is an essence created by an editor. All three positions elide from electronic texts the materiality of books and their physical differences. A more accurate perception would focus on the editorial process of choice, which is always contextual and driven by "certain interests," although these reside not exclusively in the text but in the conjunction of text, editorial process, and cultural context. In my view, the ontology card is not worth playing. There is no Platonic reality of texts. There are only physical objects such as books and computers, foci of attention, and codes that entrain attention and organize material operations. Since no print book can be completely encoded into digital media, we should think about correspondences rather than ontologies, entraining processes rather than isolated objects, and codes moving in coordinated fashion across representational media rather than mapping one object onto another.[33]

She continues, emphasizing what I think still resonates and echoing many of my concerns expressed above:

> The issue goes to the heart of what we think a text is, and at the heart of the heart is the belief that "work" and "text" are immaterial contractions independent of the substrates in which they are instantiated. We urgently need to rethink this assumption, for as long as it remains intact, efforts to account for the specificities of print and electronic media will be hamstrung.[34]

This call to action feels more relevant today than when I originally read it more than a decade ago. As we've touched upon, our current experience with "representational media" is characterized by noise, toxicity, and the fragmentation of attention. One option, as suggested by Cal Newport, and which you referenced earlier, is to "quit social media" and be judicious about how we spend our "digital lives," which appears to be a completely reasonable idea! But that approach is self-driven and individualistic; it doesn't directly impact these frameworks. This point of view is often argued with regards to print publishing—that it offers a refrain from the impact of "continuous partial attention" caused by the contemporary network and its interfaces. It is true that when reading a printed book notifications aren't popping up on the page to distract a reader. But the same could be said of e-readers, which I believe can offer a similar feeling of immersion. This idea collapses different lines of argumentation, some that are extremely valid (concerns about the chaos of our networked environments), with others that have more questionable footings (that reading on a screen fundamentally means a partial level of engagement). An alternative approach would be to challenge these frameworks with new models that facilitate the kinds of absorption and encounters we are trying to achieve.

AS: I completely agree! When speaking about the "pedagogy of concepts," philosopher Isabelle Stengers emphasizes thought as a matter of relay, not representation; that is, as she says, as a matter of "both taking over and handing over."[35] This relates to much of what we've said about publishing as a practice as well, because it underscores the situatedness of experience, encounter, and reciprocity. In this, there is no need to fetishize certain objects or media—we can attend to how each thing actually works. Indeed, what is at stake—especially in this era of post-truth—is less an abstract celebration of essences or facts but rather the careful evaluation of what a particular situation demands. Learning how to pay attention, how to trust, how to doubt, how to listen, how to speculate, connect, fabricate, nurture, inhabit, and, also, how to resist. Publishing is the transmission of relays which can spur and intensify this collective learning process, making it more useful and empowering.

1 Paul Gilroy and Adam Shatz, "The Absurdities of Race," *LRB Conversations*, August 2020, lrb.co.uk/podcasts-and-videos/podcasts/lrb-conversations/the-absurdities-of-race.

2 A Public Library was not a public library; it was a space for conversations, presentations, the sharing of resources, and for collective reading, viewing, and learning, working in conjunction

with The Public School Berlin. See: apubliclibrary.org/about.

3 THE THING was founded in New York in 1991 by artist Wolfgang Staehle as a bulletin board system (BBS). "Over the last two decades, THE THING has played a seminal role not just in fostering a generation of network-oriented activists, artists, critics, and curators, but also — and equally important — searching out ways to interconnect their diverse interests and activities. It is no exaggeration to say that the list of people and projects THE THING has supported comprises a who's who of contemporary electronic culture." For more information, see: the.thing.net/about/about.html.

4 Anna-Sophie Springer, "Volumes: The Book as Exhibition," *C Magazine* 116 (December 2012): 36–44.

5 Mark von Schlegell, *Realometer* (Berlin: Merve Verlag, 2009); Nina Power, *Die eindimensionale Frau* (Berlin: Merve Verlag, 2011).

6 The fact that bookshops were counted as *systemrelevant* during pandemic lockdowns here in Germany is a nice proof that valuing the printed book isn't a question of mere "species nostalgia." On that notion, see: Joanna Zylinska in conversation with Anna-Sophie Springer and Etienne Turpin, "The Ethics of the Book (Beyond Species Nostalgia)," in *Fantasies of the Library*, ed. Anna-Sophie Springer and Etienne Turpin (Berlin: K. Verlag and Haus der Kulturen der Welt, 2015), 112–130.

7 Anna-Sophie Springer and Etienne Turpin, "The Exhibition as a Philosophical Problem," *Graz Architecture Magazine* 14: "Exhibiting Matters" (June 2018): 135–136.

8 Peter Sloterdijk, "The Elmauer Rede: Rules for the Human Zoo: A Response to the *Letter on Humanism*," *Die Zeit*, 1999; Suhrkamp, 2001; English trans. Mary Varney Rorty (Palo Alto, CA: Stanford Center for Biomedical Ethics, 2009), web.stanford.edu/~mvr2j/docs/Elmauer.pdf.

9 Jason Read, "The Principle of Our Negative Solidarity," *The New Enquiry*, January 24, 2014, thenewinquiry.com/the-principle-of-our-negative-solidarity.

10 "Forging Feminist Futures: An Interview with Alex Martinis Roe," *EuropeNow*, January 16, 2020, europenowjournal.org/2020/01/15/forging-feminist-futures-an-interview-with-alex-martinis-roe.

11 On the socially corrosive role of binary questions (guilt/innocence, good/bad, like/dislike) driving expression on social media, see: Will Davies, "Who Am I Prepared to Kill?," *London Review of Books*, vol. 42, no. 14 (July 30, 2020), lrb.co.uk/the-paper/v42/n15/william-davies/who-am-i-prepared-to-kill.

12 See: https://k-verlag.org/books/despite-dispossession-an-activity-book.

13 See: vlb.de and kno-va.de/home.html.

14 Bernard Stiegler, *The Age of Disruption: Technology and Madness in Computational Capitalism* (Cambridge: Polity, 2019).

15 Daniel Boffey and Jennifer Rankin, "EU to Declare a No-Deal Brexit a Major Natural Disaster," *The Guardian*, September 3, 2019, theguardian.com/politics/2019/sep/02/eu-could-declare-no-deal-brexit-as-major-natural-disaster.

16 Bill McKibben, *Falter: Has the Human Game Begun to Play Itself Out?* (New York: Henry Holt and Co., 2019).

17 Cal Newport, *Deep Work: Rules for Focused Success in a Distracted World* (New York: Grand Central Publishing, 2016).

18 Triple Canopy, "Some Assembly Required," March 2, 2013, canopycanopycanopy.com/contents/some_assembly_required.

19 This approach has not necessarily been enacted at Triple Canopy in the ensuing years.

20 See, for example: "Rehearsing Hospitalities," frame-finland.fi/en/2019/08/22/programme-released-gathering-for-rehearsing-hospitalities.

21 On precarity, see: Isabelle Lorey, *State of Insecurity: Government of the Precarious* (London: Verso, 2015); Lynne Segal, *Radical Happiness: Moments of Collective Joy* (London: Verso, 2018).

22 Stefan Wray, "The Electronic Disturbance Theater and Electronic Civil Disobedience," June 17, 1998, thing.net/~rdom/ecd/EDTECD.html.

23 For a partial list of actions, see: thing.net/~rdom/ecd/ecd.html.

24 Behrouz Boochani, *No Friend but the Mountains: Writing from Manus Prison* (Sydney: Picador Australia, 2018).

25 See: adrienne maree brown, "Unthinkable Thoughts: Call-Out-Culture in the Age of COVID-19," adriennemareebrown.net/2020/07/17/unthinkable-thoughts-call-out-culture-in-the-age-of-covid-19. She is also the coeditor (with Walidah Imarisha) of *Octavia's Brood: Science Fiction Stories from Social Justice Movements* (Oakland: AK Press, 2015) and the author of *We Will Not Cancel Us And Other Dreams of Transformative Justice* (Oakland: AK Press, 2020).

26 Richard Seymour, *The Twittering Machine* (London: Indigo Press, 2019), 24.

27 Richard Seymour, "The Machine Always Wins: What Drives Our Addiction to Social Media," *The Guardian*, August 23, 2019, theguardian.com/technology/2019/aug/23/social-media-addiction-gambling.

28 For example, Twitter's original 140-character limit, which persisted until 2016, was based on the limits of text messages put in place by phone companies.

29 Bonnie Mak, *How the Page Matters* (Toronto: University of Toronto Press, 2011).

30 Geraldine Juárez, "Intercolonial Technogalactic," in *Reverse Hallucinations in the Archipelago*, ed. Anna-Sophie Springer and Etienne Turpin (Berlin: K. Verlag and Haus der Kulturen der Welt, 2017), 155.

31 For more on b-ber, see: Caleb Waldorf, "Working on Our Thoughts," Triple Canopy, December 17, 2019, canopycanopycanopy.com/contents/working-on-our-thoughts.

32 See: emergencemagazine.org.

33 N. Katherine Hayles, *My Mother Was a Computer: Digital Subjects and Literary Texts* (Chicago: University of Chicago Press, 2005), 97.

34 Ibid.

35 Isabelle Stengers, "Gilles Deleuze's Last Message," recalcitrance.com/deleuzelast.htm#.

Publishing Art Writing: A Connective and Collective Labor

Astrid Vorstermans, interviewed by Megan Patty & Brad Haylock

After being confined to home and studio for several months, the question arises: how do we connect to each other? I do not mean the deep human need to see, touch, smell, feel, hear, and love each other, but connections in a more abstract manner, in the networked labor relating to art writers, artists, editors, translators, printers, critics, academics, designers, funding bodies, distributors, booksellers, readers, and audiences. Luckily, many things went on during the lockdown as they did before: email, video conferencing, telephone calling, exchanging via digital means. But this new, confined situation produced gaps and cracks that, bit by bit, show their consequences. First of all, a deep insecurity: what will the world look like in a year's time, or further into the future? Several systems are under pressure and might crack — or are they colliding already? In priorities of life and society, how will art position itself? And what will be the effects on art writing, publishing, exchange, and discourse?

COVID-19 is real, but it is also a metaphor, a "butterfly effect." Can a butterfly flapping its wings in New Zealand cause a hurricane in Spain? Perhaps a return to simpler gestures can open up the cracks to nurture social change and find new connections.

— Astrid Vorstermans, Amsterdam, December 2020

As founding director of and publisher at independent Dutch publishing house Valiz, Astrid Vorstermans is deeply engaged with art writing and the discourses surrounding art and design. Valiz, founded in 2003 and now codirected by Vorstermans and Pia Pol, centers on publishing critical texts and engaging in discussions around art, politics, and social matters.

MP/BH: It is now almost two decades since you founded Valiz. In this time, what changes in art writing and discourse have you experienced?

AV: Art writing is a very broad field, from artist's texts, to journalism, to exhibition reviews or art reviews or writing on art market developments, to poetry, to speculative essayistic texts, to deeply researched academic texts. Academic texts, art criticism, and journalism have always been embedded in institutional structures, from universities, art schools, and academies, to (art) newspapers and other "institutionalized" platforms. These texts are peer-related, perhaps not always officially—not with the formal peer review "stamp" or process—but they are published in a context of peers who relate to them, react to them, or use them as a source. This flow of texts, reactions, and cross references forms a certain discourse.

In a good-quality general newspaper that contains an art section, art essays will be read by a general nonprofessional audience. Even here there is a "peer standard," formed by colleagues and well-informed readers. In other words, readers and writers are aware of certain lines of discourse, and they know how to position them within a wider field.

What has changed is that there are now more forms possible, many of which are not (yet) embedded in these institutionalized contexts. More and more, there are artists and designers who are writing, often in a speculative way, exploring their own voice and tone, feeding back into their own art practice. There is a long history of visual artists who write, such as the Surrealists or the Futurists, but I think it is now more common to see artists who use writing as a means to explore and investigate their other interests.

Further, in art schools there is a growing awareness that language can be a parallel universe, existing alongside visual work. For instance, at the Gerrit Rietveld Academie in Amsterdam, there is the recently formed Image & Language department, in which writing goes hand in hand with video, painting, sculpture, photography, or whatever visual discipline the student chooses to work in.

Another change that links to this is self-publishing, which has become a common practice for art students, graphic designers, and many others. Since there are so many people who publish their own booklets and writings, the parameters of art writing are changing. These writings are often part of the artist's or student's own universe, and so are not meant to reflect on art in a wider context. Although this can be rather introverted, I imagine that it does open up other ways to look at art, and modes of using language and art writing other than what we are used to, which in turn can expand more "conventional" art writing.

MP/BH: A democratization of the means of publishing is not new, but self-publishing and independent publishing have indeed seen a dramatic resurgence in popularity in recent years. Have the changing ecologies of publishing today caused you to shift your practices as a publisher?

AV: I see the two as interlinked. We are an integral part of these changing ecologies. Valiz is an independent publisher, so it is impossible to extract our practices from these developments; one defines the other, and vice versa. It is difficult to position Valiz within different "scales" of publishing. In the big, commercial book world, Valiz is a grain of sand, but in specialized, independent art book publishing, it has a recognizable place (I hope...).

Self-publishers, and other smaller and bigger independent art book publishers, have the distinct quality of being singular, perseverant, and distinctive. They are content- and socially driven on their own terms, whereas a commercial publisher is stepping into existing systems, from editing to distribution, marketing, and sales, mainly propelled by profit and the market—all this is very generously expressed.

From the beginning, Valiz has been content-driven, and it is wonderful to see that there are so many other individuals and small groups who put their questions and explorations first, and then find ways to pay for editing, paper, printing, design, etc., or do all of this work themselves. I am convinced that these explorations bring in new economic and distribution models, as well as other ways to collaborate.

The art book fairs worldwide are wonderful hubs where we can discuss and exchange our projects, and see the diversity, idiosyncrasies, singularities, etc., of our practices. Very often, these places are meeting grounds for helping each other, exchanging, linking to new and fruitful contacts, or setting up a collaboration. Let's hope that the fairs can go on again after the pandemic.

Looking back, I have tried to find common ground intuitively or naturally, but in the last ten years this is an attitude and a way of working that we, Pia and I, are more conscious of. We try to nourish this attitude wherever possible, and also address it in our program, both in publications — such as *Design Dedication* (2020), *Commonism* (2018), *Design Struggles* (2021), *Mobile Autonomy* (2015), the trancity×valiz imprint on the public domain, and other titles — and in events that we organize.

On the other hand, we also use existing book trade systems, especially in distribution, because we need to sell our titles properly, in bigger quantities, to be able to survive. I think the changing ecologies keep us sharp, prompting us to critically scrutinize how certain well-trodden paths can be refreshed, and forcing us to develop ways to follow these systems and tweak them at the same time.

MP/BH: On that note, let's go back to art discourse, recent histories, and art writing. Are there other developments you want to address?

AV: Another change, as I see it, is that art writing no longer confines itself to the art world, and it relates to much more than art history. Bluntly speaking, when I studied art history in the late 1980s, art writing was very much formed by modernism, looking at changing formalistic tendencies. Of course, there were already other starting points: John Berger's *Ways of Seeing* came out in 1972, feminist art criticism also started in the 1970s, and, much earlier, the Frankfurt School addressed social matters, including art. Plus, there were many others who sought to link societal matters to art. But I think this way of linking art to its context to look at the role of art in society, to explore conditions of artistic work within a broader background, has become more natural and common in art writing. In that sense, art writing has become more political and more activist. This comes as no surprise when looking at urgent movements like Black Lives Matter, #MeToo, and Occupy, and the knowledge that the problems in the world are growing with an uncanny speed.

MP/BH: Are there specific publishers or titles, whether on Valiz or by other publishers, that you would deem to be important examples of political or activist art writing, or are there certain art writers who are doing particularly important work?

AV: In our program, I consider Pascal Gielen a crucial and creative author of political art writing. He is a Belgian sociologist who looks at culture and art as driving forces for society at large. He analyzes how art is an indissoluble part of the fabric of society, what conditions are set and how they function, and he looks at its effects on changing structures and working conditions.

A couple of years ago, Gielen set up a research program at the University of Antwerp, the CCQO (Culture Commons Quest Office), which delves deeply into the possibilities of setting up ways of commoning across different levels in society, all informed by artists and other creative and cultural practices. In his research group, there are not only artists, or art historians, or sociologists, but also an economist, a legal specialist, etc. All of this is meant to make their work more impactful, to start from the arts and culture and try to make it work in the real world, solving practical problems along the way.

There are more Valiz authors who have a significant voice in art writing, such as Wouter Davidts, a professor of both architectural history and art history who is very creative in connecting subjects in new ways, and often invites visual artists to contribute to his academic writing. Or academic Jeroen Lutters, who has a holistic view of creativity and of what art means to society and to individuals. They are both less political—or, let's say, less explicitly political—but they change our ideas on the role and effect of art.

Then I think about other publishers who have a great program. I admire UK-based Zed Books, which publishes radical books on politics, identity, decolonization. Their starting point is politics in its broadest sense—Zed is not a specialized art publisher, but their subjects link oftentimes to the arts. Similar to Zed is Zer0 Books (now Repeater Books), with great titles by Mark Fisher and other good radical authors. Mark also contributed to a couple of Valiz books; he was a very sharp and radical writer on the conditions and intertwinements of art and capitalism, and it is sad that he died at such a young age.

Another inspiring publisher is Occasional Papers, initiated by graphic designer Sara De Bondt and her partner, curator/researcher Antony Hudek. It is completely different from the other examples above; their program is not about art writing or politics per se, but it does address art historical and graphic design subjects, and regularly covers forgotten figures or developments.

It is great that this question makes me realize that I love writing that is playful, essayistic, or speculative, and perhaps a bit "off." It is fluid and I cannot define a top ten. I like a pluriform landscape of art writing that does not need to be defined by big names or "hot" critics or philosophers.

MP/BH: Valiz often works on projects with partner organizations, such as art institutions or educational academies. What is the significance of working in these contexts, and how might these contexts affect art writing and the books you publish?

AV: There is not an easy answer to this. There can be a huge difference between projects, even within one institution. For instance, this year, 2020, I worked on two books (*Design Dedication* and *IN/Search RE/Search*) that were both initiated by the Sandberg Instituut (the Master's program of the Gerrit Rietveld Academie, Amsterdam), and the way of communicating and defining what each book should be, and the space for me as an editor and publisher, was completely different between the two.

If I need to look for a common denominator within these and other institutional projects that Valiz works on, I would say that it is the already-existing context and audience. As a publisher, you try to stretch that and look beyond that initial zone, trying to widen it to a broader discourse, and an even wider audience.

Working with an institution — and again, there are huge differences between an art school, a university, and an art gallery — has its obvious advantages and disadvantages. A disadvantage might be that an institution can be too focused on its own implicit rules and standards, linked to its organizational culture. Sometimes this means that a book needs to mirror or affirm their mission, which might not always be consistent with the message of the book. I think it is a publisher's task to open up that discussion, and try to see the book as an autonomous medium that should have its own critical place in the world, not defined by what our partner (the institution) wants to address but by how it can be compared to and contrasted with other ideas that are out there in the world. Good cooperation allows for controversies that generate discussion, and from there the book can become stronger.

I hope the significance for an institution to work with Valiz lies in that critical questioning and in trying to find a precise line of thought, structure, content, and design, and how these are going to communicate the book's message. Pia and I are trained by experience, after working on so many titles, with so many partners, over many years. We are continuously in contact with writers, editors, designers, booksellers, distributors, and other "book people," and we bring in a specific intermediary knowledge about ways in which content can be refined and made stronger, what effect structure and design has on this, and what that means for the outside world. Of course, you want each book to find its readers — not just the people of the institution itself, or their peers and colleagues, but readers in other fields and places.

For Valiz, institutional cooperation is significant in many different ways. First of all, we can of course say no, which means we only work with institutions (and individuals) we find interesting and who understand the dynamics of exchange, so we can value each other's expertise. Each collaboration is a learning process that brings in other content, and variations of how to deal with that content, with a new group of people and their own specific working processes — this can be hugely interesting, and satisfying, and it can give insights into organizational structures. More and more, I see these institutions as part of our loose "constitutional community," an ecology that feeds content, knowledge, and viewpoints, and also international friendships, conviviality, support, and new ways to deal with differences.

How does this impact art writing? I think I am too close to the processes to say how this influences art writing in general. What I do think is that art writing becomes more interesting when it finds a challenging context. On Valiz, we have set up several different series of books that explicitly try to make a platform for specific strands of art writing, such as the link between art and society (Antennae), or different and creative modes of art history and art writing (vis-à-vis), or discussions of art and intersectionality (PLURAL). Each book that comes out relates to these families and to the Valiz program as a whole; these books "dialogue" with each other. I hope the diversity invites readers to find and develop new insights by jumping into titles that they were perhaps not immediately looking for, and that it challenges writers to commit to what they are doing, and that they feel encouraged to join.

MP/BH: This is not a question about art writing per se, but we can't resist asking about publishing processes. You've mentioned being "trained by experience," and that cooperation is a learning process. Could you tell us more about your experiences of learning-by-making as a publisher?

AV: A publication is a collaborative effort, a priori. There is an author, an artist, an editor, sometimes a translator, a designer, a printer, and a publisher, and thereafter a distributor and a bookseller, all involved to bring in their specific expertise. Although this all starts with the author's (or artist's) creative work, the book is the outcome of all of these people's energy, knowledge, and time. They have to understand each other and each other's roles in order to bring out the best possible synergy and result.

The publisher is the intermediary person who connects these skills and human rhythms. Several colleges offer education where you can learn how to edit, or how to market a book, or how to guide the technical aspects of book production, but I am not sure that there is a course on "the collaborative practice of making a book." It would be preposterous to state that I know how to do this. It is an ongoing process, learning by doing, each time with unexpected angles, emotions, moments of pure frustration, humor, and fun.

An attempt to be more concrete: it all starts by trying to dive as best as possible into the other person's role to understand what they are doing, what is required, and what we are heading for, and sharing many moments of assessment along the way. It works best when the makers get to know each other in the very early stages of a publication, to discuss the image each person holds of what the book is to be — a core concept needs to be defined and agreed upon.

If an author (or editor) comes to Valiz with a plan, we always ask them to write the concept down beforehand so that it can be shared, criticized, and all collaborators can relate to it, and it can then be adjusted, get better, change. If the plan is developed by Pia or myself, we also share it immediately with the other makers so the same happens: it will be discussed with the author, editor, and designer, and examined from all sides. It is best to be aware of any differences, and to use them intentionally. It is important to not sit on another person's chair — in other words, one must be respectful of the specific knowledge and expertise somebody brings in. Not everyone is good at this, and that can cause frustration. Somebody who brings in a project —

it can be an author, an editor, or someone representing an institution—might have the idea that they are going to define the structure and the design, but the project would then miss out on the additional and different insights of the other contributors.

Pia and I see it as our role, as publishers, to steer this, to bring ideas and people together, to continue communicating about the process and goals, and to go back to the core concept whenever needed—to keep that as a spine to develop the book further and to fill in its parts and its design. We have an agenda as well: to make the book topical, urgent, as clear in its communication as possible, and to stick within the budget and to the time schedule.

Working together in such a way again and again—encountering all these different temperaments, paces, and characters, each time inventing new perspectives on how to explore subjects, how to solve problems, and how to align to each other's singularities and qualities—makes it a process of learning-by-making.

I am sure there are publishers who work completely differently, but this is how we go about it!

MP/BH: In your view, what is the publisher's role in shaping art writing and discourse? Is this view demonstrated in your commissioning process?

AV: I recently read a beautiful text by Danah Abdulla. She is a designer, artist, and writer-cum-activist who addresses decolonization in design. What impressed me in her text is the exploration of what she calls "minor gestures," namely how each—smaller and bigger—decision can define or nurture social transformation.[1] Reading this was an "aha" moment. The analogy to publishing is striking. I see publishing first and foremost as a practice, a daily labor, or a mode of working that evolves, engages, explores, addresses, solves problems, and all in all can be very mundane. But it is also a collective and connective labor, to which many individuals bring their specific knowledge and singularities.

When you ask how a publisher can shape art writing or discourse, it is through these "minor gestures" that, bit by bit, we can engender change. The authors or artists do the "major gestures": they come up with the core ideas, they work really hard on their lines of thought, they position their work in the field with others, they refine their vocabularies, and they have the stamina to pull all of it together. They are the informed specialists who know how to carve their way into difficult subjects. A publisher is more of a generalist with knowledge across a wider range of subjects, but a priori cannot carve as deeply as the author or artist.

The publisher's minor gestures are in believing, trusting, connecting, contextualizing, sorting out, bringing together, being patient, and having long-term faith in authors and in our own work. One of the minor gestures is to take good care of ourselves, to be able to read, breathe, exchange, connect, rewind, rethink, and imagine other scenarios. Beyond that, we can only exist when the books find their audiences, so it is also necessary to remain focused on how to distribute and sell them, because these activities nurture the whole. Being able to pay the bills seems far removed from the question of how a publisher can codevelop art writing, but it is obviously one of the conditions needed to be able to sustain a good relationship with authors and others. Writing and publishing are too often characterized by precarity, so it is necessary to counter-balance that with trust and long-term commitments — this is all based on minor gestures.

In many publications, especially anthologies, the commissioning process is one of "filtering." Often, there is a concept by one person (an author or artist), and then together we find out what the core idea is that they are trying to delineate. And, perhaps most importantly, what is the topicality or urgency of this subject or research, and how might we best communicate that? So, the critical questioning or dialoguing steps in again, which is why we have developed a list with core questions that try to tackle as many aspects as possible, in order to articulate what the book basically wants to address. From there, we brainstorm which people might fit that subject, and we discuss themes, other possible contributors, and further contexts.

MP/BH: How do you know when a book has found its audience? Does the book tell you, or does the audience?

AV: There is a simple or pragmatic answer to that: when we have reached the expected sales target (typically 70 percent or more of the total print run). So, book sales can tell us. But the more evocative answer is: by the feedback we receive internationally from people — at book fairs, or via email, booksellers, distributors, etc. It is great to receive emails from people and places we don't know already, people who react to specific books and who explain how these books influence their practice or thinking.

MP/BH: What do you think is urgent today in terms of publishing writing about art, and in art practice?

AV: My response to this is straightforward. The world is burning, open exchange and democracies are under threat, diversity and otherness are not being dealt with in a healthy way, many people no longer feel part of a wider community, solidarity is lacking.

My strong belief is that the arts are able to bring in new imaginaries, which can lure people into looking differently, discussing, exchanging, and dealing with others and otherness. If this is the role of art, then art writing should build a diversified platform to investigate these ideas — to understand and give meaning to what art is doing and how it counteracts specific developments in the world; to be able to disagree with each other and formulate arguments, meaning, substance; and to bring oxygen and vitality into the arts themselves, especially into the discussions that the arts are tackling.

In closing:

— Art should be embedded in society, and art writing should critically assess that position;
— Art writing can be poetic, contrary, smooth, easy, or difficult, it can have many tones and rhythms, but, in the end, it should be urgent and topical;
— A publisher has the role and the obligation to amplify the message as best as possible, and to try to spread and distribute ideas as widely as possible — to let them find roots, to allow many people to engage with them, to open up the discussion;
— And a variation on the previous point: a publisher should find or build strong contexts, and make unexpected connections, so authors, readers, and creative makers will find fertile ground to connect to content and to each other.

1 Danah Abdulla, "Disciplinary Disobedience: A Border-Thinking Approach to Design," in *Design Struggles: Intersecting Histories, Pedagogies, and Perspectives*, ed. Claudia Mareis and Nina Paim (Amsterdam: Valiz, 2021). Abdulla explains that the concept of minor gestures is a work in progress that she and Pedro Oliveira are still working on; I have liberally adopted the term.

Balancing Ethics and Economies: A Push for a New Perspective on Art Publishing

Freek Lomme

The culture of independent publishing and various forms of self-publishing has grown in recent times, into an industry that makes a serious contribution to the global publishing economy. In turn, this development has changed the landscape of art publishing more broadly. In this text, I describe changes to publishing infrastructure and discuss some of the most urgent challenges we need to face in order to foster this economy, which I call "progressive cultural publishing." I also consider how publishers can balance ethics and integrity with the competing demands on book production. I hope this honest text enables independent writers, publishers, or designers interested in bookmaking to see their ambitions more clearly, and for those currently engaged in the field to consider their responsibilities in responding to challenges.

I write this text as founding director of Onomatopee, a publisher and gallery based in the Netherlands. We produce projects consisting of both public programs (exhibitions, lectures, and workshops), which are services, and publishing, which produces products (books). I am writing this as a testimony of my vision and agenda, and on the basis of the experiences I have had over the past fifteen years. Through Onomatopee projects, we mediate between radicality, experimentation, the avant-garde, and alternative knowledge production. We aim to meet and be generous with an audience that is curious for something different, and, as our founding principles suggest, to inspire cultural life more broadly. We fund these projects independently — through our exhibition program, commissions by institutions, cultural practitioners and academics, and, evidently, publication sales.

As founding director of this small business — albeit not-for-profit — my experience is similar to that of family businesses, which are often the backbone of economies. I know every aspect of the business, having done all the roles thoroughly. I literally know how stuff works, where stuff is, and how to keep stuff going or make stuff go better. The chain of production is clear to me in all its components.

Let me conclude this introduction with two relevant distinctions to help you understand the bottom line of this text. Firstly, when I started Onomatopee with my friend, graphic designer Remco van Bladel, we were self-publishing. As we grew into the business, and came to expand our resources and capacities, we became publishers. Where self-publishing is often naïve, the practice of publishing is one where you know things, have more infrastructure, and can accordingly take on more responsibility. Secondly, although I speak of books here, it could equally apply to any other good or service of a progressive nature with the capacity to circulate worldwide, and you can therefore replace "books" in this text with any alternative product or service, including art and art writing.

The rise of an undercurrent within the global publishing economy

Traditionally, art publishing consists mostly of monographic catalogues, with print specs akin to those of coffee-table books, an introduction by a stakeholder claiming his and the institution's superiority, an essay by an acclaimed critic or curator that reaffirms the quality of the product, and so on. These books are usually produced by elites who publish to support their own cultural accomplishments. Often, they are not distributed through the commercial channels that are common to the book trade, and yet they are printed in relatively high numbers, for institutions to sell in their gift shops and give to their patrons. If they are distributed, they are often run through publishers such as Hatje Cantz or Lars Müller, or gallerists such as Hauser & Wirth. This historical backbone of art publishing shapes the dominant perception of such publishing, and remains the economic backdrop of current progressive cultural publishing. For independent publishing to exist, it has to both accept and reject the dominant sphere of art publishing—to understand the conservative notion of the book and instead produce titles that align with notions of an alternative book.

Around 2005, a group of independent publishers, academics, graphic designers, and art workers including myself formed a culture and economy of independent publishing, which slowly gained prominence on the margins of general art publishing's big business. At the time, a commonality across the art presses in this ecology was that one person performed many roles — from editing the publication, speaking to authors, and designing the book, to selling drinks at the launch event. This ecology required each imprint to have a largely DIY approach to keep costs low and remain agile, all the while retaining a high level of energy to produce projects while still traveling, being part of events, and distributing books.

This ecology grew in the mid-2000s, as small publishers took cheap flights to small art book fairs and events, found one another's blogs, and paired up with distributors covering specific continents and areas of interest. These distributors were based in Europe, North America, and Australia — continents with the means and the infrastructure to take on small independent imprints producing art-specific writing and discourse. It was through this internationalization, using the waves of global cultural capitalism, that independent culture could find more reach. Specific styles of books, types of writing, and reader engagement meant that these small publishers were able to increase print runs and find more of a market for themselves, as well as acquire new titles, commissions, and collaborations. This market, to most of these independents, meant more engagement rather than more money, and for the most part relied on publishers expending a lot of time and effort to break into said markets.

How it's made

A memory that strikes me is one familiar to many in this ecology — packing and carrying books around the world to art book events. This memory provides a tangible example of the perils of distribution. After consulting the internet, and visiting stores to feel fabrics and check on wheels, one evening I started to order a North Face trolley on my mobile phone, supposedly the one with the best wheels: "inline skating best quality." I needed a trolley to carry books around with me. The need for a good one came after too many bad trips caused by supposedly robust trolleys ending up with broken wheels while walking through rainy Basel (a recent memory) or Glasgow (almost forgotten), or finding a broken wheel at the baggage reclaim. Two trolleys and carry-on luggage are a pain in subways, but I must take trains as I cannot afford taxis.

Anyway, I started ordering the North Face trolley with my phone. At the end of the order, everything seemed to scramble, so I opened my laptop and started all over again, filling in VAT numbers, invoice and delivery address details, and all the other unavoidable data that makes our digital life supposedly so speedy these days. Once I managed to purchase the trolley, I continued doing some administration on the online management system we use. It was then that I noticed that I had paid twice for the same trolley with inline skate wheels. I called the company, which had not yet registered my first payment, and they told me they would correct it. And indeed, within the next hour, a cancellation email popped up. The next day, one hour after the scheduled delivery, the delivery guy — whom I know, as he always delivers packages for the neighbor across the street who is apparently never at home — came with only one trolley, well wrapped in plastic that was, in turn, well packaged in a big cardboard box.

What this says to me is that our independent publishing culture rests upon a reduction of costs largely achieved by the sacrifices and efforts of individuals who operate the imprints and accompanying activities. Publishers such as myself can avoid the ethical complexity or calamity of operating a more mainstream publishing business, defensively maintaining that we are circulating content we believe in. However, this does come at a personal cost — including limiting our time available for other capital-making activities.

Integrity and the economy of actors

The more recent development of a "market" for niche art publishing has meant that what might once have been regarded as self-publishing has developed a more formalized structure, akin to that of larger and more traditional publishing houses. This means that the publisher employs or manages multiple players in the field and the various aspects of production, from editing and design to dealing with printers, print specs, and distribution partnerships. This management of more players ultimately means that an independent publisher's early idealistic DIY freedoms, specifically in terms of objectives and approach, changes from being undertaken internally by fewer invested individuals to being outsourced to many parties. The positive outcomes of such changes include the fact that, with better distribution and more resources, print runs can increase, therefore reducing the cost per unit and subsequently making it possible to turn a profit on some titles. This profit becomes useful in order to fund future projects or support a community of practice. A more negative outcome is that with more people involved in a production, there is an increased hierarchy and bureaucracy to be managed, and the costs for this labor are rarely accounted for.

Following this increased profit, myself and my colleagues became much more aware of the labor needed and the labor conditions required to enable improved distribution. Onomatopee, for instance, began to produce many books with small printers in Eastern Europe, where the printing costs were much lower than those of printers in Western European countries — we found cheaper and cheaper ways of producing books using these networks and contacts. At the same time, due to high labor costs in Western Europe, we bought a shrink-wrapping machine in order to shrink-wrap books ourselves to further save costs. As an example, we are currently paying twenty-one thousand euro for the printing of a forthcoming title, but we will shrink-wrap the publication ourselves to save eight hundred euro. This is the reality of the opportunities that global distribution presents, and a real issue for progressive cultural production. Our early entrepreneurial aspirations — to remain independent, DIY, and engaged — now seem naïve; we did not fully understand the challenges of the many responsibilities one has as a publisher.

Moreover, this growth clouded our ethical judgment and all too easily we felt pushed toward free labor. I believe this is a sad reality, that many cultural producers still benefit from free or low-cost labor practices. For Onomatopee, this means that the publisher is not paid for their in-kind work, which is in fact expert labor, such as editorial advice, production support, etc., while the graphic designers, authors, and copyeditors, who are needed to produce the raw result, do receive payment.

The mission of offering an alternative service by bringing these types of smaller, niche art projects and art writing into wider circulation cannot primarily be for financial gain. Rather, it is about sharing ideas and texts that may sit outside of the mainstream or classical notions of cultural capital. This should be the objective through which to garner public support for such publications — the fact that these publishers are serving a gap in the market, and avoiding insular culture being reproduced. Public support or funding for such publications enables more people to be paid for their labor and, in turn, to expand the reach of progressive cultural pursuits.

Authors are essential players in the ecology of cultural publishing. They elevate the scope of a project and provide it with urgency and legitimacy; skilled authors coupled with a skilled editor make for a solid publication. In saying this, cultural publishing is not academic publishing, and so has the freedom to employ various styles and forms of writing, such as poetic, philosophical, essayistic, or journalistic writing, and so on. It is also the responsibility of independent, socially engaged publishers to publish lesser-known and risk-taking authors and art writing.

Independent publishers have an opportunity to create a platform for these lesser-known and marginalized art writers, artists, designers, typographers, and other content producers. A publication or other activity should, in my opinion, reflect the participatory capacity of those who have engaged in its production.

In closing

Whereas traditional art publishing largely reflects established power structures, progressive cultural publishing is the art worker's cultural equal in publishing. As independent books slowly find their way toward a wider audience, the market will change, and titles will go from being stocked in select independent bookstores internationally to being available in bigger chain stores. I hope to see wider audiences slowly familiarizing themselves with different types of art writing and different voices, beyond the cherished few we find at international fairs, with distributors willing to support this diversification and booksellers willing to endorse such activities.

Of course, the books made by Onomatopee cannot cater to everyone and evidently many of our books are exclusive in their support of the marginal. Yet, increasingly, these books do reach audiences farther afield. Consumers, funding bodies, cultural producers, and everyone engaged in this economy should be aware of the opportunities in progressive cultural publishing, and we should continue to organize together—we cannot leave this to commercial galleries or private museums. The public sector, by nature, cannot be up-to-date with progressive public interest. There may not be much money in progressive cultural publishing, but it has developed an infrastructure that provides us with an opportunity to influence culture more widely, and a supportive community of practice for a generation of art writers.

A Fiction of Our Time? China's Photobook in Absentia

Rachel Marsden

> The concept of an "artist's book" might very well endow the "book" with an air of lively revolt, which springs primarily from the artists' roaring creativity. Subordinately, it emerges from the strengths of the medium's shape and materials: among other factors, the freedom of form books permit (whether text, illustration, or collage), the sheer quantity of information they can hold, the convenience with which they are carried and transported.[1]

In China, the photobook can be first located in the discourse of documentary photography (*jishi sheying*). Coined in 1981, this compound term grounded the relationship between "documentary" and "photography" in the cultural context and social reality of China as part of Socialist Realism.[2] Initially borrowing from film, literature, and art, the prefix *jishi* was appropriated from documentary literature (*jishi wenxue*), where it was used by Chinese scholars to refer to a genre of Soviet non-fiction called "documentary prose."[3] As a practice of rereading and cultural translation corresponding to a moment of crisis in social belief in the 1980s, it was embodied by the Photographic New Wave (*sheying xinchao*) movement and the documentary turn.[4] Representing new forms of depiction and depoliticization of Cultural Revolution propaganda, practices were evolving beyond prescribed codes of portraiture, landscape, documentary, and other forms of photo-documentation and photoessays. In turn, the book as a medium *in practice* emerged in informal studio and domestic spaces in Beijing, before being curated into international exhibitions of China's avant-garde art movement in the early 1990s. A noteworthy intervention by the New Analyst Group (1988–95) created the unique "book as exhibition format" logic,[5] an approach that sought to abolish artistic individuality, the original work of art, and the concept of value as embraced by the art market.[6] The group contended that "the gallery space is not an appropriate setting for reading, but rather a situation that enables visual appreciation."[7] By the mid-1990s, in line with China's new global marketization and the rise of "experimental photography" (*shiyan sheying*), artists' books, and photobooks specifically, expanded into a conceptual practice in their own right. However, they were still positioned as complementary to exhibition-making and other artistic practices, whether as reference tools for historical context-building, as tokens of cultural engagement, or as symbols of career progression — functions usually ascribed to the artist's monograph or the exhibition catalogue as an epitaph within Chinese art history.

Since the turn of the millennium, economic and cultural reforms have developed China into one of the fastest growing economies in the world, today the second largest market for luxury goods, art, and antiques globally.[8] This has encouraged significant exchange between Chinese and non-Chinese contexts, driving China into a new era of globalization accompanied by a cultural boom in contemporary art, architecture, fashion, and graphic design. As the nation recognizes the importance of cultural innovation, it acknowledges that value cannot come from manufacturing and material production alone, prompting the national mission to be reenvisioned from "Made in China" to "Created/Designed in China."[9]

The photobook is still a developing terrain in this context, even when considered in line with marked changes in the cultural and commercial narratives of photography. These changes include the growth of associated art markets and the boom in photography spaces, photography festivals, and photofairs, including a 250 percent increase in the number of photography exhibitions between 2014 and 2017 in China.[10] The photobook's development has also been influenced by a newfound focus and investment from China's millennials, the second-generation rich (*fuerdai*) who have driven the innovation of digital technologies allowing for the do-it-yourself, low-cost production of magazines and books through small-scale presses and publishing imprints. This new social consciousness has transformed the universal legacy and cultural relevance of photography in China; the photobook provides the younger generation of artists and photographers "the freedom to approach the form in a self-reflexive way" and to create a different perceptual experience for the reader.[11]

Proving to be a unique and complementary, yet separate, cultural canon within Chinese art history, the photobook nonetheless mirrors conceptual documentary photography's increasingly fraught but determined relationship to the "real" world, producing equally paradoxical archives in China.[12] This complexity is further reflected in writing *about* the photobook—or, rather, the lack thereof within Chinese art history—and its interchangeable translations as a term of practice: the photobook (*xiang bu*) as photo album in domestic terms (for example, family photos), the photobook (*sheying ji*) as photographic collection (characterized by photographers but not contemporary artists), and the photobook (*sheying shu*) as photography book (in documentary terms). These terms also highlight an explicit connection between photobooks and photographic postcards, celebrated within documentary photography as "emblems of in absentia."[13] Establishing a vocabulary to underpin the development of the photobook conversely reveals the insufficiency of ascribing a singular approach to reading. Here, the photograph or image is largely written through a visual language, without being committed to words. This affords artists a space to question the current state of China, a space which is then open to interpretation, criticism, and censorship. Therefore, the reading of the photobook becomes as important as its writing, but can they be mutually exclusive?

> The act of reading is just another kind of writing. It is a gathering of meaning, bringing into life a world that does not yet exist, filling in the blanks between the lines and the gaps between the words with images mutated from the reader's own life.[14]

Through its material components alone, the photobook attempts to engage the gaze by creating a definite inside and outside—a container locating an alternative space—to question the dichotomy of ways visual structures interfere with modes of reading.[15] Whether handcrafted, independently published, mass-produced, or printed in custom short-run limited editions, the value of the photobook is often assigned to experimentation within conventional parameters of design, binding, and typography. Value is also accrued through ephemeral and aesthetic qualities, including "careful selection, repetition and classification" further validated through archival imperatives,[16] or, more specifically, through the artist's "direct expression of painstaking labors, of delicate feelings delicately stated, and of careful, deliberate thought."[17] Prioritizing selfhood (the self, the social, and the body), and giving insight into alternative autobiographies, mappings, and visual diaries of their makers' ways of being in the world, photobooks are deserving of respect and care for the vulnerability presented. Examinations of emotional and social trauma have become central concerns in conceptual documentary photobooks in China, identified as a unique form of "archival logic" not to be homogenized or marginalized.[18] The photobook serves as a sociopolitical response system, a mechanism to amplify hidden and subversive histories, meaning it is often understood as a non-official (independent) art practice that is counterposed to the conventional systems and markets of the art world. As such, the photobook is largely promoted to like-minded networks as a material object of desire due to its status of immediacy and "cult of authorship."[19] It is reliant on this limited audience to further contextualize and enact the artist's voice through writing — for example, photobook reviews — in order to become visible within the wider consciousness of Chinese art history. Otherwise, absence — absence of text — has the capacity to become a discourse in its own right.

> If conscious engagement of contemporary social, political, and intellectual issues remains absent in the so-called new documentaries, the reframing of documentary photography into a notion of contemporary art may end up with nothing but a play of realist rhetoric and a self-preserved photography isolated from the world photographic community.[20]

This absence is further emphasized by today's "post-" prefixed world — post-contemporary, post-studio, post-Internet, to name but a few — in which the object gaze has lost its penetration,[21] succumbing to the dominance of screen culture and the algorithmic gaze.[22] The growing popularity of the photobook as a medium and platform can be seen as a counter to technology, the latter responsible for creating a "symptom of archival impulse pervading contemporary culture."[23] In this context, I identify the material object of the photobook as a tactile act of "textography"[24] — an approach combining text analysis and ethnographic techniques to get an inside view of the worlds in which texts are written.[25] Here, textography is understood as an assemblage of texts. It presents writing, voices, life histories, and ephemera as a network of hierarchical intertextuality.[26] This network includes assumed and mundane, personal and impersonal texts, from anecdotes, annotations, and abbreviations to shopping lists and letters, always considering for and by whom they are written and experienced. Here, the image is fundamental in revealing meaning-making through an additional, coded visual language — a Deleuzian approach to a situation as a multiplicity of things, a rhizome with complex structures and no prior union.

> The genres that textography unearths, inscribes, and interprets have a richer "ground" than a purely textual study can aspire to.[27]

In action, textography is the examination of context, including consideration of the role and purpose of the text, the text's relationship to comparable texts, its audience, the expectations of the particular discursive community in which it circulates, and the underlying values of authors and audiences alike.[28] This situatedness is vital in understanding and sustaining the photobook as a field of practice. It is also important to acknowledge the tension between official (state-sanctioned, by the Ministry of Culture) and non-official (independent) art and photography practices in China, in order to fracture the logic in which art history is usually constructed and actually ask: what is the truth? As with the "book as exhibition format" logic, textography does not occupy a singular space, but, rather, comprises "a composition of parts moving/affecting/effecting other parts."[29] Textography requires the text be read as an overlapping combination of probable realities — a transcription of ordinary life seemingly presenting truths. Simultaneously, it is to be read with doubt, as no image or text is certain or whole unto itself — indeed, art and literature have often been referred to as fields of fiction.[30] Therefore, reading comes with a subtext of fiction and the photobook becomes a further refictionalization as images and the books themselves are reproduced and copied. As such, what happens to readings and writings from China through the inherent act of reproducing the image?

> We are living in an artificial world, a most unauthentic world. The nature of truth is in the end constituted by fiction [...] Nothing remains genuine. Images of images.

> The copies endless flow. We have lost a world where we can truly tell the difference between the original and copy.[31]

Beyond documentary photography, archival, and collection practices — engendered by the human impulse to collect — there has been a prolific growth of small-scale presses and publishing imprints producing photobooks in art, design, and photography communities in China. It is commonplace for these platforms to begin as independent photography magazines and zines, instigated by artists and photographers. A recent example of the progression from less formal modes of production to professional publishing practice is *Imageless* (established Wuxi circa 2016). Originally founded by Ni Liang as an independent magazine dedicated to the promotion of photography culture and young photographers in China, at the 2019 Paris Photo–Aperture Foundation PhotoBook Awards *Imageless* came into international focus as the winner of the First PhotoBook award for *The Eighth Day* (2019) by Gao Shan, designed by Guoxiao.[32] Taking its name from his personal story of adoption on the eighth day after his birth, and reflecting a desire to connect with his adoptive mother, the photobook sets out the ongoing emotional relationship between the two in their roughly-seventy-square-meter apartment. According to Shan's afterword, their relationship was characterized by coldness and indifference. Approaches to image sequencing and respectful design reflect the artist's historical knowledge of documentary photography. Concurrently, Shan employs "performative and conceptual approaches in a sophisticated way,"[33] using the camera not for cold observation but as an active tool in their relationship.[34]

Imageless joins several similar ventures, including: Jiazazhi press, library, magazine, bookshop, and fair (established Ningbo circa 2009);[35] Bananafish bookshop and gallery (established Shanghai circa 2010); *Voices of Photography* magazine (established Taiwan circa 2011) and associated platform and bookshop; Same Paper self-publishing studio (established Shanghai circa 2013) with associated bookshop Closing Ceremony; *GENDA* magazine and online platform (established China/Italy circa 2015); La Maison de Z (The House of Z) project and bookshop (established China/France circa 2015); and Brownie Publishing, which runs a magazine, cafe, gallery, and commercial printing and framing service (established Hong Kong/Shanghai circa 2016).

Shanghai has taken precedence as the site for collective practices in the field of independent publishing in China, which can be attributed to recent institutional support for, and developments within, the field of photography.[36] At the same time, there is a growing ambition to promote photography by young talent based in China on the international art stage, as demonstrated by 88Books (established Vancouver, Canada, circa 2012), an independent small press founded by artist Ho Tam. Specializing in creating and distributing limited-edition artist books through an alternative, non-profit channel, 88Books is committed to providing autonomy and freedom of expression to a younger generation of artists from China.[37] For its inaugural series, ten books by ten artists were commissioned, providing an opportunity for those artists to explore the book as an artistic medium in its own right, with all its narrative, conceptual, and formal possibilities. Showcasing current and diverse photographic practices — including those functioning below the radar of political circumstance — was prioritized, providing an insight into the lived experience of the current sociopolitical and economic situation in China.[38] Today, the 88Books publishing program can clearly be framed as a counter-archival practice, one that contests dominant representations of youth and subculture.[39]

> The archive that is produced through repetition generates an open economy in which meanings multiply and the archived event is lost. By using repetition to explore and categorize a particular subject, Conceptual Documentary photobooks similarly underscore the inability of the archive to capture and contain an event. The more an idea is reiterated and re-photographed, the more multi-faceted and elusive the "original" event becomes.[40]

However, the photobook's embrace of the act of textography cannot stand in for the absence of the original, the author, and the event — images are not substitutes for a "living memory, and neither are words."[41] More critical research is needed — through encountering, noticing, and reading the photobook — to question established forms of representation and fiction, to doubt the terms and conditions used in defining the discourse, and to reaffirm truths of the photobook on the global art stage.

> It inevitably involves doubts, querying, investigation and interrogation regarding the real world [...] the artwork is generally the result of doubting the real — not only the appearance of reality but, more importantly, its substance, or the truth. This process is full of contradictions, an infinite adventure into the realm of the impossible, since truth is by no means unique and certain. Instead, it is always unstable, uncertain and multiple.[42]

1 Chang Xuyang, "DO A BOOK," *LEAP Magazine*, issue 139 (April 2012): 203.

2 The term *jishi sheying* was first used in 1981 in the bimonthly journal *Guoji sheying* (International Photography), in the title of an article translated from the preface of Time Life's 1972 compilation *Documentary Photography*.

3 Dengyan Zhou, "Reframing Documentary Photography in China," *photographies*, vol. 11, issue 2–3 (2018): 340.

4 As termed by Chinese critics of the time, and referenced by scholar and curator Wu Hung.

5 Working under their original name the New Measurement Group, members Gu Dexin, Chen Shaoping, and Wang Luyan produced five books between 1988 and 1995.

6 Biljana Ciric, "Public Moments of Escape from Exhibition Rituals in China," in *From a History of Exhibitions towards a Future of Exhibition-Making: China and Southeast Asia*, ed. Biljana Ciric (Berlin: Sternberg Press, 2020), 121.

7 Ibid., 119.

8 Artprice, *The Art Market in 2015* (2015), http://imgpublic.artprice.com/pdf/rama2016_en.pdf.

9 Michael Keane, *Creative Industries in China: Art, Design & Media* (London: Polity Press, 2013), 149.

10 Tom Seymour, "Networks of the World," *Aesthetica*, no. 85 (October/November 2018), 24.

11 Joni Low, "Possibilities for the Page: 88BOOKS and Artists' Books in China," *Yishu: Journal of Contemporary Chinese Art*, vol. 11, no. 6 (November/December 2012): 93.

12 Ibid.

13 Colin Symes, "Something to Write Home About: A 'Textography' of Contemporary Postcards," *Annals of Leisure Research*, vol. 22, issue 5 (2019): 658.

14 Ken Liu, "A Brief and Inaccurate but True Account of the Origin of Living Books," in *Tales of Our Time*, ed. Xiaoyu Weng and Hou Hanru (New York: Guggenheim Museum Publications, 2016), 140.

15 Chang, "DO A BOOK," 203.

16 Melissa Miles, "The Drive to Archive: Conceptual Documentary Photobook Design," *Photographies*, vol. 3, issue 1 (2010): 50.

17 Chang, "DO A BOOK," 203.

18 Miles, "The Drive to Archive," 65.

19 Ibid., 53.

20 Dengyan, "Reframing Documentary Photography in China," 2018, 349–350.

21 Yve Lomax, *Writing the Image: An Adventure with Art and Theory* (London: I. B. Tauris, 2000), 42.

22 Boris Groys, *Fiction Defictionalized: Art and Literature on the Internet*, keynote lecture, Goethe-Institute New York, November 20, 2014, http://fiktion.cc/boris-groys-2/.

23 Hal Foster, "An Archival Impulse," *October*, vol. 110 (Autumn 2004): 22.

24 John M. Swales, "Textography: Toward a Contextualization of Written Academic Discourse," *Research on Language and Social Interaction*, vol. 31, issue 1 (1998): 109–121.

25 Susan M. Katz, "Other Floors, Other Voices: A Textography of a Small University Building," *Journal of Business Communication*, vol. 36, issue 4 (1999): 422.

26 Ibid., 117.

27 Swales, "Textography," 120.

28 Sue Starfield, Brian Paltridge, and Louise Ravelli, "Researching Academic Writing: What Textography Affords," *Theory and Method in Higher Education Research II (International Perspectives on Higher Education Research)*, vol. 10 (2014): 105.

29 Lomax, *Writing the Image*, 44.

30 Groys, *Fiction Defictionalized*.

31 Lomax, *Writing the Image*, 41.

32 Also, winner of the 2016 Color Shadows New Award's "Photographer of the Year."

33 Takashi Homma, "Announcing the Winners of the 2019 PhotoBook Awards," *Aperture* (2019), https://aperture.org/blog/announcing-winners-2019-photobook-awards/.

34 As summarised on *Photography of China*, http://photographyofchina.com/blog/photobooks-spotted-at-polycopies-2019.

35 From 2009 in Beijing, moving to Ningbo in 2014.

36 As further discussed in Rachel Marsden, "The Chinese Photobook: Publishing as an Ellipsis in Chinese Art History," in *The Centre: On Art and Urbanism in China*, ed. Annika Aitken, Simon Maidment, Ewan McEoin, and Megan Patty (Melbourne: National Gallery of Victoria, 2019), 98–111.

37 Summarised from 88Books website: http://www.88books.ca.

38 Low, "Possibilities for the Page," 98.

39 Paula Roush, "Download Fever: Photography, Subcultures and Online-Offline Counter-Archival Strategies," *Photographies*, vol. 2, issue 2 (2009): 157.

40 Miles, "The Drive to Archive," 61.

41 Lomax, *Writing the Image*, 51.

42 Hou Hanru, *The Power of Doubt* (Madrid: La Fabrica, 2011), 11. Exhibition catalogue produced in conjunction with *Power of Doubt* (December 18, 2011 – February 6, 2012) at Guangdong Times Museum, Guangzhou, curated by Hou Hanru.

Zooming In and Zooming Out: Life and After in Post-pandemic Publics

Nikos Papastergiadis & Hou Hanru

Nikos Papastergiadis is an academic whose current research investigates the historical transformation of contemporary art and cultural institutions by digital technologies. Here, he speaks to curator, author, and critic Hou Hanru about various crises and how they impact ecologies of culture, identity, and fields of practice such as art writing.

NP: Recent events have presented profound challenges to our conceptions of the viability and security of life on this planet. From political changes such as Brexit, to the climate fires in Australia, and now the COVID-19 pandemic, we confront radical questions about the stakes of survival and our hopes for the future. During this upheaval, we have also witnessed an exacerbation of existing social divisions along lines of race, class, and gender. Disproportionate harm is meted out to the precariat and to people of color. In these new times of crisis, environmental damage is at its extreme in rural regions, and women are more likely than ever to be victims of domestic violence. There is also a generalized crisis of collectivity: the political landscape is dominated by discourses of isolationism and authoritarianism. At a time when the world needs to come together to find common solutions, there are growing signs of hostile retreats and aggressive barricading. This context presents a new challenge to art and writing. The relationship between the two has often been cast as a kind of belated partnership. For some, art and writing walk together, like the body and the shadow. For others, they are partners in parallel quests for common answers. In times of crisis,

I think there is a need for convergence. Art and writing urgently need to wrestle and entangle together.

What sort of scenarios do you see playing out in the future? Are we going to move toward more isolationism, more authoritarianism? Will this produce a fortressed Europe? New walls being put up? New kinds of hostilities and retreats into ghettos? The advance of neo-nationalism? Or do you think, more optimistically, that current crises may stimulate new ways of thinking about place and flow? And perhaps a more abstract sense of belonging as well, a more cosmic understanding of the planet?

HH: I would start with a more optimistic embrace of contradiction. Take Zoom, as an example, because we are talking across the oceans using it. The Zoom business model has never been so successful as it has been during the pandemic crisis. We all know that perhaps 90 percent of business conferences in the world today, in 2020, are being held on platforms like Zoom. But there is an underlying security issue. According to some press information, Zoom has a back door that allowed the Chinese authorities to access its data. Some governments now ask their employees not to use it for business meetings as it poses a security risk. But the irony is that some colleagues from China told me just a few days ago that China has also started banning Zoom. Even if the Chinese authorities can potentially control it, Zoom remains a relatively open platform on which almost all kinds of conversations can continue and prosper. In particular, it can allow people in China to reach out to the world. And yet it has been turned into a battlefield for censorship and resistance. This paradoxical anecdote reveals a very interesting picture of how the COVID-19 pandemic is impacting not only the everyday behaviors of people, but also social and even geopolitical relationships around the global and the local.

We are also witnessing a really amazing mobilization of global communication, unlike anything we've seen before. Because now, not only do we have time to stay at home, we also feel an unprecedentedly strong need to prove that we continue to exist in the world. It's much bigger than the question of the technological possibilities of the virtual world versus the real world. It implies a new definition of the global and the local.

NP: You have put your finger on a very serious contradiction. On the one hand, this crisis is exposing the desperate need to connect. On the other hand, it is provoking ambient fears and other desperate acts — such as wanting to close the door because you think that the threat is from outside.

HH: Yes, it is revealing the very root of all kinds of xenophobic ideologies, as well as the will to social control and the policy of security. In general, racism is much less evident in a multicultural context. Racism very often happens in places where there's a single dominant ethnic group. People are actually scared when they imagine the possibility of invasion by a different culture. They fantasize that the arrival of the "other" will uproot their established way of living. So, xenophobia started with a fantasy that can be compared to what we call the global world today. This fantasy is vastly promulgated by digital technologies. The virtual world deeply impacts our life in the real world.

NP: It's true. Most sociological surveys have found that regions with the fewest migrants have the highest fear that migration is destroying their society. Cities like London and New York, which have the highest proportion of migrants, tend to think of migration and cultural difference as positive things.

Anyway, let's talk more about your personal and professional histories, Hanru. And let's reflect a little on your own patterns and trajectories — the ways in which your practice has revolved around, kept returning to, and quite often never been able to overcome, certain themes. In my opinion, there are five themes that structure your practice as a curator. One, faith in the capacity for self-organization. Two, the extension of democratic values into all aspects of life. Three, the validation of vernacular cultural practices. Four, a fascination with informal spaces and street life. And, five, the exploration of freedom in the so-called unregulated nocturnal times and spaces at the edges of the city.

Underpinning and traversing all of these themes is a desire to escape centralized authority and to activate a kind of cosmopolitan imaginary. You look for hope in heterotopic and heterocosmic places that are neither entirely controlled nor totally free. In the context of a pandemic, what is the time and place of hope? Are we witnessing the collapse of certain ideologies, such as neoliberalism, or a rebooting of the Indignados movement, or a more generalized and diffuse silencing of the proverbial lambs? Where do you see your own practice as a curator intersecting with current anxieties?

HH: It's true that central to my practice is the question of how to turn the tension between order and chaos, and between control and freedom, into creative action. I think we can all agree that art is about questioning priorities, it's about creating chaos in order to obtain intellectual and emotional independence and liberty. So, as we are creating, we are also promoting the existing chaos that is part of the integral structure of life. The question is how to build an institutional framework to open possibilities — to be seen, to be heard, to be shared. In other words, an institution is a location trying to provide a certain order, or an orderly structure, that can actively represent and react to our chaotic but lively reality. The tension and interaction between a museum and the city in which it is located are sources of energy for contemporary creation.

For the last decade, neoliberalism — its social values and vision, as well as its "methodology" — has become the dominant ideological influence across the world, transforming all societies and institutions in spite of their political differences. Museums and other cultural institutions are being pushed to embrace its logic. It's seemingly an irresistible or even inevitable power that mutates the very DNA of institutions, like a pandemic virus. With the arrival of COVID-19, people ironically became aware not only of the threat of the biological virus, but also of the negative effects of the social, cultural, and economic virus of neoliberalism. The neoliberal ideology and modus operandi have been seriously questioned and defied. We are entering a new phase of experimentation around how to reorganize our cultural and artistic visions, missions, and models of institutional construction beyond the neoliberal model, toward a "new world" that is still unknown. Critical reflections and experimental actions are being widely and firmly embraced. Adventures into the unknown, with an intelligent revisiting of the past for inspiration, are largely encouraged. This can certainly generate more space for freedom of imagination and expression, leading to new understandings of the public sphere — of cultural, artistic, and even political life.

There have been positives amid all the upheavals and displacements caused by globalization. It forced people to move around the world, but it also gave people like you and me the opportunity to meet. Definitively, we are living in a more open and freer world. What's more important is that, for the last few decades, we have gained knowledge and pleasure from being able to engage with more diverse people and cultures. We no longer describe the world as East versus West. More and more, we tend to talk about South versus North, South–South collaboration, etc., in order to subvert the established world system and to move toward justice and equality between people, all the while learning how to deal with this increased complexity. Of course, this requires us to assume more risk when faced with an increasing number of unknown events.

NP: How has all of this impacted the way you are planning to reopen the museum?

HH: This year we are celebrating ten years of the MAXXI Museum, the National Museum of 21st Century Art and the first Italian national institution devoted to contemporary creativity.

We have a major exhibition called *A Story for the Future*, which will represent the museum's first decade in an encyclopedic structure (referencing both Aby Warburg's *Mnemosyne Atlas* and André Malraux's "imaginary museum") and open discursive ground for the years to come. We are reinstalling our collections and organizing a series of transdisciplinary public programs, while a fundraising gala will gather funds for the collection. Many events had been scheduled for the month of May, 2020, but, because of the interruption caused by the virus crisis, we have had to rethink and replan, postponing most of the events. Now we are organizing an online festival using the same title, *A Story for the Future*, and presenting a day of marathon conversations with Italian and international professionals from the fields of art, architecture, cultural theory and policy, and so on. The festival, which will also feature images of exhibitions and performances from the museum's history, will focus on two major topics. One is the role of global museums in this time of urgency, and the other is the ecology of creative activities in a post-COVID future. The exhibition will present a constellation of ideas, images, and materials as well as "environments" in which an oral history of the museum — with talks by artists, architects, curators, and museum staff — will be "broadcast" alongside immersive moving images, providing the public with a fresh overview of the museum's activities. It will also emphasize the interaction between the museum and the city as producer of an artistic and cultural multitude — a very Italian concept of presenting the diversity of peoples and their identities in a time of intense global–local interaction and negotiation. This in turn opens up long-standing and unanswered questions around art and everyday life — how we deal with the challenges of real life, how we confront the dream of consumerism and the reality of democracy in crisis, all the while addressing the unfinished decolonial struggle and the emergency of the environmental crisis. We try to look to how creative practice can open up a new horizon, shifting between material and technological innovation and the future of humanity, between the mundane and the spiritual, and the possibility of post-human life.

NP: If we zoom in on the relationship between art and writing in times of crisis, then we start to get different perspectives to those that dominate the public arena. One of the features I have noticed among artists who are deeply engaged in writing, like Maja Kuzmanovic, is the effort to pause. She writes a great deal, and with considerable poignancy, on the need to stop and listen to the voices that exist in the margins of the mainstream. This requires a deep sensitivity to our bodily senses, and a willingness to receive and be in resonance with a wider ecology. It is a kind of cosmotechnics. However, when we zoom out, we cannot help but notice that there is a lot of discussion about the impact of the pandemic at both the personal and the political level. On a personal level, some people are using this as a time to reflect and put their life on pause while others are instead pressing fast forward. On the bigger-picture level, we've seen governments behaving in very extreme ways, including imposing controls on our bodies. For the arts, the impact of the pandemic has been quite profound. When the government swings into full lockdown mode, it not only prevents artists from being able to sell their work publicly or hold events and concerts and festivals, it also cuts out another source of income as a lot of artists support themselves by working in the hospitality sector.

When the government does intervene in the arts, it's very confused and counterproductive. At the moment, the arts are very diverse, operating across various media, adopting new modes of social engagement, collaborating with different sectors and community groups. In other words, the boundary between high art and low art has been blurred, displaced, and exploded. Amid all that noise and all that cacophony, there is a stunned and stunted reaction from the government. It would rather confine itself to dealing with iconic institutions or recognized artists who either use heritage practices or have forged very strong relationships with business partners — that is, where there's a relatively risk-free return on investment.

Do you think that the arts in this context will be even more profoundly damaged, because their ecology has unraveled? Is so-called government support a regressive step? How can we use this crisis to challenge the very ways in which we understand the role of art in everyday life?

HH: I think that this is a very contradictory situation. While many governments have reacted by offering financial support for the continuation of art activities, I think that is mostly about maintaining the business side of the arts. In France, Germany, and even the US, along with a few other countries, governments put money into supporting the cultural industries. In the meantime, there are many other countries who don't care at all. Art is not a priority for them. You can clearly see that in countries where the cultural industries are part of the mainstream, governments invest money. Interestingly, many governments had already reorganized their cultural ministries into culture and tourism ministries, like Italy and even China, long before the virus crisis. And so, investing public money in the arts has been largely justified by the necessity of rescuing tourism. However, even these investments are largely symbolic as they are not able to fill the gap.

Making symbolic gestures is an attempt to say: "we recognize the situation and support the arts and culture industry." Of course, they cannot solve the problem because the real situation is much tougher. Already many galleries and even museums are at risk of closing down. In general, the focus of government support is more about the economics of the arts industry and what it can generate, rather than encouraging the social critique that art can enforce. It's about maintaining the economic power of culture. So, when we trace back the development of art over the last century, especially in the postwar years, it is important to recall how much it has been incorporated into economic schemes and other national agendas. This includes cultural policies being defined within the social democratic system, however this trajectory has also had negative impacts — such as the taming of critical voices. Maybe it's not on purpose, but the effect is the same. So, I think it's a very interesting question, and one we have to face. Do we need public support for art? I don't think anyone can say no. But I think we should also examine how we use such support, so as not to lose the essence of our activities as a critical force, beyond just entertainment.

NP: In reality, much of the art sector has been living a hand-to-mouth existence. There is no sustainable financial model whereby an institution can be in command of assets, reserves, and income streams that make it autonomous of the state or corporate philanthropy. It has always been a meagre survival, project by project. Do you think it is also time to question this precarity?

HH: The challenge is how to produce new value every time there's a crisis. I don't think we have a clear answer, but we have to commit to a process. This is related to the question of globalization and the industry models that we have developed and embraced over the last few decades — in Europe, maybe in Australia as well. These models have led to the elevation of market forces not only as an economic resource, but also as the main ideological structure for the cultural industries.

NP: Yes, in general we see a worldwide trend in which the utility of the arts has been subsumed by values defined by the infotainment industries. Web-based art was, in the first instance, seen as a crude shadow of the real thing. Most public museums were slow to develop digital tours and interactive virtual programs. This has all changed in the past few months. With the COVID-19 crisis, a new and specific challenge has emerged: how to present your ideas and work in the context of social distancing. Already we are witnessing a reworking of public and private spheres, virtual and physical spaces, and the reformatting or translating of material works of art into digital content. It has also meant that new social media platforms have imposed new regimes of attention and duration. For art to circulate on TikTok or Instagram, for example, it must be brief and fit within specific lexicons. This also has implications for the relationship between writing and art. How long can a review be? It would be absurd to spend longer reading the review than one would with the work of art itself, in a digital format. Similarly, does the contemplative and comparative exercise of art writing get compressed by the need to contextualize everything within the here and now? I think art and writing are at a crossroads and that there will be a push toward the instantaneous and iterative, as well as the enduring allure of the longform essay.

However, apart from formal and perceptual demands, this shift goes against the grain of a major tendency in contemporary art. Socially engaged art has always sought to heighten intimacy and extend collaboration into public settings. However, in the post-pandemic publics, how will artists conduct face-to-face encounters and operate skin-to-skin exchanges? If masks, gloves, and distance become habitual features of public life, what will this mean for artistic modes of sociality and interaction? How can art generate new forms of ambient aesthetics to enhance the vitality of co-presence in these highly mediated environments? Do we need to explore the iterative potential of new media in revitalizing participation and sociality in an era of traumatic pandemics, environmental destruction, and political manipulation?

To have intimacy — face-to-face, skin-to-skin, heart-to-heart — is to provoke exchange, build bridges, make connections, and so on. In other words, it's all about interpersonal collaboration. After this pandemic is over, will people just forget about the trauma, or will the anxiety still surface and linger in people's habits and consciousness, so that they remain nervous about being in public, touching each other, having to wear a mask in order to be visible? What sort of presence do you think art will have when there is a diffuse ambience of anxiety, as opposed to the current state of trauma where people are really distancing from each other? What is the future of participatory art in a world where there's ambient fear that the virus is always coming? Is there any way that ambience and iteration, which have been features of contemporary art, can be used to facilitate a flow between intimacy and extimacy, as well as presenting new modes of public presence?

HH: This is a question that we are all now asking. I think one very important thing to do is go back to the origins of social distancing. It's not only the virus that has imposed social distancing on us. We embraced social distancing voluntarily when we embraced social media. Social media has made us much less social than ever before, which is something that we didn't really talk about. The practice of social distancing during the pandemic is amplifying the use of social media. In the short term this is helpful, but nobody can digest it in the long term. We have to find a way to come back from social distancing, and of course the most probable scenario is that when this pandemic is somehow under control, things will go back to "business as usual." The worst case scenario is that we will lose even more privacy, that by "fighting" the virus by imposing lockdowns and resorting to the most sophisticated surveillance technologies, the political elite will have learned how to limit our freedom and control our private lives in a more efficient and "legitimate" manner. I'm not very optimistic that radical revolution will happen. But everyone needs to be fighting back, including with and through the arts.

NP: You've always wanted to embrace nightlife and the "zone of chaos" as a means of being together, but right now care is being done at a distance rather than in close proximity. We have, at the moment, if not a Zoom generation, conviviality by Zoom, pedagogy by Zoom, governance by Zoom. How will this impact the way in which we see our collective responsibility? How do you imagine that, in this masked and gloved world, we'll be able to have festivals again? What sort of gatherings will we see in the short- to medium-term future?

HH: I think this has been explored since the very beginning of the lockdowns. All those musicians playing together behind the screen to celebrate and express gratitude to the nurses, doctors, and health workers was a beautiful and straightforward expression of people's desire to still have festivity. But your question is very interesting. A festival is, by definition, a carnival. Like in the darkness of nighttime, it's a moment when people can feel temporarily freed of all kinds of social constraints to come together and do things that they wouldn't usually do under the glare of daylight — an opportunity to express ecstatic sensations and fantasies. The "Zoom generation" has actually adopted the online festival model, but very carefully, reorganizing their intimate interiors before they are exposed to others. For example, 98 percent of Zoom conversations happen in front of bookshelves...

NP: Like this one — there are books behind me! In my case, they are the books that I am working with right now. I tend to keep the books for current projects just over my shoulder. I don't exactly bury the books that were part of previous projects, but they do tend to migrate to other corners of my room. However, there are some classic texts that never leave my side. For instance, Foucault and Rancière, as well as Homer and Plato. In front of me for the last few decades has been a collection of poems by Pasolini called *Roman Poems* (1986). I think I keep it close because I love the black-and-white cover image of Pasolini walking and smiling with a bunch of street kids. It fills me with both nostalgia and longing. Maybe the energy we get from the words of others, and their connection to different stages of life, is necessary for writing and for art in times of crisis.

HH: Yes, Pasolini is trendy again and would have celebrated his hundredth birthday very soon, in 2022. Many Italian institutions, especially Roman ones, are planning celebratory events in one form or another. And it's very interesting, because this kind of "setting for Zooming" is a mise en scène of a social class's expression. For people involved with culture, there are always books behind them. Other communities may have very different backdrops. Young people may have video games behind them, and so on. People organize their interiors to be presentable to the public as a statement of their social status. Pasolini's investigations revealed a strong class consciousness which, as social division becomes even more exacerbated by the virus crisis, is worth reexamining in the current context. Can we find a relevant artistic expression to convey this consciousness?

Anyway, we have to dress a little bit better than in pajamas when we talk to each other. It'd be very funny to imagine an online festival with only pajamas. Why not? This current moment is definitely prompting us to question how we might recode the distinction between public and private spaces.

NP: Yes. And it's interesting that on Zoom there is a new level of formality and informality — nobody wears a tie and the pajama bottoms are out of view.

HH: Actually, this brings us back to the early Silicon Valley dream. You may remember the first generation of the internet boom, the time of Web 1.0. That was the first time that people started talking about working from home and imagining not having to travel long distances to go to work. Many of those startup companies tried to practice working from home. In the end, Yahoo decided to bring everyone back into the office and then they collapsed, which is also very interesting.

But I don't really know how to answer your question. I put all of these phenomena on the table, a line of things in which we might be able to find some common ground, new rules being built, an in-between space where the private and public merge together. We might be living in a new society shaped by this space, one we didn't really notice before, one that is probably becoming a new norm.

NP: That's right. Museums are interesting spaces for this transformation because, on one level, the museum is defined by the objects that it holds. But, on another level, the museum is also about relationships, especially with the public. Now, ideas around engagement are being transferred from the object to the screen. Our idea of gathering now is around a screen, but it's still being mediated by culture in some way. So, there's a new challenge for museums in thinking about the aesthetics of care, as the aesthetics of hospitality are being mediated by the screen. Although these questions arise from current anxieties, they also lead us back to wider concerns about the interaction between art and technology, and, in particular, the role of AI in contemporary art. Going beyond popular fears that AI will hasten the extinction of humanity and the boosterist promises that it can be the big panacea, we need to look closely at the ways it can complement our bodily needs, perform mechanical functions at rates and scales that extend our capacities, and facilitate the creation of novel forms of aesthetic experience. In short, how do we bring AI into the sphere of human needs?

One thing is clear. We live in one world, but we are surrounded by many worlds. Whether it is inside a book or through an immersive installation, artists and art writers are always trying to open a view to one more world.

Contributor Biographies

Taylor Renee Aldridge is a writer and curator based in Los Angeles. She has organized exhibitions with the Detroit Institute of Arts, Detroit Artist Market, Cranbrook Art Museum, and The Luminary (St. Louis). In 2015, along with art critic Jessica Lynne, she cofounded *ARTS.BLACK*, a journal of art criticism for Black perspectives. Her writing has appeared in *Artforum*, *The Art Newspaper*, *Art21*, *ARTNews*, *Canadian Art*, *Contemporary And*, *Detroit Metro Times*, *Hyperallergic*, and San Francisco Museum of Modern Art's *Open Space*.

Lizzie Boon is a writer, archivist, and designer living and working on unceded Wurundjeri Country in Australia. Her practice focuses on performative and expanded perceptual possibilities of archives. She is the registrar and curatorial assistant at Negative Press. Lizzie has a Bachelor of Art History and Curating from Monash University (2018), and is currently studying psychology at Deakin University.

Kalia Brooks Nelson is the Mellon Project Director in the African American and African Diaspora Studies Department (AAADS) at Columbia University. She is a curator, arts administrator, and educator with a focus on developing exhibitions, programming, strategic planning, and curricula for organizations working at the intersection of art and education. Her academic research covers late nineteenth-century through contemporary art with an emphasis on emergent technologies and African American, transatlantic, and diasporic cultures of the Americas. Brooks Nelson holds a PhD in Aesthetics and Art Theory from the Institute for Doctoral Studies in the Visual Arts (IDSVA). She is coeditor of *Women and Migration: Responses in Art and History* (Open Book Publishers, 2019). She has served as a consulting curator with the City of New York through the Department of Cultural Affairs, and is currently an ex-officio trustee on the Board of the Museum of the City of New York.

Maddee Clark is a Yugambeh writer, editor, and researcher living in Narrm. His work has appeared on SBS and in publications such as *Sydney Review of Books*, *Memo Review*, and *Artlink*.

Justin Clemens has published in a number of genres, including a collection of essays on art, titled *Minimal Domination* (Surpllus, 2011), and a collection of limericks, titled *Limericks, Philosophical and Literary* (Surpllus, 2019). He is an Associate Professor at the University of Melbourne, living and working on the unceded lands of the Kulin Nations.

Ben Eltham is a writer, journalist, and researcher. He writes frequently about Australian culture and politics for *The Guardian*, *Overland*, *Jacobin*, *ArtsHub* and *Sydney Review of Books*. Ben teaches in the Master of Cultural and Creative Industries at Monash University. He lives in Melbourne.

Fayen d'Evie is an artist living in the rural bushlands of unceded Jaara country, Australia, and a lecturer in the Master of Communication Design at RMIT University, Melbourne. She is the founder of independent imprint 3-ply, which approaches artist-led publishing as an experimental, critical, and poetic site. Fayen is a core member of the Society of Visually Impaired Sound Artists (SoVISA), and is on the board of the Australian Centre for Contemporary Art (ACCA).

Dan Fox is a writer, filmmaker, and musician living in New York. He is the author of two books, *Pretentiousness: Why It Matters* (Fitzcarraldo Editions and Coffee House Press, 2016) and *Limbo* (Fitzcarraldo Editions, 2018). In 2021, he was a recipient of an Andy Warhol Foundation Arts Writers Grant.

Maria Fusco is an award-winning Belfast-born writer, working across the registers of fiction, performance, and theoretical writing. She is Chair of Interdisciplinary Writing at the University of Dundee, previously Director of Art

Writing at Goldsmiths. Her texts are published internationally and translated into ten languages. Her latest books are *Give Up Art* (New Documents, 2018), collected critical writings of which Lisa Robertson has said "Fusco's scintillating mobility invites us to savour a new kind of critical empathy," and *Legend of the Necessary Dreamer* (Vanguard Editions, 2017), an ambient novella described by Chris Kraus as "a new classic of female philosophical writing."

Sarah Gory is a writer, editor, and publisher living on unceded Kulin Nation lands. She works collaboratively with individuals and organizations across the arts sector, with a particular interest in the intersection of narrative and critical writing. Sarah is a PhD candidate at the University of Melbourne and the cofounder, with Paul Mylecharane, of radical imprint Common Room.

Boris Groys is Professor in the Faculty of Arts and Science, New York University, and Professor of Philosophy and Art History, European Graduate Center, Saas-Fee, Switzerland. He is the author of the books *Art Power* (MIT Press, 2008), *An Introduction to Antiphilosophy* (Verso, 2012), *Under Suspicion: A Phenomenology of Media* (Columbia University Press, 2012), *On the New* (Verso, 2014), *In the Flow* (Verso, 2016), and *Logic of the Collection* (Sternberg Press, 2021), and editor of *Russian Cosmism* (MIT Press, 2018).

Brad Haylock is a designer, publisher, and academic who lives and works on the unceded lands of the people of the Woi wurrung and Boon wurrung language groups of the eastern Kulin Nations. He is an Associate Professor in the School of Design at RMIT University, and he is founder of Surpllus, a publishing house that focuses on critical and speculative practices across art, design, and theory. He has recently coedited *Distributed* (Open Editions, 2018) and *One and Many Mirrors: Perspectives on Graphic Design Education* (Occasional Papers, 2020). His curatorial work includes major exhibitions of the work of Experimental Jetset and Metahaven.

Hou Hanru is a curator, critic, and prolific writer based in Paris and currently in Rome, where he has been Artistic Director of MAXXI, Italy's National Museum of 21st Century Arts, since 2013. Born in Guangzhou, China, Hou graduated from the Central Academy of Fine Arts in Beijing and moved to Paris in 1990. After sixteen years working as an independent curator and critic, he moved to the US and worked in several positions at the San Francisco Art Institute, until 2012. During the course of his career, he has curated and co-curated more than one hundred exhibitions at leading institutions and events around the world. Hou consults for and advises numerous cultural institutions, serves on arts juries, lectures at international institutions, guest edits art journals, and is the author of many articles and books, most recently *Curatorial Challenges: Correspondences between Hou Hanru and Hans-Ulrich Obrist* (2013). A consulting curator for New York's Guggenheim Museum since 2015, he is also a founding member of Guggenheim's Asian Art Council, a curatorial think tank.

Paul James is Professor of Globalization and Cultural Diversity in the Institute for Culture and Society at Western Sydney University. He is author or editor of over thirty books, including *Globalization Matters: Engaging the Global in Unsettled Times* (with Manfred Steger, Cambridge University Press, 2019) and *Globalism, Nationalism, Tribalism* (Sage, 2006). He is Scientific Advisor to the Mayor of Berlin and a Metropolis Ambassador of Urban Innovation.

Flavin Judd is Artistic Director of Judd Foundation. He has designed spaces in the United States and Europe and has written for exhibition catalogues and other publications. He is codesigner and coeditor of the recent publications *Donald Judd Writings* (2016), *Donald Judd Interviews* (2019), and *Donald Judd Spaces* (2020).

Sara Kaaman, Jessica Gysel & Katja Mater are editors of *Girls Like Us*, a feminist, queer publication that has been continuously changing and morphing (originally founded in 2005 and reformed in 2010). Since 2012, the magazine has published on the intentionally impossibly broad themes of WORK, PLAY, SECRETS, BODY, FAMILY, FUTURE, DANCE, ECONOMY, and BIOGRAPHY. The magazine has been collectively edited, the editorials collectively written.

Bella Li is the author of two hybrid books of poetry and art: *Argosy* (Vagabond Press, 2017), which won the Victorian Premier's Literary Award for Poetry and the Kenneth Slessor Prize, and *Lost Lake* (Vagabond Press, 2018), which was shortlisted for the Queensland Literary Award for Poetry. Her writing and artwork have been published in journals and anthologies including *Best Australian Poems*, *Australian Book Review*, *Archives of American Art Journal*, and *The Kenyon Review*. She holds a PhD from the University of Melbourne and lives and works on the unceded lands of the Kulin Nations.

Freek Lomme is the founding director of publisher and public gallery Onomatopee Projects but he also curates elsewhere at times, writes about art and culture, writes and performs poetry, lectures, and does more of the kinds of things fitting this profile.

Jessica Lynne is a writer and art critic. She is a founding editor of *ARTS.BLACK*, an online journal of art criticism from Black perspectives. Her writing has been featured in publications such as *Aperture*, *Art in America*, *Frieze*, *The Nation*, and elsewhere. She was the recipient of a 2020 Research and Development Grant from the Graham Foundation for Advanced Studies in the Fine Arts and a 2020 Andy Warhol Foundation Arts Writers Grant. Jessica lives and works in coastal Virginia.

Rachel Marsden is a curator and arts writer researching cultural translation, artistic and curatorial practices in China and the Asia-Pacific, and methodologies of radical care. She has a practice-led PhD in transcultural curating from the Centre for Chinese Visual Arts (CCVA), Birmingham City University. As an educator, Rachel is interested in practice-based research through writing and publishing, and inclusive pedagogies. Currently based in the UK, she is a lecturer in practice-based research at University of the Arts London (UAL), Governing Board Member for China Residencies (USA/China), and a member of the International Association of Arts Critics (AICA).

Nikos Papastergiadis is the Director of the Research Unit for Public Cultures at the University of Melbourne. His most recent books include *On Art and Friendship* (Surpllus, 2020) and *Museums of the Commons* (Routledge, 2020).

Megan Patty is Head of Publications at the National Gallery of Victoria (NGV), Melbourne, and is founding curator of the Melbourne Art Book Fair. She lives and works on the unceded lands of the people of the Woi wurrung and Boon wurrung language groups of the eastern Kulin Nations. She has edited numerous NGV publications including *Some Posters from the NGV* (2017), *NGV Triennial* (2017), *The Centre: On Art & Urbanism in China* (2019), *She Persists: Perspectives on Women in Art & Design* (2020), and *After The Australian Ugliness* (2021). Her curatorial projects span publishing and graphic design, and include major exhibitions of the work of Experimental Jetset and Metahaven. She is a PhD candidate in the School of Architecture and Urban Design at RMIT University.

Barry Schwabsky is art critic for *The Nation* and coeditor of international reviews at *Artforum*. He has taught at Yale University, Goldsmiths College, and the Maryland Institute College of Art, among others, and is codirector of the Saas-Fee Summer Institute of Art. His books include *The Observer Effect: On Contemporary Painting* (Sternberg Press, 2019) and *Gillian Carnegie* (Lund Humphries, 2020) as well as several collections of poetry. He lives in New York.

Anna-Sophie Springer is an exhibition maker, writer, editor, and publisher. Since 2011, she has directed the boutique publishing atelier K. Verlag in Berlin, advancing new forms of the "book-as-exhibition." In her research-based practice, Anna-Sophie works with cultural and scientific archives and collections to produce post-disciplinary ecologies of attention and care. She completed her Master of Arts in Contemporary Art Theory at the Visual Cultures Department at Goldsmiths (2007) and in Curatorial Studies at the Academy of Visual Arts Leipzig (2013). In 2014, she was the Craig-Kade Visiting Scholar at Rutgers University, New Jersey. From 2016 to 2019, she was a Visiting Lecturer at the Art Institute, Fachhochschule Nordwestschweiz (FHNW), Basel. In 2020, she received a Deutscher Verlagspreis (German Publishing Prize) for K. Verlag.

Astrid Vorstermans studied art history and worked in various jobs as a publisher, editor, and bookseller, as well as in international book distribution. In 2003 she launched Valiz, a publisher and cultural agency that traces and reacts to developments in contemporary art, architecture, and design in a broad and inventive way. Under the Valiz umbrella, she works with a large network of numerous other professionals in the arts and theory.

Caleb Waldorf is an artist currently living in Berlin. His practice operates at the intersection of publication, pedagogy, and technology, with a focus on designing, developing, and maintaining on- and offline collaborative systems. In 2007, he cofounded and is currently the creative director of the publication platform Triple Canopy. Since 2008, he has served on the committee for The Public School, an open framework for self-organized learning. Waldorf received a Master of Fine Arts in Visual Arts from the University of California, San Diego.

Index

Art Writing in Crisis
Edited by Brad Haylock & Megan Patty

Published by Sternberg Press

Contributors: Taylor Renee Aldridge & Jessica Lynne, Kalia Brooks Nelson, Maddee Clark, Justin Clemens, Ben Eltham, Fayen d'Evie & Lizzie Boon, Dan Fox, Maria Fusco, Sarah Gory, Boris Groys, Paul James & Brad Haylock, Flavin Judd, Sara Kaaman, Jessica Gysel & Katja Mater, Bella Li & Justin Clemens, Freek Lomme, Rachel Marsden, Nikos Papastergiadis & Hou Hanru, Megan Patty, Barry Schwabsky, Anna-Sophie Springer & Caleb Waldorf, and Astrid Vorstermans

Copyediting: Sarah Gory
Proofreading: Mark Gomes
Index: Nikki Davis
Design: Brad Haylock
Type family: Article by Vincent Chan
Printed by die Keure, Bruges

ISBN 978-3-95679-585-5

Distributed by The MIT Press, Art Data, and Les presses du réel

Sternberg Press
71–75 Shelton Street
London WC2H 9JQ
www.sternberg-press.com

"Writing Art Writing" by Justin Clemens was first published in: *Subtext: Artists and Writing* (Melbourne: Surpllus & un Projects, 2011), 9–13.

"The Critic as Gesture or: John Malkovich's middle name is Gavin" by Maria Fusco was first published in: Katja Hilevaara and Emily Orley, eds., *The Creative Critic: Writing as/about Practice* (London: Routledge, 2018), 207–209.

"The Fate of Art in the Age of Terror" by Boris Groys was first published in: Bruno Latour and Peter Weibel, eds., *Making Things Public: Atmospheres of Democracy* (Cambridge, MA: MIT Press, 2005), 970–977.

The editors respectfully acknowledge the people of the Woi wurrung and Boon wurrung language groups of the eastern Kulin Nations as the Traditional Owners of the unceded lands upon which the development of this volume has principally taken place.

This project has been assisted by the Australian Government through the Australia Council for the Arts, its arts funding and advisory body.

Australian Government | Australia Council for the Arts